Praise

"This new novel i
you won't want ... ... .s
and page-turning, ... an important book dealing
with important issues around our responsibility for God's
creation. And for the sake of us all, it's **a book with a message
that we can't put down.**"

–The Most Rev. Michael B. Curry
Presiding Bishop of the Episcopal Church

"**Bursting with botanical piquancy,** *Of Green Stuff Woven*
is a novel about the relationship between humans, their
environment, and the divine."

–*Foreword Reviews*

"Bascom weaves together **a complicated narrative of faith,
community, and commitment** to the earth we so desperately
depend upon. In *Of Green Stuff Woven* we understand what it
means to be rooted in radical compassion beyond our own self-
interests."

–Taylor Brorby, author of
*Crude and Coming Alive: Action and Civil Disobedience**

"You will never forget that you met Brigid Brenchley. Equally
devoted to her Episcopal flock and to the preservation of prairie
grasses, she doesn't just preach to the choir, **she inspires an
entire community to take action** by following not only her
faith, but her heart."

–Charissa Menefee, author of *When I Stopped Counting*
and artistic director of *The EcoTheatre Lab*

"This is **a marvelous novel**—morally weighty, provocative,
eloquent, funny, and very moving."

–K. L. Cook, author of *Marrying Kind,
Lost Soliloquies,* and *The Art of Disobedience*

of
GREEN
STUFF
WOVEN

of
GREEN
STUFF
WOVEN

a novel

Cathleen Bascom

Light Messages

Durham, NC

Published 2020, by Light Messages
www.lightmessages.com
Durham, NC 27713 USA
SAN: 920-9298

Paperback ISBN: 978-1-61153-336-1
E-book ISBN: 978-1-61153-337-8
Library of Congress Control Number: *2019949458*

In memory of Barney and Floyd who let me wade into trout streams and wheat fields, my threshold to the Divine.

THE PARISH DIRECTORY

Brigid Brenchley: Cathedral dean and prairie devotee

Phillip Morrow: Trial attorney, cathedral board chair and plant enthusiast

James Merlinske, aka Merlin: dean's administrative assistant and stage actor

Henry Jones: Grandfather and retired factory machine technician

Pearl Jones: Grandmother and dry cleaner attendant

Burton Taylor Smith: retired post office master and civil rights leader

Maxine Taylor Smith: retired teacher and vice-principal with old cathedral roots

Max Chase: CEO Chase Enterprises, great grandson of cathedral founder; wife is Gwen Chase

Madge Chase: Sustainable AG and prairie advocate, great granddaughter of cathedral founder

Delilah Wilson: Seasonal cathedral member, daughter of a pastor, dislikes shelters

Marianna Nichols: St. Aidan's Prairie Coordinator, retired plant ecologist

Carl Nichols: Marianna's husband, researcher for Pilgrim Seed Corps.

Simon Mellon: Director of Agape Feeding Program and cathedral accountant

Francis Burnish: Mayor of Des Moines

James Farnon: Episcopal bishop of Iowa

Dionne Farnon: Dancer, wife of Bishop Farnon

Thomas Charles: Chancellor of the diocese

Aaron Vandermann: Television reporter, has unfavorable view of prairie endeavor

Pasha Kurtz: *Des Moines Register* reporter, has positive view

Roosevelt Lane: Cathedral organist, tender of the furnace-god

Samantha Herbert: Cathedral choir conductor

Jason Mancini: Member of prairie team, director of East Village COOP Garden, leads yoga

Samuel Nielsen: Member of Prairie Team, violinist for the Des Moines Symphony

Elena Hurtado (and baby Ana): Member of Prairie Team, studies public policy at Drake

Suzanne Salz: Director of the Red Cross

Duane Myer: Urban conservationist, City of Des Moines

Dave Stone: Director of Des Moines water works

1

SIDE OATS SANCTUS

Bouteloua curtipendula, or side-oats grama, is a native perennial grass common on dry prairies and in loess soil. Tufted, flowering stalk grows 2 to 3 feet tall. Its inflorescence has many short spikes attached on one side of the zig zag flower. Its asymmetry is pleasing and distinctive—and you can pray it like a rosary. For these reasons, we have planted it near the garden benches.

–Note from Dean Brigid Brenchley's Prairie Journal

A Tuesday Morning in September, Des Moines, Iowa

Holy, holy, holy... I sit on a garden bench and my hand cradles a wire-thin stem of side oats grama grass. My right thumb and middle finger press together around the first small seed—like nature's rosary. These kernels of side oats are in size and hue like the wheat grown on my grandparents' farm in Kansas.

Holy, holy, holy. The words of the ancient *Sanctus* (first penned by Isaiah the prophet) form themselves inside me. I mouth the words. As a forty-something woman priest, dean of an Episcopal cathedral, people cut me a lot of slack about talking to God—even outdoors. I picture myself behind the marble communion altar inside the cathedral, trying to stand tall in a former male dean's chasuble, its brocaded seams hitting wrong on my frame. When interceding for a few hundred human beings, as we all chant together *holy, holy, holy,* I am often overtaken by life's mysteries: the lines of each face, or the stories behind each pair of eyes. But this morning as I sit half hidden in tall green strands, the holy mysteries are equally, if not more, evident to me in the grasses and wildflowers that move in the breeze. Only lately have I been committing them and their distinctive characteristics to heart, the way I once memorized favorite prayers or spiritual teachings. I record them in a prairie journal …bluestem, switchgrass, liatris, lady slipper… their names taste sacramental on the tongue. St. Augustine writes that we are only fully human when we're engaged with the natural world. Some people dive into the vivid layers of fish swimming in the coral reefs. Some people count birds on Christmas, noting each call and wing and colored breast. For me, it's the prairie grasses.

Above my head, the tallest buildings in Iowa clamber upward in granite and corten steel. Behind me, the squat stone cathedral, with our bells on the hour and radiant windows, sits like an historic anchor. Across 9th Street to the west, resides one of our nation's large insurance corporations. But stretching north and east is nearly three acres of tallgrass prairie, covering a square city block. Yes, we're restoring a small prairie smack in the center of the financial district. We've peeled off the dilapidated asphalt and planted species that filled Lewis and Clark with awe when they entered Iowa. Plants which, now, are nearly extinct. Plants that, we believe, are holy.

Exactly why we have this much land downtown and why we've kept it for over a hundred and sixty years remains a bit hazy to me. In my five years as dean, no one has given me a precise answer. Complicated legalities, they say. Wishes of the original benefactor, they respond, shrugging their shoulders. That's all I know. Amidst unprecedented precipitation—both snow and rain—the prairie is soggy, but flourishing. However, our city is on the verge of another flood and our graceful cathedral building is pulling apart at the seams. The fraying Victorian structure is only symbolic of the precariousness inside! Our members, if devoted and colorful, are few. Let's face it, most people don't know a thing about the Episcopal Church. This intellectual, socially-conscious expression of the faith often seems as threatened as the prairie grasses. And yet, to it I have attached my life. I left my literature studies for seminary with the conviction that people's lives are art—that a bite of blessed bread, a psalm, or a parable might actually change us. But, in an era when people assume the conservative megachurch *is* Christianity, we are as invisible to the eye as little bluestem is from a car window, as ephemeral as the prairie orchid.

Merlin, my administrative assistant and close friend, pulls his unreliable vintage Mercedes into the spot labeled "Secretary" (we reused earlier signs.) The cathedral had to keep some parking and chose a permeable paver system to capture runoff. Merlin likes this particular spot because it's near an unmarked door in the stone through which he can nip in and out from the back of his office—to clear his head, avoid a particularly sticky parishioner, or have a smoke. Merlin's full, legal name is James Anthony Merlinske. But since doing *The Once and Future King* off-Broadway, Merlin has stuck. Now, as a character-actor in our local Des Moines theater scene, everyone knows him as Merlin. I personally like his *nom de theatre* for a different reason: with his salt-and-pepper goatee, hooked nose, and large expressive eyes, he reminds me of a merlin hawk I once encountered while hiking. He often lands silently with patient, intent eyes, in my office or beside me as I roam the cathedral, to offer assistance.

Though quite tall, Merlin unfolds from his car with the aplomb of an actor, spies me and raises a hand in greeting. I walk over.

"Outdoor devotions again?" My unorthodoxies amuse him.

"Just tell them the dean is in Morning Prayer, which I am."

"Your investment in the prairie-scape's rather insatiable."

"Sanity."

"Well, if nothing else, my job is to buttress the sanity of the dean." Merlin gives me an understanding gaze. "Well...a proper place to mull over a weighty dilemma."

A weighty dilemma? Understatement of the century.

"Do you remember what yesterday was like?!" I ask him. I have been a parish priest for twelve years, and a cathedral dean for five, and I can't remember any day packed so full. "I have so much on my mind. So much to sort through..."

He nods affirmation. "Morning Prayer. I'll tell them."

Merlin twirls through the arched door with its Victorian hinges wobbling.

Monday Remembered

This is how things unfolded yesterday:

Merlin and I start our morning quite early with a seven-thirty County Organization for Disaster Assistance meeting—COAD for short. There is a steady drizzle as we crawl in his 1970 roundish 220/8 to the Red Cross offices. The car's defroster is on the blink, so it is like traveling in a terrarium on wheels. The conference room of the Red Cross Building hangs up a few floors—in the clouds.

"Evokes Zeus gathering the *Theoi Ouranioi*," Merlin quips as we sit down.

The clouds and raindrops hover and kiss the glass walls. The city is murky-to-invisible below us. I see Merlin's analogy is apt on numerous levels: around tables arranged in a huge square, a pantheon of civic power brokers is assembling: the County Supervisors' and Mayor's envoys, an engineer from the Marysville Reservoir, two FEMA leaders, head of the United Way, a commander from the National Guard, reps from City

Legal Services, various clergy like us.

Unfortunately, Poseidon and his minions seem to be excluded and resentful—out there wreaking havoc on our reservoir and roiling the Des Moines and Raccoon Rivers.

Merlin carefully pulls out a city and county map and our church directory, along with a legal pad and a cross pen. This is why I can't live without him—together we make one brain.

Suzanne, the leader of the Red Cross, enters the conference room. "Here comes Hera," Merlin continues.

"She is way lovelier than Hera!" I whisper. Suzanne Salz is actually one of my models for leadership. Thoughtful and funny, she seems able to make important decisions with a certainty of steel. A quality I find so lacking in myself right now. This collection of alpha people doesn't seem to intimidate her. She also wears gorgeous suits: today it's royal blue. Goes with her blonde bob and an emergency counsel of the sky gods, I guess.

Merlin nods, "You're right. Holds the lightning rod nonetheless."

Suzanne skillfully calls us to attention and then turns the floor over to the lead engineer from the Marysville Reservoir.

"It looks like we are facing a hundred year flood again," he begins.

"Hundred year flood, Fred, that's funny! When was the last one?" Suzanne asks with good-natured irony. "Six years ago? With each flood these designations make less sense..."

Numerous advisors speak. Nothing conclusive. We're briefed, but leave the meeting in "wait and see" mode.

Back at the cathedral, it's nine o'clock and I have taken only that first delectable sip of coffee when Simon, our deacon and treasurer, comes to my office. Slight of build, slim on hair, Simon is a saint—which I don't typically say of accountants. Of course, most accountants don't feed a hundred hungry people lunch every day. Before joining the St. Aidan's Cathedral staff, Simon was a restaurant owner. But he felt called to open the Agape Café, where Des Moines' transitional community can come for a free restaurant-style meal.

Appearing in my doorway, Simon is apoplectic. He is in this state because Roosevelt Lane, our long-time organist, has already come to him apoplectic about recent damage to the organ. Named for the Roughrider, Roosevelt displays his apoplexy in a big-voiced, bombastic style. Simon's version is thin and acerbic.

For at least two years we have been chasing a leak in the roof that is dripping onto the cathedral's large wooden organ pipes. These particular pipes are the size of mammoth tusks, polished to such a luster you can see yourself in them. I vividly remember standing in the parking lot as they arrived on a long flatbed truck from Montreal. Watching Roosevelt stomp his boots in the cold and wave the French Canadians in with his mittened hands was like watching a kid help Santa land on Christmas. Each cylinder of beautifully polished wood took four men to carry it through the halls. Then they hoisted them into place, framing the doors just inside the worship space. Suddenly, it was like coming to meet God through a gateway of the Northern Forest. And when the pipes delivered the bass notes that first Sunday, we felt them more than heard them.

Our mounting building problems threaten the important, beautiful work to which Simon and Roosevelt devote their lives. They depend on the cathedral's building and on the cathedral's money, which are both wearing thin.

So I sit, as I've done too much lately, surveying St. Aidan's accounts—exactly the reason I did not go to law school and enter my father's insurance firm.

The darker side of your humor? I ask God, as I stare at the spreadsheets.

Maybe if my own personal finances weren't so precarious— my student loans so crippling– I'd be more confident. I can practically feel the copper at my temples tarnishing.

Then I notice Merlin at my elbow.

"Two professional people to see you. *SansCorps.* Out of

Chicago." He hands me two business cards. "Were you expecting them? Represent the new hotel development." He raises an eyebrow, "They carry themselves like cash."

A man in a silk tie and a young woman in a red suit firmly shake my hand. I would guess they are about my age, in their early forties.

As a spiritual practice, I try not to project my stereotypes onto people. But these two are so airbrushed, I confess I find it difficult. I try to tell myself that their over-confidence could simply be nerves...their immaculate suits undoubtedly 'tools of the trade.'

I glance at their cards, remarking, "I went to college at Northwestern. Spent so many Saturdays near your office, at the Art Institute! Do you have links to St. Aidan's? Would you like a tour?"

"Actually we are in Des Moines on business," begins the woman in a frank Chicago way. "We just left the mayor's office. We were consulting with him and your city planner,"

"Mayor Burnish speaks very highly of you," the guy in the silk tie says with a honeyed, Southern swirl more like Charleston than Chicago "...very highly indeed."

The skirt-suit decides to get to the point. "Dean Brenchley, we have what we believe you will receive as stellar news."

"Perhaps you're aware of the new boutique hotel and shops planned for Des Moines?" The silk tie takes the baton. "The Hotel Savant is very interested in some of your cathedral's property."

I breathe.

An answer to our financial plight? Manna for the cathedral café and the organ pipes?

I smooth my nose. I have a habit of wrinkling it at inopportune times, maybe a youngest-child phenomenon. With older sisters I learned early on that, when size or other resources are limited, there is always the power of looking amused. Sometimes as an

7

CATHLEEN BASCOM

adult the nose crinkle creeps up on me unawares.

"Not the magnificent, historic church of course," the man quickly adds, maybe due to my scrunched nose, "but the adjacent piece of land to the north and east."

I sometimes fantasize about a moment like this, like picturing myself in a film. And yet when I'm living the larger than life moments, they never feel so glamorous. An equivocating mind, rattled emotions, human skin. I am simultaneously elated and deflated at the news unfolding around me. I stare at the stressful spreadsheets on my desk. I hear a bus belch nearby. I glance out the window where five-foot-tall big bluestem—green shafts edged in peacock—sway... the strands that most tether me to God.

The woman hands me an envelope.

Fine résumé stock. Tangible flecks in the paper. Embossed with *SansCorps* in gold.

It is a letter asking to begin negotiations toward purchase. Proposed price? Nearly four million dollars.

For the prairie.

2

BLUE DENVER LAWNS

Poa pratensis, or Kentucky Bluegrass, is an important grass in our landscape and economy. It is one of the most widely used lawn grasses and is also widely planted as a pasture grass. It is not native to Kentucky. ...*Poa pretensis* spreads by stolons and forms a dense sod (good for lawns) but has a shallow root system and thus needs a reliable source of water. ...On the prairie, *P.pratensis* has been an active invader

–Note from Dean Brigid Brenchley's Prairie Journal

Denver, Colorado, January 1962

Why grasses? For Hopkins, kingfishers catch fire and dragon flies draw flame, so why for me is it strands of chlorophyll that are messengers of grace? And, what people are usually more interested in, how did a secular suburbanite like me ever become a priest?

Somehow the two are intertwined.

I was born at the foot of the Rockies. Back before Denver's xeriscape awakening and arid landscaping, when hidden grids of water pipes or more modest oscillating sprinklers allowed Denver's citizens to roll out swaths and swaths of elegant Kentucky bluegrass.

I arrived upon the western edge of the Midwestern prairie as a sort of "fall crop," for my parents already had three teen-aged daughters. I was not the surprise boy swaddled in sky blue cotton that would have made such a good story. But, my Irish-American-mystical mother, the mother of three blondes, a month or two before delivery had a dream: in it a nurse placed a baby in my mother's arms—a redheaded girl wrapped in a pastel blanket—its weave the color of grass. And that was exactly the way it happened. For the Irish side, my parents chose Brigid and Quirke to balance the English of Brenchley. My mother's father, Grandpa Barney, with a droll sense of humor and fondness for his Great-Grandmother Quirke, took to calling me "Quirky"—an appellation that stuck.

As the cool night would fall over the Rockies onto their arid threshold, the *tzit, tzit, tzit* of lawn sprinklers put me to sleep like a lullaby drifting through our open suburban windows. In my childhood those elegant, blue Denver lawns seemed benevolent. My little girl skin was ivory and sensitive, with easy sunburns and eczema under the knees. But I could lie with my wavy strawberry-blonde locks cushioned upon a Denver lawn, and the turf was nearly as soft as my pastel green baby blanket. In fact, I can't recall when one gave way to the other. The grass hammocked me and carried me from babyhood to childhood.

3

BIG BLUESTEM

Andropogon gerardii or big bluestem grows 3 to 7 feet tall. Its sheath is smooth or hairy. Inflorescence: spikes, 3 to 5 at the tip of the flower stalk, resembling the foot of a bird; turkeyfoot is another common name. In Iowa, both its shaft and its seedhead display a spectrum of blue hues from teal to violet. It once covered 75% of the tallgrass prairie and was the tall totem of the region. Our Big Blue is flourishing all along Ninth Street and waving in passers-by for a spiritual, flora-fauna respite.

–Note from Dean Brigid Brenchley's Prairie Journal

Des Moines, Iowa: Monday Morning Continued

The SansCorps agents leave and I have only a half hour before our weekly cathedral staff meeting to absorb this astounding turn of events. I sit fingering the Hotel Savant letter in such shock that my coffee is growing cold. Nearly four million dollars. Fix the cathedral. But give up the prairie?

I rub the flecked stationery between my fingers and picture

a shiny new cathedral roof, its slate glimmering in the sun like a surfaced whale. I see all the pink-colored granite, tuck-pointed and polished... I see spreadsheets without any parenthesis, not one, and a fat sum at the bottom in the total assets column.

But then, as if the big bluestem grasses are tapping at the window with their turkey-feet tops, I look out my office window and see how glorious the prairie is in bloom. Textures and colors, blown in the breeze, move rhythmically toward the building in waves. My imagination takes me down into the earth to where the big blue's deep roots are soaking up rain—rain that threatens to flood our city yet again.

Fix the cathedral? Give up the prairie?

I sit in a sort of stupor, until I hear the thump, thump, thump and ca-click, ca-click of footsteps in the hallway—the members of the staff walking by to fill their coffee mugs and assemble in the nearby parlor. It sends me into a kind of panic.

Should I tell them about the offer?

It's hard to keep the possibility of suddenly coming into $3,720,000 under-wraps—especially if you are a transparent, extroverted soul like me.

As I do on many days amidst my parish rounds, I quickly carry myself over and kneel at the prayer desk tucked in a corner of my office. On the slanted wood above the kneeler, an icon of *Christ the Vine* awaits. A gentle Jesus figure in robes of crimson and blue is centered in an ocean of rippling gold. In the original 16th century Greek icon it was probably real gold leaf.

"I am the vine, you are the branches."

The image into which I gaze is actually a 20th century re-telling of the original. Jesus stands in the forked trunk of a small tree, the bifurcation point of the vine's branches. Both hands slightly raised, he bestows a benediction. Branching out from the trunk are vine shoots that hold scenes depicting various experiences of Jesus' followers. My eyes move from one scene to the next.

Three crosses on a hill of dust. Two people on a road. Possibly Emmaus.

A group of lepers, healed.

All linked to the central figure. The figure of blessing.

"I am the vine, you are the branches."

My eyes stop roving and come to rest on a watery landscape. Three men in a boat, disciples on the Sea of Galilee. Blue waves envelop the small vessel. The men look anxiously toward Jesus in the center of the icon. One of them, presumably Peter, has stepped out of the boat. He's even stepping out of the storm. In fact, he has one foot out of the picture frame, firmly planted in the gold of the Christ figure.

"I am the vine, you are the branches."

I am pulled from the sea and the storm and the faithful figure stepping out of his frame, by Simon tapping on my door. He sticks his head in to see if I am ready to join the others.

Leaning his head further into my doorway, I see he looks annoyed and pissy. Simon is very punctual.

"Coming," I say to him over my shoulder and he returns to the parlor.

So, do I tell them?

I stand, walk over to my desk and take one last look at the graceful numerals: $3,720,000.

I fold the Savant letter and carefully stash it in my blazer's inside pocket. Something about the icon imbues me with peace and with a sense that it is wisest to wait. But, I bring it with me just in case.

As I approach from down the hall I quickly ascertain why Simon looked like he was having acid reflux. Despite the closed double doors I can hear that Roosevelt is on a small verbal rampage. His oceanic voice comes rolling from under the doors and down the hall. Its full force is probably splashing right in Simon's face.

"CHASING the leaks and patching has to end. FIND the money! New slate. New roof. Not patch it! FIX IT!"

Broad, square-footed and stubborn, Roosevelt is the only organist I have ever known who loves tractors, farm equipment, and to trouble-shoot furnace problems. He is a gifted musician.

Every day of the year— except Good Friday and during his annual camping trip in South Dakota—he settles onto the organ bench like settling into a saddle. He trots and canters and gallops Mozart and Debussy and Bach around and around the cathedral nave until he gets the music right.

Simon hates conflict, but it may be Roosevelt's middle name. Compared to many clergy, church politics don't bother me. It's almost a necessary attribute for being the dean of a cathedral. But if the staff is in a hub-bub, even I can stand in the hall scared to open the door.

Today however, the peace of the icon bathes me and the potential money lining my blazer feels a bit like having on a bullet-proof vest. A steel secret. So I lunge ahead.

"Easier said than done," Simon says, with a quivery top lip as I enter the room. "Tell it to the dean."

As if watching a tennis match between Roosevelt and Simon, Merlin is looking on with a slightly sardonic brow, while folding church bulletins. "You could always play Handel..." he quips under his breath, "*Water Music...*"

At this our choir director, Samantha Sophia, throws back her head of brunette ringlets and laughs out loud. "*Water Music!*" she snorts. She takes a stack of bulletins to help Merlin fold them. "*Water Music...*" She giggles again, perhaps just to egg Roosevelt on.

"The WATER..." Roosevelt fumes, "is no laughing matter! Incessant... Dean Brigid, there's evidence it's reaching the CONTRE VIOLON!"

Now Roosevelt's oceanic blast comes straight my way, with such volume it might knock me over before I can take my place at our dining-turned-conference table. "May I remind you," he continues, now splashing coffee as he gestures, "Those are five hundred and fifty POUND PIPES, the LARGEST in the state!"

"The prairie was taking care of the runoff...we no longer had to sop up water in the Undercroft before serving lunch... until you put in those massive pipes! Now, somehow they're causing water to pour in through the kitchen ceiling! Of course music donors couldn't usually care less about the hungry people of this city!" Okay, maybe Simon doesn't hate conflict, not if it's on behalf of the hungry.

I look at these two men. I envision their weekly endeavors, like two new shoots on the vine of Christ: I picture Roosevelt playing Evensong and hear the glorious arias sung by the *Schola.* I imagine Simon, wearing his apron, spoon in hand. I see him ladling out beautiful, hearty soup to people without two nickels to rub together. While the staff appreciate the prairie, their real attachment is to the building and the people.

Deftly slipping a hand in my jacket, the folded cardstock assures me that the SansCorps agents' visit wasn't a dream. The possibility of the money makes me heady. I know I could make the staff so happy, so relieved...in an instant. They look at me quizzically, and I almost pull out the letter to show them.

"Look!" Merlin interrupts and points to a crack in the plaster on the wall across from our conference table. A bubble of water, under the salmon-colored paint, forms and like a hermit crab starts moving.

"Water up, water down...I know we're not all in agreement, but I say it has to be climate change," Merlin says, "At the Red Cross this morning, Dean Brigid and I learned that the flood threat is now very real: neighborhoods like Marshland and those south of the Fair Grounds. Anywhere in the flood plain really..."

With Merlin's words, I think of our prairie and remove my hand. Yes, Iowa conservationists have convinced me that one long-term answer to Iowa's flooding is to restore prairies and wetlands. I leave the letter in my pocket.

"SEE! There. THERE! Raise the money! Fix the DAMN ROOF!" Roosevelt turns on me again.

"Enough," I say, "I've heard and overheard you."

I give our organist a steely gaze and silently appeal to each staff member to cease and desist on this subject.

"Merlin, right after the meeting will you please put a call through to Phil Morrow's office and see how soon he can meet me?" I ask him, "Our Dean-Senior Warden's meeting isn't usually until next week, but convey to his secretary that it's urgent."

With the word "urgent," Roosevelt is appeased, and stops his bluster.

No one understands *how* urgently I want to talk to Phil! As the cathedral board's chairman, he should be the first to know of the real estate proposal. He's also adept at calming me down.

"Moving on: we need to look at the Holy Cross liturgy," I say, and Merlin hands the bulletins around, "Samantha, will we sing a capella for the procession? And Roosevelt what will you play while the children tie the flowers on the Rood?"

4
LONELY LITTLE BLUESTEM

Andropogon scoparius or little bluestem. This was once the most abundant species in the American mixed-grass prairie region. But now that the prairie is nearly extinct, it is perhaps more common as an old-field invader. Little Bluestem, as it is often called, is in some ways an unfortunate name because next to lawn grasses it is hardly little and it is only blue (blue-green actually) when the shoots first come up in the early summer. By the time the flowering stalks come out, it has turned a rich mixture of tan, brown and wine-red.

–Note from Dean Brigid Brenchley's Prairie Journal

Summer 1967

"Hi Quirky," Johnny Hull from next door waved as he mowed our lawn on certain sunny, summer mornings while I sat eating Rice Crispies at our patio table.

I waved. I have always been an animated waver, and being twice my age Johnny was an idol of mine. I was mesmerized as the lithe twelve-year-old mowed that lawn in various patterns: in long diagonal strips, like Scottish plaid, or in widening concentric circles like a Braque painting. Johnny was a hell of a little league pitcher, but I was always of the opinion that his greatest talent was his visual work in grass.

A small second backyard anchored the rear of our property –a child's garden and, as I was the only remaining young child, it was my own fiefdom: young elm with modest tree house; boat-shaped covered sandbox; swing set; a hedge of honeysuckle. I relished bringing a new friend home and sweeping my arms over the expanse of my personal backyard.

Yet, like so many American children, I was often left alone in this builder-conceived habitat tucked off Locust Street. My mother was one of those once-stay-at-home moms who was now liberated and finding herself. I was safe enough, with at least one teenage sister in the house, and I had at my disposal enough lawn to inspire hours of games. But I experienced what I would call "environmental loneliness." Perhaps it was what religious thinkers describe as the longing for paradise, the urge to return to primordial plentitude. Let's face it, that human-controlled Denver landscape lacked the diversity of plant and animal life that once lapped at the base of the Rockies: the grasses and sedges, gooseberries, cottonwoods, mule deer, prairie dogs, wild turkeys and bob cats, not to mention the bison herds and the ancient pronghorn.

I remember at kindergarten age, sitting in my barge-like sandbox, trying to pretend I was a ship captain.

"Ahoy!" I called out. I watched a lot of *Gilligan's Island*. "Ahoy!" I shouted again, imaginatively hoping for some response.

Nothing. My mother was probably studying for her master's degree and the sister assigned to babysitting was probably on the phone with a boyfriend. Johnny Hull was probably a block away in the batting cages and my backyard's blue lawn stretched like astro-turf, uninhabited. The mile high arid sunlight was devoid of mosquitos.

But then I saw them. Roly-polies nosing around in the sand. If

I poked them, they would fold themselves into mini soccer balls and I could flick them. This soccer game with the roly-polies was innocent and entertaining at first. But all I remember is that for some reason I began flicking them harder and harder.

Eventually, one of the roly-polies didn't uncurl. A sickening ennui followed, as only a five-year-old can experience it. Some days, even as a little child, existence amidst yards of Kentucky bluegrass simply struck me as too monochromatic and thin.

5

JERUSALEM ARTICHOKE

Helianthus tuberosus or Jerusalem artichoke is a species of sunflower, whose tuber is a tasty root vegetable. Its flower heads turn to face the sun. It especially likes the high ground near the cathedral apse, maybe because of the sun that bathes the rounded stone wall. I find myself humming George Harrison's *Here Comes the Sun* when I am near it. Harrison often uses sun for son, meaning God.

–Note from Dean Brigid Brenchley's Prairie Journal

Tuesday Morning Continued

My sideoats rosary in hand, having revisited the extraordinary events of yesterday that began my week, I try to shake myself awake. Despite being paralyzed by the decision placed in my lap, I face this new day.

Morning prayer?

God, you've got to show me a path.

Whimsically, I recall an old Bill Murray flick. He is hilarious as a guy with obsessive compulsive disorder. On the screen in my brain, I see and hear Richard Dreyfus, his therapist, coaching him:

"Baby steps. Take one step at a time. Baby steps."

Where do thoughts end and messages from the Divine begin? Would God really use this kind of movie to speak to me? Ambivalent on this point, the scene makes me smile nonetheless.

Okay, baby steps.

From the corporate plaza across Center Street comes a double-whirring: a tiny John Deere is eating the lawn, like a mechanical goat but louder. A bill-capped man blinks inside the plexiglass like the goat's eyes. Nearby in a circle of too-white, salt-like rocks, a lemon-vested worker also whirrs away with a petroleum-powered weed-wand removing grass from between celosia and canna lilies. On the carpet-high grass the men look god-like.

Where I am, across 9th Street, the spiderwort opens shoulder-high and the Indian grass grows higher still and I am reminded that I am small. Within our prairie's tiers bird sounds emerge from different strata: *purring* down low near the butterfly milkweed; *swooshing* of wings wave across purple coneflower and wooly verbena; a flutter of *in-out-in-in as* a colony of wrens negotiate their penthouse high on a pole. Unlike the relentless sound of the machines, the prairie murmurs a rhythm that includes pause and silence. An auditory oasis. It soothes me as I prepare for the day's important meetings.

Last night by phone I told both Simon and Phil the board chair—or "senior warden" as he is called in Episcopal nomenclature—about the Hotel Savant offer. We set a meeting this morning to carefully project what the deal could mean for the cathedral finances. But, as neither Phil nor Simon have arrived yet, I release my sideoats and prayers and decide to fit in a little weeding.

Cooled by the early morning air, I kneel near a bank of Jerusalem artichoke. Despite all the rain, the grass tops between me and the spindly sunflowers are growing blonde like straw. But down low, the mossy earth is damp, saturating my black denims. A colony of goldfinches animates the flower's stalks and flits about the stained-glass windows of the apse.

Hip, hip keee, heeeee turn, turn, tip.

Their call and flight feels like a blessing over me as the yellow faces of the tall sunflowers each seek the light. Heliotropism. Jerusalem artichoke tracks the sun. The flowers turn. They circle.

As the city starts its day and members of the cathedral begin to arrive, mimicking the plant, I try to turn first to this person, then that one, and say a short blessing for each. It's a practice I kept in my two earlier parishes. Coming to the cathedral, it has helped me to imagine concentric circles— my "parish" now is not only the people in the pews, but the leaders of commerce and government making decisions all around our old church. The dean of my seminary, who later became Bishop of New York, taught us this: he said, "If you can accomplish nothing else, you can pray for your people."

Of course, flesh-and-blood, three-dimensional humans are always more complicated than your idea of them, even your idea of them in prayer. Priests are called to love everyone with Christ's love, but no person can like everybody. Of course, Dean Mast added, "The ones you don't like are exactly the ones you must pray for the most!"

Simon drives up in his small hybrid vehicle. Exiting his car, he would wave except that he has buckets of soup in each hand, donated from the Methodists up the hill. Simon works long hours tirelessly. But he says he's blessed by the lunch guests.

"Absolutely, every day I learn about fortitude...about keeping a sense of humor in shitty, shitty circumstances," he insists. No doubt on occasion he has cause to apply this wisdom to our finances.

"Give me about twenty minutes?" he asks. I nod.

Blessed are the poor. I pray. *God bless Simon.*

A stretch limousine ambles up the alleyway and stops at the

awning of St. Aidan's rear entrance. The driver opens one door, and Max Chase gets out and circles the car to proffer an arm for his older sister Madge who has recently been in the hospital. She was in and out of the hospital before I could visit her there and, as with most old Des Moines families, the Chases keep exact personal details extremely private. So I'm not quite sure of the medical reasons for her visit. It's good to see her out.

The Chases are one of the cathedral's oldest and Des Moines' most influential families.

They are part of a cadre of people into whose laps lucrative Iowa farmland, building, and banking have poured bundles. The siblings look a lot alike: they are small of stature, their hair is the lustrous color and texture of spun white gold, and their ears are a little too large for their heads. I always think Max looks astonishingly like Andy Warhol circa 1980, though his voice and lifestyle are nothing like Warhol's.

However, although Max and Madge look a lot alike, their politics and social sensibilities diverge sharply. Madge married Peter Wallace, a nephew of FDR's vice-president. She kept her Chase name even though Peter, as well as being related to a US vice-president, was one of the heirs of Pilgrim Seed Corporation. Rather ironically, two decades ago Peter and Madge became some of the first outspoken opponents of GMOs, and Madge herself one of the greatest proponents of the prairie restoration movement in Iowa. Peter and Madge worked closely with their friend US Representative Neal Smith to get land originally set aside for a nuclear plant converted into Iowa's largest prairie and wildlife refuge instead.

For years, Madge has preferred to hide out at "the farm" and avoid the Chase Empire in town with all its politics and drama. She attends the company's board meetings—probably where she and Max are headed now—and, it is rumored, she is extremely savvy with family investments. When I became dean, Madge was seldom in the pews at the cathedral. Peter had just passed away suddenly from a heart attack, and she was in profound mourning—almost a recluse. Friends say she saw the horses, and planted her gardens, and burned her prairie, but saw few people.

However, when the idea of the cathedral's land project began to germinate, our Prairie Team leader and plant ecologist Marianna insisted I visit and consult Madge.

"It's a must," Marianna had said, "I'll drive."

I think Madge and I were both a bit nervous. In a thorough, deep-listening way she queried me. But she also felt the need to confess that in the last years she and her husband had mainly tried to follow Buddha's path, and that she had had a simple burial for Peter right there on the property.

"Those arrangements made my brother Max highly uncomfortable. He's quite a devout Episcopalian, you know."

After we talked, she took Marianna and me strolling across her prairie to harvest Indian grass, switch grass, and big bluestem seeds along with a myriad of flowers, just as she had once harvested them from the Neal Smith prairie. She gave us colorful, cotton shoulder slings, and we moved like pheasants through the grain. The process of gently cupping a sparkler-thin-wire of grass and then sliding the emerald tipped kernels off and into the pouch was rhythmic, mesmerizing labor. Memorable contemplation, and fruitful. We three worked silently for about three hours.

"If I remember right, Jesus said something about a mustard seed spreading... a little like these small prairies popping up across Iowa. Tiny but generative." Madge said.

When we left that day, Marianna had paper sacks of seeds for our downtown prairie and I had a sixty thousand dollar check to help tear off the asphalt around the cathedral.

The greatest gift of all, however, was that after my visit Madge felt inspired to come back to worship. And this time around, the Eucharist connected with her in a way that it hadn't for years. She said it touched her grief—not removing it—but soaking it in a kind of light. The memories of Peter, while still painful, became treasured transcendent pain. An added grace is to see her wily tycoon brother Max smile like a little boy when his sister resumes her place in the Chase pew Sunday after Sunday.

Now Max is a different story. He studied engineering, got an MBA, and has devotedly carried on in the line of his father and grandfather in the business of developing the city and making a profit. He's a moderate Republican who is fiscally conservative. To say he's been skeptical of our prairie project would be to put it mildly. Didn't give a dime, despite being past-CEO and current board Chairman of Chase Enterprises. When I was installed as dean, more than one of my predecessors who had flown in for the celebration pulled me aside to alert me that Max acts as the Cathedral's hidden puppeteer—pulling many strings in the cathedral politics.

However, although Max thinks a prairie downtown is ludicrous, he and his wife are very generous to St. Aidan's and to other causes. After a terrible earthquake destroyed the Anglican cathedral in Port Au Prince, Haiti in 2010, I invited their dean to visit and preach as part of his fundraising swing through the US After hearing the appeal, Max stepped forward to help rebuild both their cathedral and homes in its neighborhood. Max and I worked closely together, along with Phil Morrow, and Max's enthusiasm for the project, if a little paternalistic, seemed prayerful and genuine. He was airlifting Chase construction experts to the scene of destruction the next week.

Now he certainly appears tender and attentive to Madge—who looks pale and wobbly.

His expression is, however, rather intense as he speaks to her. Strolling arm in arm, Max is forcefully describing something.

"Steady, Max," I hear Madge caution in an older sister tone that makes me wonder if she means physical or emotional balance. Hers or his?

Instead of going into the cathedral, the Chase siblings move gingerly down the alley next to the church toward the tallest building in Iowa and the Chase offices there.

Strengthen dear Madge and bless Max and everyone impacted by him today.

As the limo pulls away, I note that the cathedral's garden entrance door is propped open. Framed there is Henry Jones, standing on a footstool. He has an oxygen machine with the tube in his nose. Henry—who has emphysema—calls the oxygen machine Fido, his faithful companion. Its roll-able tank is parked next to the stool, near a crate of curly-cue lightbulbs that sits at the ready. At nearly seventy years old, Henry's build and personality remind me of tugboats I'd watch on the Hudson River when I was at seminary. Square and determined, but starting to show wear. He has an old-fashioned anchor tattoo. Navy, Korean War.

For most of his life, Henry was a Firestone machine engineer at the plant on Des Moines' near north side. With his droll, prairie-home-companion-meets-the-honey-mooners manner, I was surprised when I learned that Henry reads Kafka. And at our weekly Bible study, he explicates scripture texts with a pragmatic brilliance: he interprets the nuances, and the texts take on flesh and blood form when Henry applies them. Retired now, Henry also gives the cathedral a couple of days each week doing handyman tasks, then afterward goes into the library to pour over biblical commentaries. Says he can't get enough of the stuff. At least until the dust and mold of the old books get to him. Recently, he and his wife Pearl joined St. Aidan's Green Cathedral Committee, and Henry has been methodically transforming the building ever since: energy audit; double-pane windows, as we can afford them; even wonders about a green-roof over the flat Sunday school wing, though he knows there's no money for that item, despite Max Chase's hefty annual pledge. Today it looks like it is light bulbs.

Facing his form in the door, I close my eyes, soaking in how much I appreciate this member of our flock.

Henry is salt and light! God, bless Henry.

Looking up, I see Phil, winding my direction on one of the

garden paths. Seeing this man, my simple prayer rounds as dean become infinitely more complex. Dressed in a soft suit—muted blue like the sea—with necktie pulled loose, Phil reaches out and touches the seed heads as he careens down the path, the way a child would do. Nearly fifty, with sandy hair and quick sarcasm, he has a look—though maybe it is just his glasses—that merge John Lennon and Bill Gates in a fashion I find pretty fine. He studied in Boston and New York but came back when his lawyer father suddenly died. It floored me when Phil, this well-known trial attorney, joined the Prairie Team. But I soon discovered he is a closet naturalist. He can distinguish big and little bluestem early in spring. Something, even with my years in the Flint Hills, I still find tricky.

About a year ago, after one of our board meetings, I glimpsed his screensaver: large emerald green fronds with Jackson-Pollack-like splatters.

"So, Phil," I'd asked, "What are those gorgeous leaves?"

"Bromeliad," he'd replied with a self-conscious grin, "my favorite plant." I somehow didn't imagine trial attorneys had favorite plants!

"My old man loved sailing in the Virgin Islands—to get away from his legal work and headaches. As a teenager, I'd spend most of the time ashore, fascinated by the flora. I've been photographing bromeliads for years."

Despite his East Coast education and professional success, there's a surprising humility about Phil—a bit like rich Iowa soil turned over for planting. Maybe his failed marriage was the spade work? That would be my guess. Phil and his first wife divorced before I came to be dean.

Sonya was the Episcopalian originally, so I've always wondered why he stayed in the parish and she left. What kept him?

Whatever the reason, I'm thankful. I can find any number of men physically attractive. But seldom, if ever, do I find a mind and spirit that allure me, too. No one really since my graduate school lover Daniel Goldberg. I think maybe the attraction is mutual but am in no way certain. Now, as Phil strolls down the path, oblivious of me kneeling in the grasses, I have to face that I find him alluring: body, mind, and spirit. Admitting this to myself, I am suddenly washed over with sensations that I haven't experienced in years—like body surfing in Hawaii. For a second, I just let myself tumble under! The abandon is glorious. But then I try to grab hold of the earth; I literally hug a stand of big bluestem near its base.

Dear God, this is ridiculous! I don't have psychic space for this now. A parishioner? The bishop will flip. AND, I'm in the middle of a parish crisis.

Mostly, my prayers are one-sided.

But, occasionally, as the mystics say, *something* comes from Beyond.

Of course, I'd heard the phrase a thousand times, recited it at weddings a hundred times; I could easily explain it away psychologically. But my raw experience is that it emanates as if from the ground:

Love is patient.

Phil almost walks past, unaware of my crouching form. "Brigid?" He actually startles when he glances down.

I can't help but laugh, a crinkled-nose-giggle no doubt—it's so hard to catch a trial attorney off-guard.

"You certainly are the industrious cathedral dean!"

He offers me a hand. I take it, but look down to knock earth from my wellies. Seeing that I am weeding, he looks down at his suit with a little confusion.

"I'm afraid I'm dressed for court later today. Did I get my holy tasks crisscrossed? I thought it was to be spreadsheets for breakfast and grass-trimming over lunch. With this court case, I won't make it back for the Prairie Team work."

"I was just killing time," I say, composed enough now to look into his face. "Simon is waiting for us. He knows about the *SansCorps* offer by name, but no details."

"*SansCorps*," Phil whistles. "Bit of a conundrum. Probably best to keep it close to our vest, at least for the moment. You know the news will spread like wild fire when it's out!"

He folds his arms across his chest and looks pensive. His eyes pass over our acreage and I glimpse a man who's been around the block despite his youthful exterior. For a moment, his dimple sags and pulls his mouth downward, like the weight on a fishing line. As the cathedral's board chair, Phil will encounter even greater pressures than I will while we decide what to do about the hotel and the land. Though we share the leadership equally, the people allow that the dean will be "spiritual" which often translates as impractical. But the board chairman is to frugally watch over our financial interests. If we accept the four million, there are many members who, like King David bringing home the Ark of the Covenant, would gladly strip naked and dance through the streets of Des Moines. Phil and I could both be ecclesiastical heroes! But Phil is even more committed to sustainability and plant diversity than I am. He's politically savvy and environmentally sensitive, and I can't imagine working through this issue with anyone better than him.

Lost in thought, together we silently move down the path to the cathedral.

I feel balanced, my burden lightened, walking side-by-side with Phil Morrow.

Thank you for Phil. Whatever it means, give me patience. Not my strong suit.

Together we enter St. Aidan's where Henry has the door propped. Henry's grandson Nicholas is with him. Henry and Pearl have five grandkids and Nick is the youngest. Everyone else in the family works, so Henry says it falls to him to be Grandpa-sitter. He doesn't seem to mind.

"Hello Henry. Nick. Looks like two professionals here," Phil says, and he tousles Nick's hair as the boy and his toy truck circle by.

"Replacing dimwits. Putting in these," Henry says and holds aloft a bulb, "enviro-swirl-cones, we call them, because Nick says they look like ice cream." The grandfather flashes an amused smile, though I notice he has bags under his eyes. "Gift from Pearl and me. I took your sermon to heart." Hank winks at me. "Do not hide your light under a bushel, you said. Put it on a lampstand for all the world, you told us. Well...corridors around here dank as hell! Dean Brigid, you keep throwing light from the pulpit, and I'll try to throw some down the hall. 'Course, it's slow work with this rug-rat along."

Nicholas, not unlike his determined grandfather, is tenaciously pushing a dump truck around and around Henry's metal stool. He is built like his yellow truck, square and low to the ground, with significant traction. His blond hair is standing up on end from the static created each time he goes under his grandfather's oxygen cord. Henry's eyes sparkle, despite having to lift the oxygen hose at every circuit.

Henry has an unlit cigarette in his mouth—likes the aroma of tobacco that much, I guess.

He recently quit smoking. Doctors' orders. One of whom shares a pew with Pearl and him on Sundays. Not too long ago, Dr. Lancaster soundly upbraided Henry when he caught him stealing a smoke with Merlin after worship. Having stood a time or two shoulder to his white jacketed shoulder, hovering over Henry in a hospital bed, I couldn't really blame Doctor Charlie for his frustrated outburst. In fact, the scolding may have had some effect: Henry hasn't had a bout in the hospital in months; his emphysema has been holding rather steady.

"After all those years," Henry says, turning a bulb the last bit, lifting the coiled tube for Nick to pass under, and taking the Marlboro from his lips, "watching the plant belch black into the air ... want to do something to turn back the tide."

Phil and I give him a thumbs up and move down the hallway to Simon's office door.

When we go in, I simply hand him the embossed envelope containing the offer and initial negotiating price. Phil and I stand on one side of Simon's desk watching him unfold the parchment. We don't say a word. Sometimes silence is the only human response to thresholds.

The sun glints off the thin strands of blond atop Simon's rather bald head. Then, this man who works himself every which way to the bone, be it on accounts or in the kitchen, looks up at us with incredulity. It is the incredulity of a sunrise.

"Are you kidding me? Nearly four million dollars? We could fix the roof and feed a hundred more hungry people—maybe each day!" Simon's child-like relief tweaks my great ambivalence. Simon notices: I must look slightly nauseated and conflicted. "But...that would mean losing the prairie wouldn't it?...all you've fought for...all that's grown there."

Blessed are the poor, I pray. *Consider the lilies*, I pray.

Phil thoughtfully interjects, "It will be a delicate decision. So, we'd better become as informed as we possibly can." There is a small table in Simon's office and Phil strides over to it, takes off his ocean-blue jacket, and rolls up his sleeves, "Let's get cracking."

I join him and so does Simon, calculator in hand.

When we work through from every conceivable angle of what the offer might mean, and leave Simon's office, Henry has pretty well completed his light bulb project.

"The light is making a real difference already," Phil says, chin up, surveying the long hallway. "Hank, you're a master. I know its complicated changing out these Victorian fixtures. Cost me a pretty penny in electrician bills at my house to convert just a couple. You're saving us a lot of money as well as reducing our carbon footprint. Thank you."

Nick Jones has parked his truck. All three feet of him stands up and eyes Phil. "We're going fishing. Wanna come?"

Just then, Merlin pokes his head out of his office. "Dean Brenchley, a reporter from Channel 13 is on the phone. Would like a TV interview this afternoon. About the prairie, in the prairie. That is if the rain holds off."

I stare at Merlin somewhat surprised. Merlin and Phil know I am a media hound; I tend to take any publicity for the cathedral or the prairie that we can get. Still, strange timing.

"Channel 13?" Phil muses.

Channel 13 is the local FOX affiliate. Didn't show with the other press when the mayor and bishop came for the ribbon-cutting. So why now? The hotel already has me stressed, and media is stressful, too.

"The life of the gainfully employed," Henry quips, seeing my ambivalence. "If we do get a dry afternoon, Nicholas and I are going fishing. Brigid, want to chuck it all and come with us? Unfortunately, we can't fish our usual spot, the river is too high by us... over the banks. But we'll find a spot."

I relish the idea.

Merlin is a sport and sort of gives me permission. "The interview wouldn't be until about three. You have some flex in your calendar."

The vision of me with Henry and Nick and a line in the water seems to give Phil a real kick. "I guess its pastoral care. Brigid, you've got to make your parish calls..."

The Jones clan lives in the Marshland Neighborhood, aptly named. They were flooded out in the last deluge and the cathedral had to help them re-build their home. I don't say anything about it, but suddenly the concerns of the COAD take on flesh and blood form: Henry and Nick Jones. Pastoral care? At this moment in time, Phil may be right.

"What do you say, Dean Brigid?" Henry continues to cajole me. "You've bragged about your luck with rainbow trout! Try your hand at bass," Henry says and winks at Nick.

"Why not!" I say and give Nick a scrunched nose laugh. "But I only know about flies and worms. Not a thing about these Martian-looking midwestern fishing lures."

Then I turn to Merlin. "All right. If I can relax my nerves fishing first with Henry, I will wash up and return and do the TV interview. You can tell 13-News I accept."

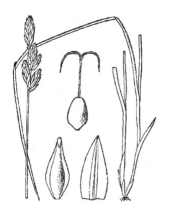

6

FISHSCALE SEDGE

Cyperaceae heteroneura chalciolepis, or fishscale sedge is a subalpine plant, found at 8-13,000 feet in mountain states like Colorado and Wyoming. It has black, heavy heads, either erect or drooping. Found in wet places. Marianna always says to the Prairie Team members, "Remember: sedges have edges that's how you can distinguish them from the more-rounded grasses."

—Note from Dean Brigid Brenchley's Prairie Journal

Elk Falls, Near Pine, Colorado, July 1969

At dawn, the grass was cold with dew when Grandpa Barney revealed to me that there was actually hidden life teeming under the bluegrass lawns of Denver. As the sun rose, a peppery sweet fragrance fell on us from the nearby honeysuckle hedge. At age seven, I was old enough to take a flashlight to the dark shed and locate the garden trowel my grandfather needed. Grandpa Barney took the trowel and indented a square outline in the lawn—like the cut-out marks for paper dolls. He then edged out a square of turf resembling the carpet remnants I sat on at my progressive school.

"You see," Grandpa said, "although the grass feels thick, it's not deep. Under here is a whole world in the soil where the worms live." He broke up the earth a bit and then thrust his hand into the rich, porous earth. It was alive with moving creatures—worms leaving air paths and nutritious soil in their wake. Soon we would be heading southwest up through sandstone, granite, and pine toward Kenosha Pass for the summer fishing rituals.

Byron "Barney" Ward, the one who nicknamed me Quirky—in his double-breasted Cary Grant suit, a cocktail in one hand and with Grandma Helen in a full-length mink on his other—would appear unlikely to be my key to the natural world. My favorite photo of him was taken at the fountain in Trafalgar Square in London: short in height and wiry, he wore a jaunty tweed sport coat, a brushed, olive-hued brim hat, and a winning smile. He was a news reporter-turned-insurance-gentleman who traveled well globally. No, to most people Grandpa Barney would seem a strange choice as a mentor in things out-of-doors.

Yet, he was one. For Byron Ward moved to Colorado because he felt most alive in the mountains and he was an avid and adept wet-fly fisherman.

All week Grandpa Barney had carefully tied his red-headed Varian flies. But, we also needed live bait. He stuck his quick hand into the earth and removed night crawlers.

"Oohhh," I said, "Yuck!"

Grandpa, who was also a gardener, explained to me how good the worms were for the earth.

Then, converted to compassion, I expressed remorse at scooping them into the coffee-can-equivalent-of-a-death-sentence. But Grandpa spoke with reverence about the web of life and a worm's regal place in it:

"Oh, not at all. You see, Quirky, the worms eat dirt..."

"What?!!"

"Then the fish eat the worms, and we eat the trout, and then we have energy to till the ground, which turns into the nutrients the worms love to eat in the soil—one big circle."

He imbued such a respect in me that all the way up Deer Creek Canyon I eyed the coffee can as a holy artifact, a Folgers-red-and-silver icon of the web of life.

The Elk Falls Fishing Ranch was a reach back into an earlier mountain era. The coffee can *was* a portal to the living web of the Lower Lake. My favorite spot was the paint-worn, half-submerged dock jutting into the water. To get there I had to tightrope walk a way through grasses, sedges, and forbs that were very different from what they called grass in Denver—anything but thin and monochromatic! To reach the dock I waded into the itchy and feathery stalks—some above my head. Unlike the controllable grass people bought and rolled out in the city and suburbs, these grasses intermingled in a riotous combination of sizes, colors, and textures. Their names evoked mountain creatures. I would walk over tufts of mutton grass, carefully cup a squirrel-tail seed head and then stick it to my shirt. Once, I tried to wear the drooping seed head of a fish-scale sedge like an earring and it sliced my hand like a paper cut.

These grasses were home to many creatures. Sometimes I heard the rustle and splash of a beaver pushing off, its brown nose leaving a V-shaped wake across the water. I *was*, forgive me G.M. Hopkins, stopped dead in my tracks by the dragonflies. Though Grandpa Barney assured me they were harmless, when I saw them swooping in and out of the grasses like small jeweled helicopters, I had a hard time believing they were peace-keepers that would not in fact sting like the easily angered wasp. Dragonfly fears and all, I nonetheless dove with relish into the tall grasses woven at the lake's edge.

Once I maneuvered my way between the grasses and the dragonflies, pranced over the faded planks of the bridge, and finally reached the dock, I would dangle my feet in the brook-fed water. I discovered that, like the grasses, the surface of the water was also alive: small, moving, concentric circles rippled as bugs landed and trout fed and the decoys of bobbers were gracefully placed in tandem by the fishermen. Here, the malaise of the suburbs fell off. I felt full, not empty.

We spent most of our time at the Lower Lake where live-bait was allowed. But Elk Falls Fishing Ranch boasted two trout lakes. The Upper Lake was reserved for fly-fishing only. The Upper Lake was completely different than the lower, and once Grandpa Barney had his fill of bait fishing—if the snow was gone and the summer high—we'd take the car "up." As the engine strained with the elevation, we left the grasslands behind.

Sometimes Grandpa Barney suddenly slowed the car to a crawl, whispered and pointed. If the car motor was quiet enough we would see, peering at us from behind the well-placed pine and spruce, the majestic elk for which Elk Falls Fishing Club was named. Then, almost as quickly as I caught sight of them, the herd disappeared— in one flowing movement—as if into thin air.

Near the Upper Lake, we entered a truly alpine context and the landscape became like a sculpture or giant Zen garden. Here there was little grass or none at all. On the banks of the Upper Lake Grandpa himself took a more central mythic role. With the silent concentration and devotion that another man might give to a Bible or rosary, my grandfather would unfold his fly case, gaze, ponder, choose, and then affix to his line the fly that spoke to him. Then began his active homage to the creation, and to the next generation. Grandpa Barney, God, and the fishing club had an important covenant: no grandchild of his would exist without the privilege of, at least once in their lifetime, reeling in a fish.

My first solo trout. I was mesmerized by the water rippling under my bobber. The yellow plastic globe had a brown zig-zag stripe on it, like the one on Charlie Brown's cartoon shirt. That evening, as the sun was setting, it was as if the Creator was playing with a well-loved Spirograph. Expanding and over-lapping circles on the water turned from blue to fuchsia to lavender to coral all in a matter of minutes. I was tired and was about to give up on catching any fish, when the nylon line under my left hand suddenly began spiraling outward. The Charlie Brown striped bubble completely disappeared. I became disoriented, but then re-focused to where my pole was pointing, like a long fiber-glass finger.

Before I could even look toward him, Grandpa Barney's Arnie Palmer rain jacket brushed my sleeve. Like a hawk after fish, he had instantly swooped silently to my side. "That's the way. Steady. Steady." His wrinkled but agile hands cupped mine on the reel, but then he thought better of it and let them fall to his side. "You can do it, Quirky. You're big enough, strong enough. But set the hook. Set the hook. What I mean is give it a little flick to the side with your pole."

With some trepidation, a little too quickly, I jerked the rod left, and Grandpa grimaced. Not pretty, but it worked. Everything in front of me went taut. I sensed by the reverberations in my hands that the fish knew it was hooked. It started darting, like a hurdler under water. My pole bent over like a willow.

Grandpa Barney's eyes sparkled. "Got him. Now reel, Brigid. Firm and steady. Reel. Reel, steady."

The fish was strong for a seven-year-old, unfathomably strong. But the line was stronger, and the communion between grandfather and grandchild stronger yet. Eventually the trout tired.

"You did it, Quirky. You bring the trout to shore. I'll get the net."

My grandfather was not a man of prayer. Yet, with the rainbow fish in the hammock of the net, Byron Ward exuded a gratitude that bordered on the holy. His face manifested a gratitude for things beyond himself: for a child, and a fish, and cold air that assured him that he was alive.

We pointed the car east, with some ambivalence, toward our city. At the foot of the Rockies it spread out like scattered diamonds on billiard felt. I fell asleep as the Malibu coasted toward lower elevations, the empty Folger's can at my feet. I fell asleep imagining the beaver, the dragonflies, and the tough old trout bedding down in the tall grasses for the night.

7

EDELWEISS #1

Flora von Deutshland Osterreich und der Schweiz 1885 by Otto Wilheim Thomè or edelweiss. My grandmother loved edelweiss both outdoors and in art. She owned a botanical print—which she bought on a tour of the Alps in the 1960s and later gave to me when she had to move from her sprawling ranch-style brick for her current shoebox apartment in assisted living. Grandma Helen bought the botanical print simply to remember the flowers she viewed in the alpine meadows, but it seems it was rather rare and valued in art circles.

–Note from Dean Brigid Brenchley's Prairie Journal

Tuesday Lunchtime

Merlin and Simon return to their offices and Phil, Henry and Nick leave the cathedral to live lives in the world. I spend the rest of the morning hours on the phone recruiting clergy from around the diocese to help with various elements of the Diocesan Convention liturgies.

This particular year, our Iowa bishop, James Farnon, has invited the bishop of Swaziland and Brechin in Scotland—our companion dioceses in the Anglican Communion. The bishop and his staff have some exquisite and creative worship planned... but I have to oversee many of the nuts and bolts. Such is the role of a cathedral dean.

Thankfully, at noon I get to clear my head. Every Tuesday, our Cathedral Prairie Team does gardening over the lunch hour. Phil is a regular, but today he'll be at the courthouse instead, which makes me pleased we already spent time in the same room. I shed my kitten heels and pull back on my well-worn Wellington boots. I brought them home from Devon years ago, after grad school and before seminary. Once-green, they now hover in hue between pistachio and peat bog. Memories of trekking across Dartmoor, as well as traces of Colorado sandstone, Kansas lime dust, and black Iowa mud layer the boots' uppers— like a geologist's cut, they reveal my earthy history.

My first footfall just hits the grass as Marianna, our prairie's coordinator, zips up in her small truck. Usually, I am so glad to see her, but today I confess I shudder. As leader of the Prairie Team, Marianna is the last person I want to tell about the purchase offer. Agile for her age, she reaches into the truck's bed and lifts out a plastic rain barrel. The incessant rain this year hasn't slowed Marianna down! She dons a robin's egg-colored rain coat and a hat with a cord under the neck. It makes her seem on perpetual safari. A plant ecologist, from a long life lived outdoors, Marianna has crow's feet at the corners of her eyes and is perennially tan.

When I first learned of Marianna's training and approached her about overseeing the prairie, she took a week to think about it.

"Yes," she finally said, "but I need two hundred dollars to drive to Chicago and consult with people who keep the Oak Savannah on the North Side—grounds of an old TB sanatorium. If they can do it on that urban site, we probably can do it even downtown, considering Iowa's soil."

"It's a deal."

One of the best deals I ever made!

Marianna is tough. Being her pastor, I know it comes in part from extricating herself and three children from an abusive first marriage, raising them alone while earning her PhD and surviving on macaroni and cheese. Later, Marianna married again. She and her second husband Carl were caretakers for the Cal State Research Farm. But they returned to Iowa when Carl was offered a research job with The Pilgrim Seed Corporation. Marianna worries he has "gone over to the dark side." She isn't one to mince words. Not with Carl, not with me. Getting a shovel from the truck, Marianna sees me and waves.

"The big blue is really taking off this year," I say, as she strides in my direction.

"When I was growing up in Western Iowa, " Marianna remembers, "there were buffers of bluestem... blue streams and rivers of grass. Strange, planting it downtown. Still, it's proving it likes the soil. Probably senses that its ancestors thrived on this spot for a thousand years. So...have you spoken to the city about the permit?"

Marianna has been badgering me to get authorization for a prairie burn, says it is the right time in the prairie's life. I relish the prospect, too, especially if we do it as the deacon chants "the Light of Christ" at the Easter Vigil! But I don't relish the uproar the idea will unleash.

"Marianna, it is the cathedral members I'm worried about. You know anxiety will run rampant when we set a fire around this historic landmark!"

She says nothing... just stares at me like she is identifying a plant species. Her crow's feet look like a bird's talons clamping tighter.

"Blame it on me," she says. We'll protect the building, and next summer the congregation will see a green carpet come up through the ashes like Resurrection itself."

Next summer? I sweep my gaze across our acres.

What will be here next summer?

I picture a backhoe brought in by the developers. I hear the ripping of the deep roots. I picture myself in my office, like Lady Macbeth, trying to rub the green blood from my hands.

Marianna, with her head slightly cocked, looks at me quizzically. She puts up with my daydreams because she's decided they make me a better preacher. "For such a brave girl, you are a coward," she says, "Start the process!"

Without us seeing him, our oldest Prairie Team member Burton Taylor-Smith has arrived and gallantly waded into a soggy circular pond to tend horse-tail plants. The bamboo-like shafts are not easily cut, especially by a man who sometimes supports himself with a cane. The older gentleman is getting frustrated, whipping around with a bent horsetail lodged in his clippers.

Marianna, afraid he is going to fall, races to his aid. She tells him to throw down the clippers and shows him how you can just pop out the spent, dry plants grasping one shaft at a time. He tries it. *Pop.*

"Like pulling a gray hair from its follicle," Marianna tells him, "You and I both know about that."

I smile and, spying some encroaching foxtail grass, I kneel to do a little weeding.

Elegantly tall, with a close salt-and-pepper beard, Burton served as postmaster in the Oakland neighborhood just north of the cathedral. I was shocked when some of our matriarchs took me to lunch and told me of the African-American hub that once thrived there. Businesses, and blocks of middle class homes, owned by people whose ancestors fought for the Union in the Civil War. In the early 1960s, the powers-that-be built I-275 right through it. Burton was central in organizing the resistance. The Episcopal dean at the time was solidly Civil Rights and fought alongside, viewing the massive ribbons of concrete as a segregationist ploy. But, it was a losing battle. Now in place of the neighborhood is a no man's land on both sides of the freeway. Concrete. Sad-looking lawns. A few ratty auto establishments.

Burton has the government pension, as does his wife Maxine, who had been a teacher and school vice-principal. They had the means to move to the suburbs and did, but not without bitterness. Still, every Sunday, Burton and Maxine cruise in their white Lincoln down that same freeway—Maxine at the wheel because Burton can no longer drive—to worship at St. Aidan's where Burton was baptized.

These two finish at the pond and move my way, Burton dripping slightly.

"Dean Brigid," he says as he takes off a glove and shakes my hand, "you know, when I was a cathedral chorister, right where you're weeding"—the older gentleman looks into the air above my shoulders and with his two hands blocks out what only he sees—"there were brick apartment buildings there. We'd race out after choir straight to Lucky's Burgers around the front. Then horse around on the fire escapes hoping to catch sight of a lady of the night from the third floor." He laughs. "I don't know if there was really a bordello there, or just the imaginations of boys."

When Burton signed up for the Prairie Team, I could tell how much he loved working outside.

"Well, I really wanted to farm," he told me when I queried him.

"Seriously?" I asked. He's so suave it's a little hard to imagine. "Burton, you?"

"Yes. Maxine's Taylor-side farmed for some generations. First land down here, Willowbend Farm they called it. Then moved near Ankeny. It was just a small town then. Don't let on, but Maxine's got some white blood through those people. When Maxine's parents moved to California, it fell to us to help her grandparents who were still on the farm. I was my happiest working weekends there: no envelopes *ad infinitum*; no lines of impatient people; no drunken postmen screwing up their routes. Just air to breathe. But Maxine, no, Maxine she never took to the idea of being a farm wife."

For Burton, putting in prairie where the tenements once stood was like recovering a dream. He and Maxine contributed the grass seed, and the county let him drive the tractor and drill it into the ground.

"What's our plan?" I ask them, stuffing the mischievous foxtails into Marianna's weed satchel. "Give me directions."

"We won't get much done today, I'm afraid. Elena and Jason are bringing fourth graders," Marianna explains. The Prairie Team often hosts school field trips. Received a REAP grant to do so. "Burton's to tell the history of the neighborhood and I'm to introduce them to our native plants. With all this flooding, we've decided to focus on the root system."

"We've got some twine. We'll have the kids cut root lengths," Burton adds. "One inch for lawn grass, three inches for corn, two feet for little bluestem, eight feet for spiderwort.That is, of course, if they don't strangle each other first."

"Here they are!" Marianna plants her shovel and removes her gloves.

Two yellow school buses rumble to a stop. We hear shouts and giggles as nine-year-olds of all shapes and colors explode off the bus and run into the grasses. I see them and the real estate decision punches me in the guts. I doubt the Hotel Savant will be doing much for the neighborhood children.

"You okay?" Marianna asks.

I rub my stomach, "Just a sensitive GI track today," I fib.

"You may as well just get lunch," Marianna says and excuses me. "Little gardening now."

I heave a sigh of relief. I am terribly transparent—one of my greatest strengths and faults. And both Burton and Marianna tend to read me like a book. So, I gladly head to the refuge of my house for a short break. If solitary, I can't spill any beans.

I push into the bungalow and throw my valise with the SansCorps letter in it on the sofa. Until recently, entering the bungalow felt a bit like entering the backroom of an art gallery or antique shop. The previous owner installed wondrous skylights—the reason I bought this house—and the wall space and mantle of my small dwelling has teemed with paintings, prints, and ceramics. A convergence of factors renders me the keeper of the family heirlooms. From seven to ten years older than me, my sisters all have minimalistic, Scandinavian tastes. I am the only one of the four of us that likes old stuff.

That's variable number one. Variable, two, three, and four: our only remaining grandparent, Grandma Helen, finally left the sprawling brick ranch on S. Oneida Way, the same year that my parents decided to downsize and move to Hawaii, the same year I became dean and bought the bungalow. Instead of sorting the sometimes extravagant accumulations of their adult lives, these three realized it was much easier to rent a moving van together and ship it all to me. I really didn't mind. My father has always said, "If you want the finer things in life you have to pay for them," but I have always delighted in obtaining the finer things without paying for them.

And, over the course of my spiritual life, I have come to repeatedly question: what are the finer things anyway? Living alone, it's been a comfort to wrap myself in strands of family identity. Each morning when I wake up, pad into the living room for prayer or to work on a sermon, this item or that brings memories. The house is less lonely.

I get out of my dripping raincoat and go to the kitchen to warm some roasted red pepper soup. I see that my phone machine is blinking. I keep the outdated device for church-related calls mainly. Also family.

"Quirky, it's Bonnie. I guess Grandma's sores have healed enough that she can make the trip after all."

My sister Bonnie still lives in Denver. Except for the three months my grandmother stays with our parents and my uncle on Oahu, Bonnie is her main caregiver. Once a year my sister—we other three call her 'Bonnie the Saint'—puts our grandmother on a plane to visit each of us. Grandma likes autumn in Iowa, before the snow starts.

"I am still not sure the trip is wise," Bonnie on the box continues. Grandma is ninety and mainly gets around in a wheelchair now. "You'll see for yourself how thin and weak she is, but Grandma Helen is adamant. She wants to see you. I e-mailed you the flight details. Make sure you get extra help to get her through the concourse."

My dear, dear, zany grandmother.

I finish the soup and return to the living room, settle on the sofa, and remove the letter.

Dated this 5th day of September

The Hotel Savant desires to enter into conversation with The Cathedral Church of Saint Aidan about purchase of the property:

774 High Street

Lot 47 of Willowbend section

Initial offer: $3,720,000

Dear Lord. Almost four million. I pull up the calculator on my iPhone and rehearse Simon's equation. Even if the board would move to treat it as an endowment, which is probable (Des Moines is so socially liberal but fiscally conservative that *Forbes* magazine even featured the trait) we figured an annual 5 percent draw puts about $186,000 into the operating budget each year. Over two years we could fix the roof, launch a creative communication campaign to attract new members, and raise staff salaries.

Staff salaries? I look across and stare at a blank wall. Or rather, I should say, it stares at me. It has only been an empty square of ivory this week. I think of Grandma Helen coming, and I wince. What graced this spot was one of her most beloved botanical prints: an old German lithograph of edelweiss. At her age she may not notice, especially if I move something new to fill the space. On the other hand, last time she visited she was still so sharp. She'll notice.

I would say our family is a fairly good case study of America's downwardly-mobile middle class. Like a microcosm of the cathedral's struggles. When I didn't enter my father's insurance firm but went instead to seminary, my father wasn't bitter. But he saw the writing on the wall and merged with a national insurance firm that had been courting him. He retired early. But the long and short of it is that the new company pretty much swindled him. After living the high life for decades, my parents have ended up with a very modest retirement income. They moved to Oahu because my mother's brother had a garden apartment they could use. My mother adores her brother and my father puts a good face on things, "Hawaii is living in paradise," and all that. But underneath, we know he feels like a failure. They can hardly afford plane fare to come see us. Grandma could have been more help, except that the cost of assisted living takes everything she has—for life. And hers has stretched out a bit.

Being a priest has been more satisfying than I would have ever imagined, and yet every now and then, I am haunted by guilt. If I had joined the firm, could we have turned it around? At forty-one, I am full of second-guessing. I have large student debt from seminary, too. If I'd gone to law school, I would have some hope of paying it back. But as a priest? Not so much. In a world of real poverty and food insecurity, racial injustice, climate change, and terrorism, I am ashamed by my relatively inconsequential worries. But still, trying to make ends meet both at the cathedral and at home is like trying to tunnel out of prison with a silver spoon.

So, I am selling off the family paintings. Antiques, too. Most are not worth much. Eclectic. Various styles and eras. Art of landscapes and flora dear to my grandparents and parents. Grasses and greenback dollars painted together, one flesh. My sisters don't care if I sell them. But I haven't told my grandmother nor my parents. Now Grandma Helen is coming to visit.

Raises for the staff? I finger the textured letter.

The blank wall stares me down. She will notice it right off! I imagine wheeling her into the living room and Grandma Helen saying, "Where is the edelweiss?"

God, why did I sell that one? One of her favorites, what with our memories of edelweiss. What was I thinking?

God and I both know the answer: it was worth a good price and I had a big student loan payment coming due.

8

EDELWEISS #2

Leontopodium alpinum or edelweiss is a well-known mountain flower of the Asteracceae (daisy or sunflower) family. Each bloom consists of fuzzy, ivory-white petals in a double star formation. Its growth in early season is hard to distinguish from grass. As a scarce short-lived flower found in remote mountain areas, the plant has been used as a symbol for alpinism, and as a national symbol especially of Austria. Scientists underline the fragility of this cold-loving plant in a time of global warming, as cold-adapted mountain plant species are gradually replaced with warm-adapted species.

–Note from Dean Brigid Brenchley's Prairie Journal

On Either Side of 1965, When the Movie Premiered in Denver, Colorado

In reality, before my hands ever read the nodes of grass like braille, or bent a meaty shoot of sedge, the weave of living things was planted in my imagination by art. Children's literature and movie matinees were like shovel and spade. The earliest green strands of all were lines of flowing words on a page, swirls of film on a movie reel, ribbons of notes running across a musical score, carried to me by my mother Marilyn and her mother, Grandma Helen. These earliest plants were pussy willow, nasturtiums, and, of course, edelweiss.

Consciousness cut through sleep like a canoe pushing into still water, and I had a book in my chubby arms. My favorite book: *Pussywillow*. My post-nap cheek imprinted with the pattern of the hobnail bedspread, and white, John Singer Sergeant type light cascading through sheer curtains, my grandmother sat reading.

"Again, Granma?"

"You don't think that kitten is getting tired?" Grandma Helen asked, looking over her reading glasses. "So many conversations with the goose this afternoon?"

Grandma Helen left *Doctor Zhivago* on the chair in the sunlight.

At this stage of life, Grandma Helen was large but still striking. In appearance and style she resembled Myrna Loy in *The Thin Man* movies. She was dressed in a silk robe and a hair turban reminiscent of her days as a flapper. Plumeria wafted over me, as if Hawaii just got on the bed, and I pushed the cardboard golden book into my grandmother's hands. This was no ordinary golden book: when stroked, both the fluffy catkins and the kitten on the book's cover were soft to the touch. It is the story of a kitten that gets lost in a pond-side environment and somehow gains its name by discovering pussy willow.

On another day, my face was hot to the touch from a fever. My mother cradled me on her lap and read to me from a woven peach-colored volume of *Winnie-the-Pooh* given to her as a kindergartner on Feb. 2, 1937. She was in a terrycloth robe about the hue of the Milne book. My mother was all about peach and coral, in clothes, lipstick, and nail polish. With mousier features and light-brown hair, she felt unlovely next to her stylish, jazz-age mother. But she was lovely in her way, especially in peach, and she did smell lovely... of bath talc and Channel No. 5. She was the only one in my family who really practiced religion. She had been moved by a clergyman involved in civil rights in Topeka around the time of Brown v. the Board of Education, and she kept a small leather Bible next to her bedside. It was even more worn than the *Winnie-the-Pooh* volume. Mother sang in the Episcopal church choir, and, on this day tending me and my fever, her rich, melodic voice placed Piglet in my consciousness. Piglet, the muse of growing things: haycorns to eat, violets to cheer up Eeyore, and the mysterious nasturtiums.

Nasturtiums were not even an image or a concept but simply a beloved sound for something that grows.

"Christopher Robin gave me a mastershalum seed, and I planted it, and I am going to have mastershalums all over the front door," said Pooh.

"I thought they were called nasturtiums," Piglet said timidly.

But these books, with their garden aesthetics, were just precursors to The Movie, my first movie.

Almost every Saturday Grandma Helen took my older sisters to a matinee. Denver boasted some very large and elegant movie houses indeed. When it opened in 1961, The Cooper Cinema had the biggest movie screen in the world and was only one of ten Cinerama theaters in existence—theater screens designed to wrap halfway around the audience.

I held my Coke and settled in. The faux velvet of the movie seat was almost as comfy as my mother's and grandmother's laps. With the most gentle of orchestral sound, the screen filled with feathery cirrus clouds. My feather-light, three-year-old self was transported high in the air, and then taken in descending flight like a falcon, down, down. First, the peaks and snowy caps of the glacial zone became visible through the clouds ...then appeared the montane zone of granite outcrops and slopes of pine, ash, beech and oak with a blue expanse of water at their base.

Finally, Ted McCord and academy award-winning photographers and photo editors found their subject: a spinning Julie Andrews.

I quietly gasped and reached for a fold of Grandma Helen's mink coat, "Granma," I nudged, "She's as big as three yous!"

"Quirky, *Shhh!*" my sisters said in unison, glaring at me over their row of knee-socks.

Tilting back, I tried to absorb this gigantic screen full of grass. I was barely three feet in height, and upon that thirty-eight-foot high Cooper screen the twirling Maria was fourteen feet tall. A hundred-foot wide expanse of green grasses with almost imperceptible ivory and yellow flowers surrounded the audience on three sides. Green. Everywhere I looked. Left. Green. Right. Green. Straight ahead. Green. Up. Green. Okay, down was brown and dark and sticky with popcorn. But otherwise, filaments of green were growing everywhere. I was heady with the grass. So was Maria. She was spinning and spinning.

The scene, shot on-site in Austria, occurred at nearly the same altitude as Denver. But any native Colorado child immediately discerned that these were not our mountains. For the Rockies, though equally majestic and punctuated with aspen and pine and the occasional meadow, are most basically tan and terracotta-colored, sandy and rocky. With double the annual precipitation, Maria's mountains wore a refined robe of European grasses and wildflowers.

Grandma Helen, who had been to Austria and Switzerland on a botanical tour, after the movie explained to us that in modern languages the term *alp*, *alm*, *albe*, or *alpe* actually refers to the mountain pasture where cows graze in the summer, not the mountain peaks like most Americans think. If the cameramen had zoomed in for a close-up on the strands below Maria's dancing feet, they would have magnified the stuff the Alps are really named for: perennial grasses, legumes (like the Austrian pea), cushion plants, lichen and mosses, trumpet-like blue gentian, magenta alpine carnation, rusty alpine rose, yellow arnica, glacier buttercups, and of course, the edelweiss that

Captain Von Trapp loves. She showed us the photos, and I thought the edelweiss looked like a vanilla-starred dandelion. Tilting back, at those proportions, it was a lot to take in at age three. "Granma," I asked, "Who is she dancing for?"

My sisters again glowered at me, fingers to their lips.

"Dancing for?" Grandma Helen asked. She paused and pondered so long that I thought maybe my sisters had cowed our grandmother and she wouldn't answer.

Finally she whispered back, "God, I suppose." A lapsed-Irish-Catholic-turned-Episcopalian, Grandma Helen said, "I think she is dancing for God."

The next minute on the screen, my grandmother's idea seemed confirmed: Maria stopped her twirling and bowed her head. There on the mountain she appeared to be in deep communion—presumably with the One whom Grandma called God. From deep inside I thought I knew *whom* my grandmother meant. Then the bells from the convent in Salzburg rang out and scattered Maria's prayer. Maria left her holy mountain and ran to the good sisters below.

Newspaper magnate and theater patron "Dame" Helen Bonfils—as locals fondly called her—printed an exciting announcement in *The Denver Post*: the following summer the community musical production in Cheesman Park would be *The Sound of Music*. Bonfils and the organizers converted three outdoor swimming pools into sets and seating.

The biggest news? Children from across the city were invited to audition—one simply had to rehearse a song, bring a parent or guardian, and come to The Browne Palace Hotel on a certain Saturday.

I was such a natural born ham, everyone in the family agreed that I should try out for Gretel. Grandma Helen first learned to play piano as a girl in her Irish American, Kansas City enclave, when parlor singing was at its height. As young adults Barney drove Helen around in a car with bullet holes that they won together in a dance marathon. They roved the speakeasies and all-night jazz clubs of Kansas City to hear players like Charlie "Bird" Parker. The jazz musicians had inspired her style and Grandma Helen still played with flare. Her long fingernails and multi-faceted amethyst ring added percussive clicks and clunks, especially way down the bass clef.

"Raindrops on roses, and whiskers on kiddens," I sang.

"Try to say the 't' in kitten," Mom coached, "it's not a 'd'..."

"Brown paper packages ...all tied in strings...these are a few of my favorite things," I continued.

Grandma Helen joined in to give some drama to the interpretation. She had done a lot of musical theater as a younger woman, too. "When the dog *bites*, when the bee *stings*," she emphasized. Then she stopped and turned, glass fobs dangling. "You have a sweet voice and get the notes just right. But make it bigger!"

"RAINDROPS," I sang-yelled.

"No, no. Not louder, bigger." Grandma Helen stopped playing, musing how to explain. "You want your voice to fill the room," she said and stretched out her arms. "Imagine someone you love, like maybe Grandpa, sitting way in the back seats. And you want your voice to carry the song to him—like a birthday present."

I pondered that. "Then not the kitten song. If I'm giving it to Grandpa. I want to sing the mountain song."

My mother and grandmother looked at me blankly—probably because every song in *The Sound of Music* seemed to them the mountain song.

"The one the beautiful, grouchy man sings. It makes him cry. You know, he sings it, and then they run from the bad guys, and then the mountain saves them."

The women still looked confused. So I had to sing it:

"Small and white... clean and bright."

Quickly, Grandma Helen flipped the music on the piano to *Edelweiss.*

We practiced that song. As I sang, I remembered the green

on all sides and inside me—the grass and the mountains and the ivory-starred dandelions. I sang like I was giving Maria's mountain to Grandpa Barney. I pictured him beaming, hands open to receive the gift. Grandpa loved the mountains more than anything. Mom and Grandma nodded and smiled.

I had been to The Browne Palace Hotel once before. As a toddler I had circled it in the back seat of our second car, my mother's De Soto, on a most notable occasion: my mother drove my giggling sisters and friends, pursuing the Beatles' limousine. Very like in *A Hard Day's Night*, these girls—who were all mini-skirts, eyelashes, and legs—eventually pushed out of the De Soto to chase John, Paul, George, and Ringo into The Browne Palace. I stood, chubby hands pressed against the car window, watching teenagers stream by.

From the outside, the seven-story red stone structure of downtown Denver's historic hotel was a triangular block, anchoring the three-way corner of Broadway, Tremont and 17th streets. The exterior was really rather plain, and this was my first time inside. As Grandma Helen and Mom led me through the revolving glass doors, the rough exterior gave way to a mesmerizing lobby. It was like cracking open a geode! Designed by the dean of Denver architecture, Frank Edbrook, the atrium of The Browne was like a seven-tiered tea rose. Light filtered down through the geometric stained glass of the ceiling, bathing the 12,400 square feet of swirled onyx in gold light.

Despite my tomboy leanings, I had consented to don a dotted-Swiss green dress with a lacey apron, and from the minute we crossed the threshold, it was obvious I was not alone. The seven tiers of the Browne's lobby had become a *living* rose, for ascending up the grand staircase and around and around each level of the atrium—outfitted in frilly dresses, louden-colored socks, and *lieder hosen,* with their musical scores under their arms and adoring adults at their sides—were hundreds if not thousands of children! It was like one huge Chinese dragon of Denver's youngest citizens, all eager to sing. It took hours, and hours—with people taking lunch shifts at the Ship's Tavern or even an extra break for high-dollar high tea in the lobby café below.

Grandma Helen looked up the staircase and laughed out loud, "I don't think I have ever seen so many children together in one space in all my life!" She and Mom exchanged a glance, "It's the Von Trapp family reproducing like rabbits."

Grandma Helen looked down toward me. "I bet your whole school is here, Quirky. Do you see anyone you know?"

In fact, I did. My gaze drifted down from the mesmerizing ceiling, and I spotted a neighbor friend hanging on the bannister a few spaces up. There was also an impish boy, probably trying to land the part of Kurt, who sent a paper airplane at me from three floors up. Suddenly this felt like the biggest birthday party ever.

Mostly, the whole day was heady, exciting, fun. However, at one point I stared ahead at the trail of children and parents edging up the grand staircase, and realized something was profoundly wrong. Where was the grass? Where were the small daisy-like flowers? Most importantly, where were Maria's mountains? How in the world could they try to make *The Sound of Music* without the grasses and the mountain where Maria meets God?

I might have tried to extricate myself from Gretel's lace, right then, except that it was now nearly my turn to audition. With tired knees and head, I ascended all those onyx steps to sing *Edelweiss* to a very weary looking man in a bow tie behind a grand piano. Suddenly, this was not Grandma Helen and her clicking ring in the basement, with an open box of Russell Stover's candy. This was a proper theater audition, with a kind enough but erudite stranger in seersucker trousers. I felt slightly nauseated, staring wide-eyed at him. His smile was frozen and he was surely in pain as he nodded for me to begin. I tried to fill myself up with green. I tried to imagine the mountain, and the ivory stars of edelweiss, and how much Grandpa Barney would love it. But I just kept seeing this strange man who was waiting behind the ivories. My voice came out like the rasping of two china teacups rubbed together in the atrium, and about as thin as that fine porcelain. I sang, and he handed me back my score with a wan smile. My mother took my hand and we left.

But the beautiful thing was it didn't really matter. I lived in a child's universe, where the moment of knowing—Boy, I did not sing as well as I did in Grandma's house—was forgotten almost the moment it was thought. At home I got to tell my older sisters about the millions of children, and the chocolate crème puffs for tea, and about the cute boy's paper airplane that circumnavigated three levels of lobby. Once we descended the grand staircase, I never worried once about not getting a callback to be Gretel. After all, no play could match the sheer fun of just auditioning at The Browne Palace with Grandma Helen and Mom as my coaches. Besides, once I'd got the true picture, the whole enterprise seemed flawed: the play was to be performed in Cheesman Park. Cheesman Park! I had been to Cheesman Park. Sure there was a lot of Denver lawn there, but not a mountain, nor any edelweiss in sight.

9
SWITCHGRASS

Panicum virgatum L. or switchgrass is common on wet to
moist prairies; also on roadsides, stream banks, and other
moist open places. Grows in big, leafy clumps. Flowers
are borne singly at the end of the branches; grain is hard
and bony. The leafy clumps last through the winter,
though dead, and their yellow color provides a touch of
brightness on dark rainy days.

–Note from Dean Brigid Brenchley's Prairie Journal

Tuesday Afternoon and Evening

My life is always tangled up with the grass...even on the air!
I muse as I stand watching myself on television. The large TV
is ludicrously big for the bungalow. It was a gift from a woman
physician parishioner thrilled to have a woman priest. She had it
delivered on my first Christmas as dean. Despite my house being
filled to the gills, I cleared a space next to my Hartford chest,
and I confess that after long days of pastoral rounds I regularly
collapse into the screen's massive, imaginative arms. But now, on

the shiny broad expanse I am face-to-face with myself.

It is ten o'clock and time for the Channel 13 news. The virtual me being interviewed is not the size of Julie Andrews on the Cooper Cinerama screen—thank you Jesus—but is almost as large as the flesh-and-blood me watching and drinking a glass of merlot to calm my nerves. I am back home after a stressful afternoon and evening.

I could easily lose ten pounds, but decide I look reasonably attractive for forty plus. Yet, what matters is that the prairie plants framing me on every side are stunning! Indian grass and switchgrass fan their graceful plumes beneath the church's bell tower, various sunflowers and pearly everlastings are beginning to bloom in profusion. I am filled with awe to see it.

But my ears are not pleased by the interview. As it unfolds on the screen, angst unfurls in my stomach.

Who knows who might be watching? Well, I guess You may know... The mayor, the bishop, a million different parishioners! Phil?

I sip the merlot. Considering the afternoon and evening I've had, I need a drink! And the newsreel has me reliving all that's happened in the hours since I last sat on my couch with the Hotel Savant letter and missing Grandma's Edelweiss print.

Crossing the Des Moines River driving toward Henry's favorite fishing spot, I see muddy fingers grope the top edge of the earthen banks, and the water's usually placid flow is galloping along. In fact, when I reach Henry's Riverside Park, the spot where we said we would rendezvous literally doesn't exist. The river has jumped its banks here. A few picnic tables stand, knee deep in water, their benches invisible. Swallows fly in figure eights around them as if analyzing potential real estate.

No Henry. No Nicholas. No fishing poles.

I drive north just a bit to where the river is still contained in its banks. The water is so level with their top edges it looks like

I could just walk across. Still no grandfather and little boy. I find a pull off, look up and down the river, and decide to call Merlin.

"I don't see Henry here..."

"Didn't you get my message?" he replies, a little annoyed. I see now that I have a voicemail alert. "Henry says the river is too dangerous for Nick. He actually sounded shook up. Said, ironically, they'd have to take a rain check."

"The river has even left its bank at Riverside Park, no buildings to bother, but foreboding nonetheless. Remember how you circled Marshland at the COAD meeting... well, I am seeing the threat up close. Okay, I will just head back to the cathedral soon."

"Since you're in the vicinity, can you pop into the Marshland Bakery and bring some cream puffs back to the office?"

"Of course."

Merlin generally watches his diet...but Marshland cream puffs are one of his downfalls.

I stand outside the car for a little while gazing at the river, slightly disappointed not to fish. I rub my forehead. I can see that Henry's a wise grandfather: the crests of the waves are like horses shaking their manes and it is way too easy to imagine a little boy like Nicholas losing his footing just to have his small frame tossed around by those white-capped steeds. Maybe dragged under. Henry and Pearl, as well as Nicholas' family, live in houses not far from Riverside Park.

Lord, is the water this high and fast in the Jones' neighborhood too? I see why the engineers at the COAD are worried. I'm worried too. Then a car putters up. It's Henry and Nicholas.

"You stay in the car," Henry tells Nick, in his factory foreman's voice.

The little boy slumps, arms hanging out the car window, a pout practically disfiguring his face.

"Brigid. I was afraid Merlin might not get you the message... sorry for the wasted trip."

Henry turns to face the river. If the reservoir engineer is worried, and I'm worried, Henry absorbs the state of this waterway next to which he has lived for about fifty years with true cause for worry.

"Confess I don't like the look of it..." he shakes his head, "that last flood was bad, and this looks like her sister." The older man gestures toward the boy, "After all those light bulbs, Nicholas feels gypped. I promised him some fishing." Then a twinkle returns to Henry's eyes. "But I have an idea—Madge Chase has told me for years to come to her horse pond. Says there are bass there. Maybe we make a 'pastoral call' to Madge after her stint in the hospital and ask to fish too?"

"Henry, it's a great idea! Merlin knows my calendar and can help set it up. And, I have another idea..."

I walk over to the car where Nicholas and Fido the oxygen machine share a seat. "I'm bummed about the fishing, too."

"Grandpa said..."

"But I have to go to the Marshland Bakery and get cream puffs for Merlin. Want to come? If we can't catch fish we can at least eat donuts."

Nick pulls up his dangling depressed arms and smiles, "Grandpa, can we?"

"Treats are on me," I say.

"Then what are we waiting for?" Henry nods.

Back at the cathedral, Merlin and I do some proofing of Sunday worship bulletins. The cream puffs make the tedious task more festive. Then, I change out of my fishing togs and into a clerical collar and slacks, and before I know it the TV-13 team arrives.

Waiting for me is a middle-aged television reporter named Aaron Vandermann. I recognize him. I am guessing at this stage in life he would rather be a news anchor instead of covering irritating little stories like this one. He is nicely tan, but has hair a little too blond, cut a little too short, such that you're not quite sure what's hair and what's scalp. The expression on his face is a thinly veiled sneer. I try not to let that throw me as he centers me with him in the cameraman's frame.

"Rolling," the head behind the camera says.

"Why would anyone want to plant a prairie downtown? In the financial district?" Aaron Vandermann asks me.

Now my brain races. The question and his tone confirm the sneer I had hoped I was only imagining. Moreover, Max Chase said these exact words to me when the architects and I presented the vision to the parish. Verbatim. Chase. Word for word.

"We see it more as returning the land to its earlier state, rather than planting," I reply.

I'm rattled at this launch. But a breeze makes the switchgrass, goldenrod, and fading liatris sway all around us. The switchgrass tops are like the feathery tops of sparklers; elegant, exploding bits of flora. Realizing they are centered in the camera's frame too, I pray:

May the beauty of the grasses come across to people, wherever this thing goes.

"In Iowa's land between the Missouri and Mississippi Rivers," I hear my voice explain, "for almost a thousand years tall grasses and wildflowers reigned." Imagining it, my mind fills with green paintbrush strokes, like a richly textured abstract painting. Maybe a Rothko. A Rothko green. "But when European settlers arrived, we began to tear it out, to plant crops. Corn. Soybeans. Corn." The green-stroked canvas quickly fills with yellow squares. "We roll out highways and parking lots." Rothko Green turns to Rothko Yellow-Maroon-Green inside my mind. "Today, just one/one-thousandth of our original prairie remains."

Vandermann looks a bit impressed with my rhetoric, but goes in a new direction, "Do I understand that your cathedral has received money from the Department of Natural Resources?"

I nod. I am proud of our partners.

"Isn't the use of government funds a basic breach of the division of Church and State?" Vandermann asks. "Should taxpayers fund a church landscape?"

Now I get a bit angry. We are all part of the city and many of us have left behind old notions of compartmentalized citizenry. I think of the raging river. I think of Merlin and I and other clergy up at dawn to attend COAD meetings. We are all one fabric.

"This prairie is small, but we keep thirty swimming pools of water out of the Des Moines River every year," I tell the camera. Then I look more pointedly at Vandermann. " I imagine you are reporting on the fact—even today— that our river is jumping its banks just north of downtown? I'd say this small prairie is a great investment of public money."

I am persuading myself. I have lost land before; I don't want to lose this patch.

"Well, if we're speaking of investments. Does your church care about unemployment, hunger? I understand you have a feeding program in your basement. This is prime real estate! What about economic development and new jobs? Isn't that of more help to people than grass?"

Economic development...

Shit. The Hotel Savant offer. Is SansCorps... behind this? Now I have little doubt.

Sweet Jesus, the reporter knows, doesn't he?

10
WINTER WHEAT

Triticum aestivum or winter wheat was brought to Kansas by German-Russian Mennonites—it transformed the high plains. Who thinks about the fact that wheat is grass? Of the fifteen crops that stand between us and starvation, ten of them are grasses.

–Note from Dean Brigid Brenchley's Prairie Journal

Section 7 & 8, Emmett Township, Norton, KS, April 1970

For my paternal grandfather, Floyd Brenchley, grasses were not the lace around recreation, nor were they *objet d'art;* they were sustenance. It was with Grandpa Floyd that I learned that grasses are edible.

In stature and style, no one could have been more different from Grandpa Barney. Whereas Barney was short and wiry, Floyd was over six feet tall with long limbs. He had a tanned, serious face of sun-and-wind-induced wrinkles, and a forehead chalky white from years under a round-brimmed Stetson. My paternal grandparents lived on a wheat farm near Norton, Kansas. I have a treasured photo of Floyd and me when I was an elementary kid. His lanky arm is draped around my auburn strands and we are dressed in identical blue overalls—except that mine have hippy embroidered flowers. He was both bemused and amused that a ten-year-old girl from the city would don bib-denims. He pulled me a little awkwardly to his side for the photo, and he smelled like sunlight and starch and the tang of chewing tobacco.

Whereas Grandpa Barney's mouth was central to his personality—from it proceeded jokes, rollicking laughter, a whistle, a grin—Floyd's mouth sort of disappeared into his face, perhaps due to lack of use. He spoke instead through actions and through his eyes. They were a foggy-blue color like the water of the English Channel from whence the Brenchleys originated. There was often a pensive, faraway look to them—the eyes of a midwestern sea captain who had stared too long across the swells of grain and seen men drown in their depths.

Why exactly Grandpa Floyd's forbears left the Brenchley Sons-of-the-American-Revolution identity to homestead on the Great Plains isn't documented, but we ennoble ourselves with the likely story that we were "Free-Staters" called to cultivate Kansas and keep it out of the hands of slave-owners. We do know that soon after she arrived from New England, Floyd's grandmother was hit by lightning while pulling clothes off a line. We also know that her son, Grandpa's handsome fiddle-playing father, abandoned his wife and two tiny children. Floyd was three and his sister a baby. Then the Dust Bowl struck. Any trace of blue blood New England identity withered and blew away. My Grandfather Floyd's life was much more like that portrayed in the ballads of Woody Guthrie than of a long-lost descendant of the first governor of Vermont.

Grandpa Floyd married Grandma Jennie. Her real name from her Friesland immigrant parents was *Tishka Rypkema*—but from day one this practical girl of four feet ten inches demanded the appellation "Jennie." When they married in 1925, the harvests were good, and metal implements were easing the labor. But by 1933 the wheat harvests were the lowest on record, the worst in thirty-eight years. My grandparents ended up saying farewell to more than half of Jennie's first-generation-Dutch siblings who headed west to Paradise, California, to pick fruit and survive. The Brenchleys stayed.

In the worst years of the Dust Bowl, my grandparents would search for the silvery-green leaves of lambs quarters surviving in the shade of locust trees. They would cut, boil, salt, and consume them. It is only now, at seventy-plus years, that my father, Floyd and Jennie's only child, can enjoy spinach—so akin is its taste to that tenacious weed that helped keep them from starving.

Perhaps it was the memories of the Dust Bowl that floated behind Grandpa Floyd's gaze. Or, perhaps, it was the wreckage of his marriage. Floyd and Jennie mainly stayed apart. They slept separately. Grandma in a hot frilly bedroom near the kitchen, and Grandpa on a three season porch made bedroom full of muddy work boots and coat trees of coveralls. The reason given was his love of sleeping in the cold, but it was obvious even to a child that their relations were frosty. Together they looked about as happy as the couple in Grant Wood's famous *American Gothic*.

However, by the time of my childhood the Great Depression was long over and Floyd and Jennie were living proof of The New Deal and the Agricultural Adjustment Act. They were empowered to purchase a half-section of land. Moreover, they paid off the fifty-year mortgage in six years. They lived in a ship-shape, white farmhouse trimmed in forest green. We thrilled when its form, book-ended by cottonwoods, graced the horizon as we crested the hill on Rural Route 3 north of Highway 36. There was also a sizable, blood-red barn and numerous red out-buildings: the tractor shed, the chicken coop, the low-slung building crawling with kittens and their mothers. Dust no longer choked the air and blew under the doors. In those boom days before the eighties farm crisis, what the wind tossed back and forth were golden acres of wheat.

Just as my out-of-sync age had me riding with Grandpa Barney to favorite trout-fishing hideaways, the need to find something for this caboose-child to do often found me in his red

Ford pickup riding around with Grandpa Floyd. My memories of those rides have a recurring pattern: *one,* Grandpa Floyd stops the pickup and gets out to silently gaze; *two,* I get out my side or jump out from the truck's bed and gaze as well, with no comprehension of the object; *three,* finally I either ask or he offers an explanation about the object of our attention.

In one such recollection, we were returning from eastern Kansas and the object of our interest was some especially plump and green sweet corn.

"I love corn, with lots of butter! But sometimes it gets stuck in my teeth," I said to him. "Do you grow corn on the farm?"

"Corn's the fattest grass. It often makes the wallets of the farmers fat, too." Grandpa and I both noted the black earth and size of the nearby modern farmhouse. "We put in a few acres. But corn's a thirsty crop. Not much rain in Norton County. We do dry-land farming. For us, it's the wheat—turkey red and scout and parker. We owe *that* to the Russians—they brought us winter wheat. And of course we have the cows.They eat the grasses that grow on these plains. But, mainly, it's the wheat."

The Brenchleys kept about a dozen dairy cows—white Holsteins for milk, smaller brown Jerseys or Guernseys for cream, and fifty beef cattle. I can see a small group of Marcel Marceau faced cows following my grandfather into the corral as the sun was setting—a line of shadows like a German woodcut. The herd of Herefords would wade knee-high in grass between fields.

Today, ranching gourmets seek to turn the grasslands north of Norton into a kind of Napa or Sonoma, recovering the nearly lost art of grass finishing by capturing the tastes of little bluestem or sage or side oats in the meat. Then, I only knew that the hamburger on the farm was lighter and sweeter than the cellophaned stuff we bought in Denver.

Yes, I realize now that farming was Grandfather Floyd's trade, his area of expertise, and he would take time, standing beside his pickup, analyzing what others were doing. We all knew that he distrusted the locust-like oil pumps that were beginning to dot the landscape. My father with his interest in the finer things urged some test drilling. But Grandpa Floyd declined. It didn't help my father's cause that the neighbors had started "thumping for oil"—a portly father and son who owned most of the surrounding land but refused to sell any of it to the Brenchleys. I intuitively didn't like them for their farmstead was dotted with abandoned vehicles.

"Besides," Floyd said, "the Texans already have three times as many cattle as anyone else. These oil companies come up north like buzzards—like the wheat fields are dying."

On the other hand, he seemed to like sunflowers. I remember he took our whole family out to see a nearby field of hybrid sunflowers. Their yellow-bonneted flower faces were turned toward the sun and were filled with edible seeds. It was an innovative idea by a young hippy-farmer who had moved back from Oregon to try farming on his grandparents' land. You could tell the new crop positively enthralled my grandfather. I even think he smiled. This was a creative variation on the growers' theme and not some dirty departure like the oil wells.

But, there was one, interminable, chin-scratching pause at the edge of a field. I could tell it was a moment of both levity and gravity. My father stood, dressed in a Denver Broncos running suit, pushing the blond hair from his eyes to look into the sun. He whistled. He and Grandpa Floyd were riveted by a first-time encounter with a large center-pivot irrigator. To me it looked as alien as the despised oil pumps, and I stayed in the truck for a while, immobilized by an uncanny sense of dread. To a little girl it seemed massive, like an iron centipede that walked, spreading water. Nonetheless, I could see clearly the source of the men's fascination. While the soybeans across the road were lower to the ground and brown in places, the irrigation contraption left in its wake emerald circles of almost-perfect crops. I believe in that moment I observed in my grandfather simultaneous awe and consternation. As he stood, Stetson in hand, rubbing his white brow, I believe he knew that he stood with humanity on an ethical threshold.

I have one last memory, when what my Grandfather Brenchley stood and gazed at in the field was me. In the fields nearest the farmhouse, I ran and danced in the waving winter wheat. Often the wind in Norton was strong and one-directional as if the Creator had a huge blow-dryer aimed across the plains. But this day there was just enough breeze to tussle the wheat—cool, frisky and rhythmic, and my body followed suit. The sunlight, the new green strands, and the benevolence of the weather released all my inhibitions and I danced. The early wheat played gently about my shins and knees, akin to seaweed in the ocean. Like the green strands, I was moving, moving, free.

My grandfather must have been sent to find me for dinner. As he rarely spoke, I am not sure how I was drawn from my earth-trance to see his lanky form. I had surely been a laughable spectacle.

To cover my embarrassment, I said, "I was practicing square dance, like you and Grandma did the other night. Would I do a 'do-se-do' when I swing up the line?"

My Kansas grandfather's gaze communicated a pleased understanding. His whole life had been a kind of waltz with the edible grasses of the prairie. That was a year or two before they had to sell the farm.

"Chassé," he said in all earnestness. "I am pretty sure it would be a Chassé."

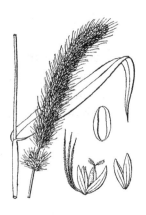

11
FOXTAIL

Setaria faberi or giant foxtail grass is a perennial plant that likes disturbed areas. The inflorescence is a long awned, nodding spike with shimmering greenish or purplish coloring. Once established, foxtail is extremely difficult to eradicate and in some countries it is considered a weed. Somehow it keeps sneaking across the street from the insurance complex to infiltrate and harass our little bluestem.

–Note from Dean Brigid Brenchley's Prairie Journal

Wednesday Morning

Dismayed by the interview, I click off the TV and fall into a favorite Ward wingback chair. It has raised, tactilely interesting maple leaves and the high back hugs me safe in Iowa winters. I wonder—will I have to sell this chair before Christmas? How else can I swing the flight to Hawaii to see my parents? Exhausted, and with a little wine on board, I have just enough energy to reach for the small Christ the Vine icon that waits on the lampstand, the twin sister of the one at my office.

"I am the vine, you are the branches."

On the background of rippling gold, Jesus from the vine offers his benediction. For a moment, I gaze at the forlorn-looking apostles in the boat feeling I am one with them on the watery chaos. A Mystical Theology professor at Northwestern taught us to simply open our gaze when praying with icons. "It is then," he said, "the Risen One gazes upon us. We are the object of this deep communion with the Divine."

I hope this is true as I nod off in the chair, cradling the icon.

I have only slept about three hours when the phone rouses me. The digital clock reads 3:17 a.m.

"Oh, God." I say to myself and hit the speaker button.

A familiar computer voice, "This is PDT Security Services." Loud static. "We are reporting a burglar alarm at St. Aidan's Cathedral. 755 High Street. Will you respond?"

"Again?" I shake my head in dismay to disperse the sleep cobwebs, "Yes, yes. I'll respond."

I reach for the clerical collar I'd removed and placed on the lampstand, and knock over the remnant of merlot.

Soaking up the spill with a nearby tea towel, I more fall onto the floor than kneel. *Protect the cathedral. Anyone inside. May it be nothing. Oh...and keep me from alcoholism and wine stains on the carpet.*

I drive in a quasi-zombie state downtown. Living in the near, old brick suburbs, where the trolley line ended in 1910, it takes me eight minutes flat to get to St. Aidan's in nice weather—twelve minutes crawling through an Iowa blizzard. The mottled, ivory bark of the sycamore trees of the boulevards are luminescent in my headlights and almost lull me back to sleep.

A young PDT security guard with a flashlight meets me on the west cathedral steps. St. Aidan's threshold feels like the gangplank of a Victorian ocean liner. I often feel like a sea captain working with a small band to steer the grand old vessel ever so slightly toward The Light, trying to avoid the fate of the Titanic. The security guard points the flashlight at the substantial double doors, wooden and glossy red with swirled ironwork hinges.

"This is the door where the alarm got tripped."

Together we push through. Inside, the air is a delicious chocolate color. The guard silently leads and we inch into the lofty interior of the nAvenue Ivory slabs of light from surrounding office buildings come cascading down from the rose window. One hundred and sixty years of dust dance in the splintered rays. I almost forget to be scared.

We move slowly down the center aisle. The guard throws a beam with his flashlight down each pew: left side, then right. Then the next pew, left side, then right. Nothing.

We approach the altar area and the guard's light catches the crucifix suspended there. St. Aidan's cross carries a humble, human Jesus whose arms stretch out like a sheltering elm. At Holy Communion it is as if we gather under limbs of the Real Presence. Moving cautiously up the few marble stairs, I can tell my adrenaline is high: the pads of my toes sense the polished stone through my shoes, and I am acutely aware of the jangling of the guard's keys.

We hear a slight stir. Stop in our tracks. The guard's beam crisscrosses the dark, and then lands on a figure bundled under the altar itself, wrapped in a blanket and some material like burlap. I can just make out the profile. It's Delilah.

Usually quarrelsome, like many of us, Delilah looks sweeter as she sleeps, her mouth slightly open. One of our transitory members, she lives in Des Moines from May to October, and we let her claim St. Aidan's as her summer mailing address. Delilah suffers from bouts of paranoia and hates the shelters. I let out my breath and reach down to gently shake her.

"Delilah."

Delilah moves onto all fours and throws off the burlap. About sixty, she is wiry and has leaves in her afro.

"Delilah. How did you get in here? I've told you before, Merlin's told you a million times: you can't sleep here. What's—"

"You know why!" Delilah says. The shelter has expelled her repeatedly for breaking the smoking rules.

"Well, you can't smoke in here either," I tell her. "Burn down this old church and they'll be hunting you like hounds. Delilah, if you keep breaking and entering, I'll have to call the real police."

"You call yourself a woman of the cloth? Don't you read the Psalms?" Delilah shakes herself awake by shaking her fist at me. Her volume increases like an orator. Her father was a minister— Episcopalian with a Pentecostal twist—somewhere in Kentucky. "*And I shall dwell in the house of the Lord all the days of my life.* That's what I was peacefully doing, until you bothered me! Dwelling in God's house. How am I supposed to follow when you lock the doors?!"

A dwelling place for Delilah. Economic development. I hear Vandermann's words as I look at her shielded under the arms of the Jesus elm.

Lord, would money invested in a downtown hotel ever reach someone like Delilah? Make her lot in life easier?

"Shall I escort her out?" The PDT guard asks. I am fiercely tired, painfully tired, and I contemplate just letting him deal with her. But the cathedral clock chimes four o'clock.

"No. I know her well. I'll help her find somewhere to sleep." We three walk out together.

"Delilah," I say, "Let me take you to the shelter in my car."

"Hell."

Now I am getting annoyed.

"That place is Hell," she continues, "You'd send me to Hell."

"It has beds and showers."

"People googling through the shower curtains, bedbugs in the mattress, I'm sleeping in *Paradisio*. Dante. You read it? Not purgatory. Not hell." She still has the burlap piece and I realize it is one of our grass seed bags from the garden torn to fit. "You want to deliver me to Hell! But if you're going to kick me out of God's House, I'm sleeping in Paradise out back. Even if the vaults of heaven are open like the days of Noah. About to wipe us away. Call yourself a woman of the cloth!"

A triangular tail of burlap dragging behind her, she moves toward the prairie. I nip into my office and grab two long-forgotten coats left by parishioners and follow her. The prairie will be water-logged and chilly, but I can't let her sleep alone.

My ears awaken to an orchestra tuning before the performance. A bus on High Street rumbles and fills the air like a bassoon. From the freeway a cluster of car horns debate like clarinets. Moving stiletto heels—a drum solo on pavement. A few human voices, over the top, words imperceptible. A man laughs. All filtered through the gauze of the prairie. Farmers swear that in August you can hear the corn growing at night and, as the sun clambers through an opening between buildings, the geo-phonics of the prairie itself whisper underneath it all: stems crack like dried shells and seed heads ripple like tissue-paper with the breeze. From my cocoon of green, I listen to the city starting its day.

When I finally open my eyes, I see a robin bathing in a puddle near the iron bench on which I am curled, droplets lapping down its wings. A rabbit moves through the grass, periodically chewing. Delilah, who was sleeping on a bench across from me, has gone. Probably to the Catholic Worker House for breakfast. The powdery, peppery smell from a nearby patch of prairie sage tingles my nostrils, though in my just awake trance-like state I see clearly that foxtail grass, very invasive, is sneaking its way in amidst the sage. I'll have to alert Marianna or better yet weed the patch this morning. I pull in the saged air and turn onto my back. The pinnacle of the Chase Building is impressive at this angle, all granite against topaz. *Ouch.* It has been a long time since I slept outdoors.

As if from nowhere a mug appears, coffee laced with milk, in cathedral china, and I pull up onto my elbows. Merlin holds two mugs steaming in the morning light and sits down.

Letting the steam from his mug curl up toward his nose before sipping, he turns his large, discerning eyes on me. "Delilah?"

I nod and take in the warm coffee gratefully. "3:17 a.m."

"Her schedule painfully resembles that of a four-week-infant," he murmurs.

Merlin responds to these security calls whenever I am on vacation, and he also engages with Delilah almost every day: watching for her mail, getting her the occasional sandwich with his petty cash, being startled when he comes to grab a tome in the cathedral library and she suddenly talks to him from where she is napping under the big mahogany table.

"We escorted her out from under the altar!" I tell him. "Refused to let me take her to the shelter. *Paradisio*—that's here, the prairie. The shelter is pretty much one of Dante's circles. But this is paradise, so ..."

"Why are you still here?" Merlin asks. "Go home."

"Too much to do. I need to get my article finished for the newsletter, meet with Artemis and Marianna about Holy Cross preparations. Besides, I couldn't sleep anyway. Did you watch the TV-13 interview?"

Merlin nods. "The ten o'clock news is one of Ivan's rituals. We watch religiously. He's always secretly hoping for unexpected coverage on the Botanic Center. And with the flooding, he's obsessed with the weather." Merlin's partner is the director of Des Moines' Botanic Center, an author and horticulturalist. He has written over twenty gardening books and has a jonquil named for him. "No," Merlin agrees, "the prairie spot was not as favorable as we'd like, but it was TV-13 after all."

"I don't even want to hear the reactions on Sunday."

"Oh, you won't have to wait that long. The message machine already held a few choice inquiries when I arrived at seven."

"That reporter, what he said about the prairie word-for-word was like a parrot of Max Chase. It was like the Chase Corp. scripted Vandermann's questions."

Merlin ponders this awhile. "Stranger things have happened."

"Or, even more possible, SansCorps. Do developers leak to the media things like their offer?"

Merlin strokes his goatee, "In New York City? All the time. Real Estate development was a kind of new beat."

My shoulders slump. "You want to know what's ironic, I adore a fine hotel. Worldly weakness of mine really."

"Cathedral deans are civic leaders. Not easy, but it's what you signed on for. You vowed to pray and work for the common good of this city. I remember, I typed up the installation service. Then, in front of about five hundred people, the mayor handed you a city flag, remember?"

"Yes, I remember. The common good... about four a.m., Delilah fell asleep, snoring away, and my brain kept wrestling with what is the common good? Do you think a swanky hotel would ever bring economic blessing to someone like Delilah? Could it change her circumstances?"

"It seems unlikely the Hotel Savant will hire Delilah as concierge," Merlin retorts, "but we feed others at the café who might benefit. Plenty of construction workers and cooks out of work."

"Maybe we should accept," I just put it out there.

A breeze moves the grass tops. Almost tangible patches of sunlight linger in the prairie, like carpets we could roll up and drag inside for inspiration during worship.

"You will make a prayerful decision," Merlin says.

"Thanks for the healing cup," I say and hand him my mug. "Hold any calls, unless it's about the levee bursting or a parishioner near-death. There's some weedy foxtail I need to attend to before I come inside."

"I know, Morning Prayer," he says, moving toward the building with an Elizabethan wave.

I have barely started pulling out the silky, long-awned foxtails—they are deceptive because they look elegant and soft but actually cling to clothes and lodge themselves in animal fur— when I notice Merlin's tasseled loafers on the path.

"It seems you are suddenly very popular." He's amused, but tries to be calming. "A reporter from *The Des Moines Register* is on the line. Saw the television spot and would like to follow up with a news piece. About the prairie."

I look sky-ward, half-praying-half-cursing.

Oh no, this reporter knows about the Hotel Savant, too? Why me?

I'll often go two years without such an experience. But maybe the prairie is a thin place?

More than hearing, or thinking them, I fathom these words:

What have you got to lose, except earthly memory of these grasses?

The Creator is not giving me a lot of wiggle room.

I look at Merlin, "Yeah, yeah. Civic leader and all that ... Okay, set up the interview."

Merlin has tried to impress upon me the wisdom of shutting and even locking my office door when I'm elsewhere in the cathedral. But I must have left it slightly ajar when I grabbed the coats for Delilah and me at four a.m. Upon return to my office I almost jump out of my pumps as the form of Max Chase rises from the sofa to greet me.

"My dear dean," he says, in his usual measured tone, "forgive my unannounced arrival.

You look well."

Max had been reading. He places the documents in a leather folio, takes off his readers and stows them in his inside breast pocket, stands and offers me a refined European greeting to both cheeks. Perhaps it's my pupils adjusting to the light, or maybe it is because I am exhausted and self-consciously disheveled having slept outside on a bench, but Max's coiffed hair shimmers eerily—he looks more like pop painter Andy Warhol than ever!

Now, perhaps a quarter of my male flock wear bowties for work or worship. But theirs seem machine-made next to Max's Turkish-rug bowties. Max wears ties of fine materials and hypnotizing complexity—a lot like the man. They draw one's attention away from his face.

"I am well, Max," I say, very intentionally raising my gaze from his tie to the intelligent gray eyes floating in the bud-vases of his glasses. "At least well enough. Though I'm worried about this never-ending rain. And you and Gwen? How are you?"

"Dean Brigid, it seems we stand on a threshold," he says, "of incalculable wellness. For the cathedral congregation. For the city. For us all."

In conversation with Max, it often feels as if his phrases have been strategically scripted ahead of time. It takes me a minute to absorb the fact that he is talking about the hotel. My heart leaps and sinks in one movement as I perceive where Max is headed.

"I imagine you are aware that Chase Enterprises is involved with all the burgeoning plans for downtown. And now, a further opportunity. To raise employment through economic development right in the core of this city that you and I both love and serve."

Dear God. Employment. Economic development. Max did script Vandermann's interview!

"Gwen and I, my sister Madge, and all at Chase have a vested interest in the success of The Hotel Savant complex." Like a seasoned politician, Max adds gravity with a pause. His gray eyes survey my face for comprehension. "We have the contract to sell and lease the attached restaurant and retail spaces. We understand that St. Aidan's is being invited into the project in a fashion beneficial to all sides."

Every dean in recent history has had their Max Chase moment. Earlier deans had their earlier Chases to negotiate. Burton and Maxine told me that the Chases and other cathedral families gained substantially from the freeway development and that Dean Wilson had major conflict with Max's father at that juncture. But for the last thirty years, Max has held the reigns of the Chase dynasty, so Chase moments have been Max moments.

"Dean Brigid, the Savant will be a fine hotel, unexcelled by any Des Moines has to offer. The plan is to bring in artisans from Europe. There will be an art gallery, and spas, and fine cuisine."

Nice. His description makes it sound like my own personal favorite: The Broadmoor Hotel. Maybe we should ask for more than four million? A lot more.

He continues, with the exuberance of a child, "It will be a

jewel in the crown of a renewed, gentrified downtown Des Moines."

To date, most of my interactions with Max have been pleasant enough. In fact, despite the warnings of earlier deans, I believe his spirituality is genuine and his compassion expanding. I sense that Max is a more gentle man at sixty-five than, rumor would have it, when he was at forty-five.

"Max, of course we wish blessings, both spiritual and financial, for you and your family. But this is complex. You yourself advised the cathedral board on the legal parameters of the prairie installation. And Madge has given substantially to it."

"Dean Brenchley." Max looks like I have somehow missed the memo he thought he had sent deftly and eloquently. Max obviously likes control. Some of the old ladies of the parish have quietly informed me that while making his millions Max's father was a raging alcoholic. They think control shapes Max's reality because of a childhood of maneuvering that chaos. Max continues in a cool tone, "I cannot comprehend how you or other cathedral leaders would even consider turning down an offer that will finally bring financial security to this house of worship."

"Max, last night on Fox 13 News..."

"Of course, I saw it."

"I shared how our prairie absorbs thirty swimming pools of water a year. Have you seen the flooding in Marshland? It's a real concern."

"Brigid, those are Mayor Burnish's worries. Not yours. Leave them to civic officials. You are a spiritual leader being given a chance to emerge in cathedral history as a turning-point dean. Earlier deans would envy you. Use these resources to repair the cathedral structure, fund new initiatives. When they laid the foundation of this cathedral, my great grandfather and great uncles dreamed of such a time."

No doubt he's right. Accept and my tenure would warrant a few pages in the next chapter in cathedral history. Perhaps merit an oil portrait for the foyer alongside important deans and bishops—all of them male by the way.

"Increases in staff salaries will follow." He places these words like a consummate bridge player counting and collecting tricks. "Of that I am sure."

Max will increase our salaries. One simple plank of Max Chase's platform of church politics is to always give an annual pledge identical to the current dean's salary. A very generous gift that sends a not so subtle message to the cleric about the potential cost of crossing him. Thus the deans and their Max moments. It's a velvet bribe, but a bribe nonetheless. My head swims. It is alluring.

Turning point? What is the turn you want? I silently ask God.

Then, a foundational Franciscan teaching also arises in that part of me where I receive these things, something I stumbled on in Italy when I finally decided to go to seminary: a line from Clare of Assisi's letter to Agnes the princess of Bohemia: The Laudable Exchange?

"It may be a Laudable Exchange," I say.

"Excuse me?" says Max.

"The Great Laudable Exchange." I have often thanked my stars that Grandpa Barney and Grandma Helen encouraged us to memorize poems, favorite sayings, Irish toasts. I know Clare's words by heart: "To leave the things of time for those of eternity. To choose the things of heaven for the goods of the earth.' Max, life is sometimes about giving things up. What if God's way is the prairie?"

Who reads cathedral histories anyway, I think.

"The Laudable Exchange?" Max responds, looking assured that I am nuts and also now dangerously annoying. "The logical exchange is trading a scrappy few acres for nearly four million dollars!"

He is so in the loop; he even knows the offer amount. Probably gave SansCorps an appropriate figure to begin negotiations!

What came to me in the prairie now returns, rising from that open *shakra* the Hebrews call the heart: *What have you got to lose? Except earthly memory of these grasses?*

"Max, when your great grandfather laid the foundation stone, like Willa Cather and Lewis and Clarke, he probably saw hundreds if not thousands of acres of tallgrass prairie. All of it now nearly extinct. And prairie plants soak up this never-ending Iowa rain. Our own parishioners may suffer again and again if we don't steward our land better."

Max's eyes are like steely magnets fixed to me in disbelief, and I am slightly frightened. "Dean Brenchley, Gwen and I have been pleased to help our cathedral when times are lean. But if leadership refuses to capitalize on other available resources, we will feel our generosity taken for granted. Do you think we want to be a permanent subsidy? On the other hand, should we be financially blessed through a business partnership with the Savant we will share with the cathedral as we always do. A laudable exchange, I think, and logical."

I am exhausted body, soul, and mind. In this minute it would be so much easier to just ride Max's persuasive wAvenue I imagine the cheering crowds in church—maybe just two Sundays from now—as Max and Phil and I hold aloft a blown-up fake four million dollar check—the real one in the bank. I can see the cameras flash. Hear ululation.

But then Max overplays his hand.

"Other long-standing cathedral families—the Lehmans, the Reynoldses—whom I've consulted, see it as Gwen and I do. They also may well choose to leave the cathedral if its leaders, in folly, ignore this opportunity."

The Irish half of my blood boils. I hear no evidence that Max cares a tat about what is holy, no evidence he's seeking God's opinion. His spirit has turned mean, and I wonder how much he really cares for this congregation. Orchestrating an exodus of families? Who the hell does he think he is? These are my thoughts, as yet unspoken. I feel them form and roll around in my mouth; I taste them, like good Irish whiskey.

Luckily, uncannily, before I spit them out, the swirl-cone light-bulb on my desk inexplicably jiggles on. An electrical short? A message from God? Or, humorously, from Henry? *Deus ex machina* with the message to "cool it"?

This time my nose definitely crinkles; I don't tell St. Aidan's largest donor to go screw himself. But instead, I do laugh out loud! Suddenly, the long-standing fear of my own Max moment evaporates. In fact, the minute he intimates he'll take his pledge and leave, I feel a bit giddy—realizing my Max moment will soon be in the past. With the serendipity of the light bulb, I know I won't be controlled by Max and his money.

Max's countenance frays. Mysterious light bulbs, humor, and my odd values are bridge strategies he had not counted on. His eyebrows arch from under his metallic wave and I think I see a small tremor of rage registered by his bow tie.

"You would refuse four million dollars to maintain this building," Max continues, "something solid, made of stone and sweat and generations of worship...for grass? Grass can go up in smoke. Some kid flicks his cigarette on the way to Court Ave..." His pewter eyes hammer his pause home. "I would not, dear dean, put your faith in the staying power of grass."

Having now topped his bribe with what may be a threat of arson, Max straightens his trouser legs and rises.

I am relieved to see that Merlin's tall form fills the doorway.

"Mr. Chase," Merlin says, "Mrs. Chase is in my office. Says you are meeting to go to brunch?"

Max makes sure I am clear. "I will be at the cathedral board meeting Tuesday and urge the acceptance of the Hotel Savant's offer."

No European kiss this time.

12

SHOWY GOLDENROD

Solidago speciosa or showy goldenrod blooms later than most goldenrod. It is indeed one of the most glamorous of the genus. Feathery plume and dense clump of deep yellow flowers atop attractive red stem. Native to eastern Colorado and filling my memories of the Broadmoor, it is also doing nicely beneath our Kentucky Coffee Trees, as it tolerates part shade.

–Note from Dean Brigid Brenchley's Prairie Journal

The Broadmoor, September 1971

Grandpa Barney whistled as we followed the Valley Highway south along the base of the Rockies. I was never sure if the highway bent west or the mountains galloped eastward to meet us, but after we passed Parker and Castle Rock, the peaks loomed, the color of peacocks, large and very near. Grandpa Barney was chauffer in the mustard-colored Malibu. Grandma Helen, Mom, my sister Barbara, and I were the entourage. The twins, Bonnie and Bev, were now in college and not with us.

Earlier that summer Grandpa Barney had a scare. One day while trout fishing at Elk Falls, he doubled over in excruciating pain. My father rushed him immediately down the mountains to Swedish Hospital. Once there, he spent a week undergoing tests. But, except for some loss of appetite, he assured everyone that he now felt fine. Quite fine.

The windows cracked, a mild mountain breeze flirted with us. September in Colorado often blends sunlight and fresh air into the kind of weather golfers dream about at night, and Grandpa Barney had his golf sweater packed. Goldenrod yellow.

Our destination? The Broadmoor Hotel.

The Broadmoor was built by Spencer Penrose. A ne'er do well son of the influential Pennsylvania Penrose family, "Speck" finally hit it rich in mining and created the lavish hotel. In the Maxfield Parrish rendering that Penrose commissioned, landscape and dream converge. The mountains are saturated with red-purple hues, and the lake (which the artist conveniently moves from behind the hotel to the front) is a luminescent, glazed teal. Encircled by the mountains and the lake, the arms of the hotel beckon like one of Parrish's neo-classic goddesses. The invitation is eternal; the place appears timeless. Our own Mount Olympus.

Erected on the threshold of the Rockies just above Colorado Springs, the hotel was designed by architects Warren and Wetmore (of Grand Central Station and Ritz-Carlton fame) to conform to the landscape of the Pike's Peak region and at the same time to include features from the finest European resorts. Spencer married the refined young widow Julie Lewis McMillan, daughter of the mayor of Detroit, well-educated and well-traveled in Europe. She loved art and music, and was a Catholic of ever-deepening spiritual devotion. As World War I made travel to the great spas of Europe less tenable, together the couple sought to permanently lure America's elite to the Colorado Rockies instead. The interior of the hotel represents Mrs. Penrose's tastes more than her husband's. With Parrish's mythical rendering as its logo—a siren call for the wealthy back

East—they opened the hotel's doors on June 1, 1918 and "the party began."

Our particular party began fifty-three years after the first white-gloved bellmen stood at the hotel's glass doors. Members of Colorado's insurance industry gathered there every September for their annual convention. Like vassals summoned from the four corners of our economically-booming state, as if by Lord and Lady Penrose themselves, actuaries and agents would drive over snowy passes, across windy plains, and through Denver traffic jams for the event. A newly-minted CEO of his small Denver insurance firm, my father Bruce was one of these vassals—his Dust Bowl childhood a distant memory. The men would arrive first, get some semblance of business out of the way, and then wives and families would join them.

As we made our approach, the sun fell behind the mountains, wrapping all in twilight.

Instead of checking in at the hotel, we met Dad and his friends at The Golden Bee, a well-visited tavern just off the Broadmoor's grounds. The pub was packed with middle-aged men in sports coats, sunburned from a round of golf. It took us a while to find Dad in the crush.

At first I felt overwhelmed, almost nauseated: hot bodies, a wood-paneled windowless pub, having to dodge pivoting elbows raising pints of English ale or snifters of scotch. But Grandpa Barney snaked his way back to the bar, and like a court juggler returned with martinis and Shirley Temples, olives and pretzels for us. Then he snagged a stool and stood me on it to see above the crowd.

Almost immediately a very large man in a red vest sat down at the piano to play, and with my monkey's-eye-view, my mood radically changed. This man had dark hair on his knuckles and looked too boulder-like to sit on the proposed bench. But he rolled up his sleeves, and his furry fingers were as fast as he was huge. They were all over those keys. First he played Dixie Land tunes and then, when a horn and a bass arrived, they played newer jazz like Brubeck, Davis, and Coltrane. Grandpa Barney and Grandma Helen were elated. They coaxed him into old Irish-American chestnuts like "When Irish Eyes are Smiling" and "Danny Boy" and everybody sang and sang. Grandpa Barney turned his brimmed hat sideways and vaguely resembled Jimmy Durante. And when the trio did a minimalistic "In the Mood," people got on their feet and jitterbugged. Those hairy fingers traversed the ivories until nearly two in the morning.

I awoke in a nest of down pillows and cloud-soft sheets, thinking I heard ducks. No, maybe it was bees? The Golden Bee was still buzzing in my head: the songs, the martinis, the Shirley Temples, and above all the music—flowing, flowing, flowing. I had never been in a piano pub before, and I wondered if it was a dream.

When I opened my eyes, Barbara and Mom were getting dressed.

"Breakfast," Barbara said. "We're meeting Grandma. Lake Terrace Dining Room."

Barbara, brushing her waist-length honey-colored hair, was now in high school and delivered these details with great authority, as if she knew all about this Lake Terrace Dining Room. I couldn't even quite remember where I was. I shook my head again, like Pooh trying to rid himself of the honey bees.

I rose and grabbed my purple culottes. I was all about purple at age nine. Then I confirmed that the night of Seven-up, maraschino cherries, and music wasn't a dream—for an embroidered bumble bee still stuck to my blouse. Everyone who entered the pub got one.

We pushed out the leaded, pane-glass doors of our room and found ourselves in a sculpted, mountain Shangri-La. Cheyenne Lake was once a natural body of water, an oasis for foothills creatures and area tribal peoples. But the Penroses had encircled it instead by a promenade that reminded me of Captain Von Trapp's villa in *The Sound of Music*. Bronze unicorns, Grecian gods and androgynous nymphs burst forth from beds of showy goldenrod and sprayed arcs of water that sounded like quiet timpani. A shiny, wood-hulled boat pushed across the surface of the lake, steered by a man in a cravat.

My ears upon waking had not deceived me: all along the shore there were small fleets of ducks. Ducks accustomed to human admirers, for they never pushed off. They allowed me to draw so close that I could see the iridescence of the mallard's green head feathers, catching sunlight like Mom's emerald ring. And most fascinating of all, around the ducks and out in the middle of the lake, tufts of steam were rising, like swirls of frosting on a cake. I touched the water.

"It's heated," Barb said, joining me. "All winter they heat it— for the ducks and the fishermen. Can you believe it?"

As usual, I had recently spent two memorable weeks in August on my grandparent Brenchleys' wheat farm. I'd spent long days outdoors with the farm animals, tromping through fields with vegetative odors filling my nostrils, sticking my finger in the icy hole to drain the ice cream maker and taste the ice cream made of the milk from my grandparents' own dairy cows.

But poised on the edge of the Broadmoor's stately lake, that life now seemed homespun and strange. I thought of Grandpa Floyd and the duck he had given me that made do with the muddy cow pond. I could imagine Grandpa Floyd standing on this shore in his overalls shaking his head, suspicious of these kept ducks. I was both suspicious and enthralled. Looking closely, I did think maybe these ducks looked a little bored, with no natural predators and being fed breadcrumbs by tourists. Still, a heated lake!

"How do you know these things?" I asked Barb.

"I've been up an hour or two. You know how I love breakfast. I'm starved," she said and pulled me from the lake. "So come on."

From there we entered the mezzanine. Each area of The Broadmoor was like entering a new dream sequence. Over a hundred Italian artists had been imported to custom-craft each room. Barb and Mom made a bee line for the restaurant. But a familiar sound lured me.

Elevators. I had to peek at the gilded elevator hub sitting at the very heart of the hotel. The foyer had an arched ceiling, and above each elevator were circular moldings that told stories in the style of Della Robbia— a panoply of subjects that were meaningful to Lord and Lady Penrose. I looked up, neck straining: there was a pantheon of classical gods, surprisingly there was a lithe Indian woman in headdress. Victorian, winged cherubs made an appearance as well as a regal Virgin Mary, and Jesus, showing his heart. They all floated in one harmonious *bas relief* universe, as if history was laughable and had been overcome.

"We're ordering," Barbara said fuming, finding me gaping near the elevators.

Grandma Helen sat at a table looking out at the lake. She was in a lilac-colored suit that complemented her silver hair. A friendly Austrian waitress was placing a plate of eggs benedict before her. Fresh, steamed asparagus graced one side and a spear of pineapple and strawberries anchored the other.

"Oh, Katarina," Grandma Helen exclaimed to the waitress, "it's like a Mary Cassatt still life. It may be too beautiful to eat!"

She and the waitress were already friends.

"I ordered you French toast, with glacéd bananas," Mom said. "Where were you?"

"The elevators. More beautiful than our church. And the people get off under Indian princesses and babies with wings and boys with no clothes."

"It worries me that Barney decided to play all eighteen holes, so soon from the hospital," Grandma began.

But she didn't go on, for our friends Arlene and Kathy Falck and the men arrived, ablaze in the naïve colors of 1971—in golf attire straight from my forty-eight crayon box: Dad was in robin's egg blue, which, with his wave of blond he could just pull off. Erv Falck, though by far the best golfer, donned a more modest, sage-green Izod. Grandpa Barney was in a goldenrod cardigan. They were aglow over the golf game. My father actually hated golf. In Dust Bowl Western Kansas in his childhood and youth, there was no rain to grow crops let alone golf greens. Golf was something he had come to as an adult because insuring small businesses and highway contractors and other insurance companies was Dad's niche, and the deals were often introduced, sealed, or celebrated on a golf course. It all made Dad extremely tense. But that day, The Broadmoor had worked its magic: Dad enjoyed reasonable success; Erv won a trophy; and Grandpa— though his total wasn't so good—had sunk a hole-in-one. Of wiry build, Grandpa Barney didn't have much power. But he knew his own strengths and weaknesses and had this almost Charlie Chaplin-esque technique. He'd point himself way left at the tee to compensate for his slice. After a sideways arc, like a baseball curve-ball, his white orb often landed inches from the hole. This particular day it went in. To achieve a hole-in-one at The Broadmoor by this method was a real feather in his cap.

"Barney," Erv said, "You were just in the hospital. How do you do it?"

"Maybe martinis and lots of love from Helen," he replied, and winked at my grandmother. "Of course, being doubled-over in a hospital gown and getting barium enemas does make a guy long to play golf. I'll admit hitting that flag was like the kiss of recovery to an old man!"

With this new wave appearing at the table, we basically had to start the meal again.

Usually I was a quick, impatient child. But as I bit into sweet, soft toast and brown-sugared fruit, I let the tastes and textures linger, as well as the sounds of the dining room. At the tables around us, people were conversing and laughing. There were old people. There were other children. I could hear broad, western monotone sounds, but laced as well with unfamiliar French, German, and Italian phrases. It was as if the Alps had come over to have coffee with the Rockies, and those on all sides were enjoying it.

The spell of The Broadmoor was undeniably and unapologetically about the pleasures of wealth. For us, the appeal was strong. We were middle class people. Yes, increasingly upper middle class—but the elegant lifestyle of The Broadmoor was not our norm. We had none of the boredom with wealth of the truly affluent.

But beyond the fantasy of wealth, visits to The Broadmoor held a promise far more potent: immortality. Here, it seemed, time opened up. Here, The Broadmoor pledged, one could luxuriate in time. Time for leisure. Time to do whatever each one pleased. In a way, money provided time to escape from time. In a family where I sometimes felt lost and forgotten, the hotel meant time for relationship too, for connection.

We all lingered at the table, in droll turns imagining how we might spend the day.

Barbara would read *War and Peace* on the French chaise-lounge in our room. Dad would venture into the invigorating pool. Mom and the Falcks wanted to explore the shops. For my part, I looked forward to feeding the half-wild-half-pet ducks all the eternal afternoon long. Various family members saved me their uneaten toast for this purpose. I would attempt to discern if they liked their fake lake, or desired an escape to a farm pond.

As Grandpa Barney and Grandma Helen described their plans to try lawn-bowling, which they'd heard was all the rage with the older set in England, I actually put my head down on a linen napkin in a patch of sunlight. At nine, I was not used to pub life 'til two o'clock in the morning. I shut my eyes. I could faintly hear the ducks. I saw them floating up some feet above the lake on swirls of steam. I saw the piano player pull up a chair at our table and tuck into a large stack of pancakes carving at them with his hairy fingers. I saw Jesus and the Kiowa princess come in from the elevators.

They joined our table, offered us Russell Stover chocolates, and we all ate. And every center was coconut, which was Grandpa Barney's and my favorite.

Of course, no visit could ever quite live up to that first. It was as if the filtered camera lens was changed out each visit, and the clouds and sparkles incrementally paled and turned grainy. The next year the Broadmoor trip was still fairly luminescent. But the year after that, we chose not to start at The Golden Bee. The year after that Grandpa Barney had spent most of the summer in the hospital and he needed to save his strength. He was in no shape to play in the golf tournament. Instead of his goldenrod sweater, he wore an oatmeal-colored jacket. We sat on a bench and gazed across Lake Cheyenne. The ducks cheered us somewhat.

"Grandpa," I asked, "since you can't golf today, maybe you'd like to fish? I heard we can rent a boat and fish from it."

He didn't want to hurt my feelings, but Barney slightly grimaced. His stomach always ached now in a battle with what the doctors would finally decide was Crohn's disease. They had removed substantial lengths of his intestines.

"I like the restaurants, and the golf, and the martinis at The Broadmoor," Grandpa Barney said, "but *never* the fishing. The fish are flown in, and haven't got a fighting chance. We'll go to Elk Falls again. Next spring, when the snow melts, and the hummingbirds flit." He assured me and brushed my cheek with his thumb. "But not here. No, to fish here is like Spencer Penrose serving you trout on one more silver platter."

A stocky, mustached old man with an ivory-handled cane tottered toward us and nodded. "Interlaken," he said. "You ever been to Interlaken?"

Grandpa and I shook our heads.

"Not quite so many wild flowers, but otherwise, this is America's Interlaken."

We were to meet Mom and Grandma Helen on the far side of the lake, outside the Pauline Chapel, a place of prayer that Lady Penrose had built when her daughter and new granddaughter were under house-arrest in Belgium in WWI. To stand, Grandpa Barney put one hand on the bench armrest and one on my shoulder. I was twelve years old, getting strong, and aware he was in obvious pain. I noticed how thin Grandpa Barney's legs had become, like bones under cloth. In that moment of awareness the Broadmoor dream began to wash away.

It only got worse, as he struggled to take steps to circuit the lake. The tottering old man from Switzerland easily outdistanced us. We found Grandma Helen by herself on a bench. She had never looked small to me before, never. But she did that day, her face like the translucent Limoges porcelain she loved. Her mink hat was askew. She looked like a lost child. Though when she saw Grandpa, some light returned to her worried face. He smiled at her.

Mom emerged from the chapel, where she had undoubtedly been praying about my grandfather's health. But unlike Grandmother, who seemed to carry her worries clutched in her handbag, you could tell from Mom's face that she had gone inside to meet with God and came out strengthened. I realized that in this one way my mother—whom I had always seen as smaller in every way than her mother—was larger. I also knew that my grandfather was very ill.

For me, at that moment The Broadmoor's stucco-and-tile façade cracked. The bronze nymphs and unicorns appeared ageless, but Grandpa Barney was not. Penrose lied. Money couldn't purchase immortality. Maxfield Parrish's glazed layers were washing into the lake.

13

PURPLE LOVE GRASS

Eragrostis spectabilis or purple love grass is a perennial warm season grass. It reaches heights of one to two feet even in the driest, poorest of soils. The seed heads bloom mid-summer in shades of light to bright purple, giving an overall purple haze to the landscape.

–Note from Dean Brigid Brenchley's Prairie Journal

Thursday, 7:00 a.m.

One thing about the encounter with Max is that it has shaken me out of my paralysis and galvanized me into action. I have realized that I need to talk to my best advisors and learn what the people I serve make of this situation. So yesterday I asked Marianna to set up time with the Prairie Team, and Merlin to arrange time with Phil to further prepare for the board meeting. I need to warn him about Max. I proposed an afternoon meeting, but Phil asked if dinner was acceptable. Due to his court case, of course. Dinner with Phil? That sounds more than acceptable.

So, it is early morning and I am trying to cross the Des Moines River to get to the community vegetable garden. Marianna didn't lose any time in gathering the troops, and landed on this spot. At seven o'clock no less! And of course, traffic is crawling along. Usually, Thursday is my "Sabbath," when I rest and write my sermon. Jewish theologians have called Sabbath a cathedral in time, and I wish I could keep it, but am aware this is "just one of those weeks."

Paused in traffic, I survey my environs. I have lived in a number of locales and cities: Colorado, Chicago, Exeter in England, the Flint Hills of Kansas. But I am endeared to Des Moines. The small city is in an era of urban renewal that reminds me of the Denver of my youth; there's a creative, collective spirit. Also, Denver has the mountains as its aesthetic focus, and downtown Des Moines gazes into its river. Only lately have I come to see that a river can be more powerful than 14,000 feet of granite.

Behind me are a few blocks of high-rises. Across the river, which is still running pell-mell north to south, the city offices spread. The mayor's office with two side wings sits like a benevolent lion, stone paws outstretched amidst beautiful flower beds. Unfortunately, right now those beds are like wading pools. A small team in matching purple jackets is working to pump out the accumulated water. Upstream, I can just make out Wells Fargo Arena, like a concrete whale that has pulled itself onto the bank. Beyond it winks the cut glass geodome of the Botanic Center. I can imagine Ivan inside in a flurry of activity, preparing for tomorrow night's gala.

Downstream, the beautifully restored World Food Prize Building has a long line of middle schoolers exiting yellow buses, waiting for a tour. But there is also a long line of adult volunteers placing sandbags.

My usual route, the Grand Avenue Bridge, is blocked off due to the rising water. Some geographically misplaced gulls are happy, careening over the waves and perching on the orange barricades. But the closed bridges have messed with motorists' paradigms and our usually modest early morning traffic is in a tangle. It is not raining, but the air is tangible, like a cirrus cloud sits on the city.

High atop the river's eastern slope, safe from the rising water, the Iowa State Capital beckons. The building is what I would call, paradoxically, "staid-rococo"—built by reserved Midwesterners flush from the wealth of exquisitely fertile farmland. Its crown looks vaguely Slavic or Turkish with four garlic-shaped domes that stand sentinel around the central neo-classical dome.

The large community garden is in the reclaimed river bottoms just south of the capital.

Jason, one of our younger members, oversees the garden, and some others were already planning to be there for seed collection and sorting before heading to work. The community garden land, inundated by the last flood, now hosts a quilt of raised beds guarded by a strengthened levee. I am glad to see this steep-sloped levee holding fast, and that the raised beds below are thriving.

The city owns the land but leases it at low cost to Jason's non-profit. A mix of east-side immigrants—Sudanese, Mexican, and Vietnamese—grow their favorite vegetables here, alongside the basil and kale of hipsters and the tomatoes and radishes of elderly gardeners. Organic is one rule. Absolutely no chemicals. The gardeners put money, as each is able, into a kitty. They share both seeds and produce. Membership "cards" are t-shirts or bumper stickers that say "Veggies for the People" in four languages. The group also sponsors events on the land: cooking and nutrition demonstrations, bike rides, kids' days, fitness classes, and an occasional political candidate. As I pull into the gravel lot, I can see Jason leading yoga on a kind of terrace halfway up the levee.

Burton and Marianna have already arrived and are settled at a picnic table, eyeing piles of seeds. So is Prairie Team member Elena, an Ecuadorian student from Drake University, with her one year old baby Ana. Ana reaches her chubby hand, with its sterling baby bracelet, toward the seeds. No yoga for the four of them. I see another team member, Samuel, is with Jason's class. Phil can't come because of his trial. Except him, the core gardeners are here.

"What's this all about?" Burton asks me pointedly, taking a long draught from his coffee as I join them at the picnic table. He looks tired, wrinkles across his brow. If painful for me, I realize that seven o'clock meetings may be a real struggle for Burton at age ninety.

He doesn't wait for an answer, saying, "I saw that television deal. We want the real scoop. Best to tell us. Get it over with."

I have been dreading telling these, some of my closest friends, about the hotel. But as my own opinion takes form, I am more ready. Burton has always been a rock of support for me. When I first came to St. Aidan's, I did a year of home or workplace visits, making my way alphabetically through the parish directory. At Burton and Maxine's, the one-hour visit turned into a three-hour lunch. Burton shared hysterical, and poignant, stories about being the token African-American man on the cathedral board in the 1960s and 70s, when it was still an all-male body of Des Moines' power brokers. In those days, the Chases were but one of many such families. He said he was often relegated to play bartender. His droll storytelling style had Maxine and me crying; I could hardly eat for laughing. Maxine would say, "Oh, Burton," and that would just egg him on to another story. A lot has changed, he told me. But not everything. He said that I was the first white priest who had ever come to their home.

Burton centers his wizened gaze on me, and Marianna and Elena look silently but keenly at me as well.

"Okay. Brace yourselves," I reply. "But do you mind if we wait for Jason and Samuel? Is yoga almost over?"

We look over and Jason has arched backward into a bridge pose. His firm body reminds me of a piece of Jean Arp sculpture: solid fluidity.

"Have you watched Jason do this?" Burton asks me. Sometimes Burton rolls his eyes at Jason's ideas and antics. But this morning Burton's tone holds genuine esteem. The old man once played sports and recognizes the obvious athleticism of Jason's poses. "It's like there are no bones in his body. Drops forward, palms to the ground. Puts his heels behind his neck.

Confess I'm impressed!"

"Like prairie dropseed," Marianna says. "Every time we look over, they're touching the ground with a different part of their bodies."

As we look on, the human bridges meld onto their mats. Then they sporadically rise, gesture "Namaste," and like the man in Jesus' healing story roll up their brightly colored mats and start moving toward life in the city. Samuel joins us, while Jason attends to some of his student-admirers, most of them young women his age.

"Do this often?" Burton asks Samuel.

Samuel nods, "You can't imagine what tucking a violin under your chin for hours every day does to your neck and shoulders!"

"Eagle pose," Jason says as he walks over, "do it every day. At home, too."

With a sweatshirt hoody tied around his waist and flip-flops as shoes, Jason's attire evokes an Asian prince.

"So, what's the skinny?" he asks as he sits next to me on the bench. "Something's up. There are rumors on the street."

Of course, if anyone would hear of the offer first it would be Jason. Not quite thirty years old, he nonetheless moves in lively social circles.

I stare at the faces around the table. Momentarily the sun has clambered up above the statehouse, imbuing the remnant fog. We sit in textured light. The I Am the Vine icon surfaces in my mind's eye again. One fruit of prayer with icons is that the image will appear to you amidst daily life. The mystics say to take this as a sign of the Risen One's presence. I savor the communion I share with these people. Laboring side-by-side in the prairie, we have told one another about heartbreaks, job promotions, and lost loved ones. Like the figures on the vine, our lives are connected.

Thank you for them, whatever happens next.

I have feared that this hotel offer, from out of the blue, could bring division. With my own relatives miles away in Colorado and Hawaii, these people are like family to me. I realize I have put off telling them this news out of fear—that my closest relationships could be damaged. But the time has come, and by their rapt attention the preacher in me knows there will be no rhetorical preamble this day.

"The cathedral has received an offer of $3,720,000 for the prairie garden."

"What?!" Samuel is the loudest.

Elena raises her hands skyward, then steadies teetering Ana.

"From whom?" Marianna's voice sounds the most indignant.

Burton simply shakes his head.

"So it is true," Jason says. "The Hotel Savant and its shops? That was what was floating around during salsa dancing at the Social Club."

"Yes. They need a certain amount of land for parking—city requirement."

At the word parking, Marianna erupts, "Slather the earth with asphalt again? Send the oily water to join the nitrates in the river and help poison the Gulf?!"

"So that the One-Percent can slip between silk sheets no less. Prayer Prairie turns Trump Tower," Jason snorts. "Brigid, the grasses and the forbs are just taking hold, just beginning to thrive. You can't rip them out now."

They speak what I feel. Nonetheless, I do want the proposal weighed carefully. This group is my most steady, if unofficial, counsel of advice. With trusted friends, I want to risk some transparent probing.

"You've seen me beg, borrow and steal for our prairie. But this is a lot of money: we could endow the building, fix the roof. Or endow the feeding program?" I say, "Burton and Samuel, you are both on the board. Would the board do meaningful things with that much money if we did sell?"

Burton, still shaking his head, does however hear the reality behind my queries, seems to accept an earnest humility in me.

"We're all fine, Christian people, even most of us board members," he replies. "Sure, we might do some good with it. But if we take the hotel's cash, I can promise you the biggest chunk will go to organ pipes and champagne brunches. I've seen it happen before."

"I have an idea," Jason's eyes light up. "A petition. Collect signatures. There are a lot of people who do understand and appreciate prairie."

"People like to hang out there for sanity, what with frenetic work days," Samuel adds.

"Drake students and faculty would sign," Elena says as Ana coos. "In my grad classes we talk of how we absolutely need more green space in American cities, not less!"

"Elena and I will fly into action and have a ton of signatures by the board meeting," Jason says. "St. Aidan's always says it wants to connect with young people."

"A petition might in fact have a positive impact," Samuel tells them with middle-age moderation, "though... it's a pretty hard-boiled group."

Marianna just looks angry; her eyes are like a hawk's. Burton looks like he's having acid reflux. They don't seem to share the wave of optimism the younger team members are riding.

"My, my, my," Burton says finally, "I should have known. I've seen greed grab that place before. Same-old, same-old. The grass seed Maxine and I donated... all of Marianna's work...down the drain."

Burton's bitterness punches me in the gut. As I listen to the resignation in the older man's voice, it's like the deck of our ocean liner is compromised and everything is sliding downward. I realize that my openness to exploring the options has him convinced that I have decided to sell; maybe he suspects the money has me under its spell. I frantically run up deck, trying verbally to rectify his misconception.

"Burton, we don't have to sell. I was just exploring options, garnering collective wisdom. If we're sure the prairie is the common good and God's vision, we can fight for it! As the dean, I'm willing to say no. I hope we can count on that from you and Samuel."

"Where the hell is Phil?" Burton asks. "Head of the board.

Where will he land?"

"He's at the courthouse. Big trial. But I think he is willing to work for the prairie, vote no to the money, too. We're going to discuss strategies further this evening."

Burton looks suspicious.

"Is there a prayer in the world?" Marianna asks, appealing mainly to Burton. Burton addresses us all with oratorical intention.

"Listen. I've served on the cathedral's board five different times over forty years. There isn't a chance in hell those merchants and aristocrats are going to turn down nearly four million dollars! They'll think the old glory days are back and pull out their silk stockings and dancing shoes. Probably already have their claws in Phil."

"Burton, you told me yourself that St. Aidan's is a different place today," I respond.

"Brigid, we won't have the votes. Plain and simple. Count 'em. Max Chase has probably already secured them."

I blanch. My stomach burns at the mention of Max. I can't believe he threatened me, my salary, maybe even arson.

Burton reads my reaction, "Dear Lord, he's already shown his hand, hasn't he?" I can't reply, but nod.

"Well, it may be a new day," Burton continues, "but *it's easier to get a camel through the eye of a needle than to get a rich man through* this scenario! Our whole neighborhood didn't matter and the prairie won't mean crap. Especially if Max is in the mix. Just like his father. It's not worth wasting our time. We may as well bring our shovels down here."

I never anticipated this. I don't think Phil did either. We have been completely counting on Burton's leadership if we move to refuse the offer. He is respected in the parish much more than he knows.

"Burton, what did Jesus say next?" I ask him, my voice shrill and desperate. "You know the end. *With God all things are possible.*"

Burton places a fist, knuckles down, into a plank of the picnic table and uses it as a prop to raise his six feet 3 inches frame to his feet.

"We have a few days before the board meeting. But you tell Philip Morrow that I want to talk to him. I want to hear from his own lips where he stands. I will also take Samuel's advice and pray about it. Yes... we all better pray about it."

One by one people rise from the picnic table. Workday lives beckon.

Thursday 7 p.m.

The twilight is velvet soft with a cool lining. The first evening in weeks it seems without rain. A waiter moves with a taper and the table candles emerge one-by-one like fireflies. I have settled myself on the patio of a favorite restaurant near the cathedral, with its green awning and its border of shoulder-high boxwoods. I wish my state would allow me to savor this evening of lingering warmth. I take a swill of cabernet and try to calm down, to lie back and disappear in an eddy of Sonoma aroma and flavors. Forget Aaron the sneering, Delilah the breaking-and-entering, Henry in harm's way, Marianna the transplanting, Max the menacing. Forget them all! Why didn't I become a cloistered nun?

You are such better company.

I cradle the bowl of the wine glass and dive into that eddy. But Max Chase—shimmering hair, magic-carpet-tie, and thinly veiled threats—is alive in my head. Unshakeable specter. I can't help myself and I mentally rehearse my Max encounter. Adrenaline courses through me with a fine Quirke indignation as I remember it. I take another draught and close my eyes, trying to submerge under the notes of cherry and spice. But Max is still there, inside, leering at me. I am incredulous that he actually threatened me: "Some kid flicks a cigarette" and "I would not put faith in the staying power of grass."

God, did Max actually mean it? Would he ever act on it?

"Dining *al fresco* in September," Phil pulls out the chair and sits down across from me. "Exquisite."

Just to see him buoys me a little.

"This trial was a bear. But we won," he informs me. Wrinkles at the corners of his eyes show his fatigue, but otherwise he's riding a wave of quiet ebullience.

Despite my stressed state, I am truly happy for him.

"A drink, sir?" the waiter asks.

"Tonic with lime."

"Another wine?" I nod. "We're celebrating... or trying to."

Phil surveys my mood. Next to his wave of courtroom satisfaction, no doubt I am a complex coral reef. I fear the tone in which I said "celebrating" was not unlike the tone I use when announcing that I am "celebrating" a funeral.

"My intuition says it might be good to de-brief your day? Then maybe we can revel in my win."

I give him an apologetic look.

The waiter brings bruschetta and our drinks, and I breathe for a moment. The trial-worn Phil is caste with a mellow luster from the table lamps. The ambience reminds me of Kauai at night, and I almost think I hear surf.

But then, the specter of Max appears, like a torpedo through the water, as Phil adds, "Burton Taylor-Smith called me over my lunch break and read me the riot act about this hotel offer. Accused me of greed and knuckling under to Max Chase. What's that all about?"

"Well, Max Chase visited me unannounced yesterday. It's the main reason I had Merlin set up this meeting. I wanted to fill you in."

At this, Phil's intelligent eyes cast across the boxwoods.

"He knows all about the SansCorps offer," I continue. "Chase Enterprises is the partner to sell or lease the restaurant and shop space."

"Holy shit. You're joking?" Phil reads my face, "You're not joking." He tosses back his tonic like it's a shot of bourbon. "Of course, I should have anticipated this, the Chases are everywhere.

That does weigh down the balloon."

We sit together in silence. The bruschetta on my plate looks like a small volcano of tomato, onion, and basil. The best in town, but I haven't the strength to raise a slice.

"He's threatened to stop his pledge if we refuse the hotel."

Now Phil's jaw looks like there is a jawbreaker rolling around inside, and his eyes inquire—the kind of scrutiny with which I imagine he cross-examines witnesses. "What do Max and Gwen give. Really?"

"Currently? $79,465. No cents."

"What? You have everyone's pledge memorized?"

"Just Max's. It's easy because he always matches the dean's salary exactly."

"The bastard."

"Until today I've always vacillated on that point. He and Gwen give even more to the food pantry and the symphony than the cathedral. If you remember, Chase Enterprises re-built a wing of the cathedral and a whole neighborhood in Haiti."

Phil doesn't look convinced, mumbles something about a tax write off, and takes some bruschetta. I poke around at mine and decide I should tell him the worst.

"He's already spoken to Hal Lehman and the Reynoldses, who will back his demands, and now, I'm not sure—it could be stress, me losing my grip—but I think Max threatened to have the prairie set on fire."

Phil almost chokes. "Like arson?" he asks with a cheek full of baguette.

"It was an offhand comment, or that was its form."

"He's a master at that," Phil says.

"He said that whereas the cathedral building was solid and should be endowed, the prairie might go up in flames at any time, with some kid's cigarette on the way to Court Avenue."

"Calculating bastard." Phil downs his tonic and throws the lime so hard some ice ricochets to my side of the table. Veins stand out on his neck like a topographic map. I have transferred the tyrannizing Max-dragon to his brain.

Considering how angry he looks, his next words surprise me.

"I don't like it," he says, "if the fight for the prairie could put you in jeopardy. Your livelihood even. Maybe we should just accept the Savant's offer."

I think about all the paintings and antiques I won't need to sell. Maybe buy a painting of my own choice. Treat Grandma Helen to an extra trip to Hawaii. But then I come to my true sensibilities.

"You know, forty-eight hours ago I would have said yes. But, I was with Henry and Nick Jones two days ago and I believe their neighborhood is truly threatened by the flooding."

"Again?"

"It's not certain. But the Army Corps of Engineers is worried, and I can't quit seeing the torrent of water we'll send back down to the river if we sell. I adore those rare plant species and I adore people in our parish in the vulnerable lowlands."

I take a bite of bruschetta at last. Delicious. I add, "Besides, Max is starting to really piss me off."

Phil smiles. The dragon seems finally banished. Phil seems to see only me; seems to like what he sees.

But, I suddenly realize that he might bear consequences, too, if we don't sell. "What about you?" I ask him. "Could Max harm your practice?"

"I could lose some clients," Phil admits. "But, I took on Rudy Giuliani once. Relatively, Chase's reach is limited."

"Giuliani, the past mayor of New York City?"

"As a grad student at The New School. It was land issues then too. I was heavily involved with Green Thumb and the Green Guerillas."

I grin, "The Green Guerillas?"

"It's a network of community gardens all over the boroughs. The plots had been leased for decades. A real boon to neighborhoods. But Giuliani gets into power and moves the properties from the Parks Department to the Department of Housing. Then moved to auction them off. Highest bidder!"

"Wow. Puts our prairie politics into perspective. What

happened? Is that the end of the story?"

"People were furious. Enter Green Thumb and Guerillas. We staged protests in front of the mayor's Office."

With a wry, embarrassed smile, Phil reaches into his wallet and hands me a frayed photo. "You are sworn to secrecy."

I see a younger Phil with shoulder length hair—looking very like John Lennon of the White Album period—peeking out from a vegetable costume.

"Lettuce," Phil explains, and I laugh out loud. "We marched singing "Lettuce Overcome." I was a bit self-conscious about that choice. Did not want to mock earlier civil rights activists. But since Lou, a peer African-American protester, suggested it, I sang, too. Giuliani was hot. Actually pulled some of us into his office and read us the riot act: 'This is a free market economy, boys. Welcome to the era after communism.'"

"God, you really do look like John Lennon, early Yoko." Phil looks amused. "Nice green legs, too. But they didn't sway Mayor Rudy?"

"No. But we were a big hit with the press. *The New York Times* was all on the side of the vegetables! Two NGOs swooped in and bought most of the lots. The Trust for Public Land. Also singer Bette Midler's group. Kept them as gardens."

Hope returns. Max and his threats explode like a fireworks dragon. Our entrees come.

"More wine?" the waiter asks. I actually consider a third.

"It won't take the headaches away, you realize," Phil says. "Only make them more literal. Believe me, I know. I'm in recovery."

The waiter waits, perhaps feeling awkward.

"I'm fine," I say, and realize that I am.

14

CANNABIS

Cannabis sativa or marijuana is an annual, dioecious, flowering herb. The leaves are palmately compound or digitate, with serrate leaflets.[9] The first pair of leaves usually have a single leaflet, the number gradually increasing up to a maximum of about thirteen leaflets per leaf (usually seven or nine), depending on variety and growing conditions. When Colorado became a state, both hemp and cannabis were legal. Mexican migrant workers in the sugar beet fields brought marijuana first to sell in Denver to augment their scanty income.

–Note from Dean Brigid Brenchley's Prairie Journal

Saint Clare's Academy, Early October 1976

I rolled grass into a joint for the first time about a month after Grandpa and Grandma Brenchley had to sell the farm. I inhaled the sweet verdant smoke while hidden under a large stand of Russian Sage at the base of the statue of the Blessed Saint Clare, companion of St. Francis. Being September, the tall, aromatic plants allowed room for three young girls under their wispy bowers, andits pale purple petals dusting their hair like snow. Hiding from real life felt good. Not only was I watching Grandpa Barney deteriorate physically as I entered adolescence, but everything was changing. All of my sisters were in college, and I was no longer the baby but the only child.

My Dad was making very solid earnings and I was enrolled in a pricey Catholic school.

The graceful Clare figure, hovering above an oasis of drought-resistant perennials, was the centerpiece of the circle drive of St. Clare's Academy. Ever since they arrived in Denver from Santa Fe in 1852, to educate the youth of this wild, gold rush town, the Sisters of Perpetual Adoration had been ahead of their time. To them, a firm faith and progressive thinking went hand in hand. God was to be found everywhere, after all, so why not experiment and explore?

Of late, Sister Julian, who looked like a thinner, kinder Jane Fonda and taught us horticulture, was the living example. She was obsessed with saving the precious water of the convent and of the American West for that matter. She was on a mission to return the acres of St. Clare's private school grounds back to the flora and fauna God placed there before their Order first arrived. Of course, the Mother Superior put her foot down about changing the field hockey fields or the school's famed grass tennis courts. But Julian was allowed her signature piece: she tore out the geraniums and verbena that had always graced Lady Clare, and instead planted this large fountain-like island of natives.

This outlandish choice for our forbidden activity was the idea of my friend Michelle. Michelle was one of these wealthy, half-delinquents who convinced me and my best friend Monica that it was "safest to stash the loot right under the nuns' noses." The nugget of this truant's wisdom was to light up immediately beneath the lily whiteness of the Blessed Clare herself.

I reached into the Ziploc bag that Michelle offered and pinched a sample of the mysterious, fragrant particles. It was as if I held some of the farm between my fingers. It reminded me of the parsley and thyme Grandma Jenny cut from her kitchen garden and used to lace her casseroles. That very summer before the heart attacks, I had seen pot growing wild on the Brenchley farm. Grandpa Floyd had stopped his Ford pick-up at the edge of their western pasture and strolled, with me tagging behind, a few paces to a corner of barbed-wire fence. Leaning against the bottom wire, four or five plants were reaching large, spread-fingered leaves toward the sun.

"Rogue hemp. Marijuana. The government once paid us to grow the stuff," he told me. "Makes strong rope. Now, I guess some kids run out from town and cut it to smoke, and the State wants to pay us to kill it." Grandpa, fond of his tobacco in various forms, bent down to count the number of thriving plants. He straightened up and said with a twinkle in his eye, "I think I'll just let it be."

Nonetheless, I was pretty sure my grandfather would not want me, at thirteen, to be smoking the stuff. Especially not at school. But moving the grains between my fingers, I thought of the farm. The sadness weighed me down. Why didn't time just hold?

Make it be the beginning of summer again.

Luxurious days, away from the city, running around the green countryside in the blinding hot metal of Grandpa Floyd's red pick-up. Soaking up the sun. Going mindless. Breeze tangling my waist-length locks. Time slowed down on the farm; it moved with the sun. Unlike the hubbub of Denver, I could almost feel myself living there—more natural time than the fake-eternity we purchased at The Broadmoor. On the farm, it was the free slow-and-easy time that you could count on. Eternal time woven into creation itself. That's what I thought in June.

But, a month later, in the teeth of the heat of July, the severe pain and nausea hit Grandpa Floyd. He was in the upper pasture changing out salt licks for the cattle. He swung one of the blocks down from the truck and a shot of pain surged up his arm and into his chest. The first heart incident, five months earlier, was in calving season and had been so light Grandpa Floyd just thought he was murky from lack of sleep. He had ignored it. But not this time. It was a good thing that Floyd's friend and neighbor Vern was along. Took him straight to the ER in Norton.

"Quirks, you need more than that," Michelle told me. I had never known a white girl with an afro before I met Michelle. But it fit. She wore a lavender headband that pushed the fro skyward and it matched the tiny sage petals now collecting in her curls. Michelle was unpredictable, like her hair.

"Where did you get the stuff, anyway?" I asked.

"Randall."

"Randall? Your father?" Monica exclaimed. Monica knew Michelle as a neighbor. Monica and I exchanged looks. Monica's father Capper was cool. He flew his own private plane. But he was not that cool. Bruce, my father, was positively medieval in his thinking when it came to things like pot or anything else illegal.

"Randall keeps it in his desk drawer. 'The fine Columbian,' he calls it, just like in Steely Dan. In fact, he keeps joints in the fourteen-karat gold cigarette case out on his desk. Some of his business associates are very hip."

Michelle peered at my embryonic joint. "Brigid, you'll never get a Rocky Mountain High that way."

I pinched some more leaf between my fingers and let it fall into the textured paper. I rolled and licked it, mimicking Monica. I stared into the flame beyond my nose, breathed in, and thought of The Sale. It made me sigh—a sweet, smoky sigh.

The Sale, as they called it, was something of a blur. It was akin to later experiences I had of shock. I had woken later than the rest of the family, let the screen door of the farmhouse slam behind me, and once outside in the usually quiet farmstead I discovered swarms of cars and pick-ups and more than a hundred milling people. Men stood around in indigo overalls or sienna colored jackets. They eyed, pointed, picked up items, and conversed together in pairs or clumps. They were quietly, or not so quietly, estimating what they'd pay for various pieces of Floyd and Jennie's sixty years of existence—all strewn out in the sun. Disoriented and out of body, I searched the crowd for my grandfather. I finally picked out his tall form and ran toward him, but then halted. Up close I could hardly recognize him. Grandpa Floyd's face was the gray-white color of the ashes that we cleaned out of our Denver fireplace. Standing near my father and the auctioneer, Grandpa Floyd's lanky limbs hung limp. He looked like one of the specters in the movie *Scrooge*—The Ghost of Farming Past.

I sucked some smoke in and held it in my mouth. I edged down the base of Blessed Clare, made a pillow of cypress mulch, and closed my eyes.

The auction of the animals had been worst of all. Grandpa Floyd stood, as I imagined was the custom, near the gate as each group of animals came into the corral and members of the crowd made their bids. First were the Marcel Marceau-faced Hereford calves, then the steers. Then the twelve Guernsey and Jersey dairy cows, and finally the slightly-wild pony that I had just gained enough skill and confidence to ride, along with Trixie the ancient quarter horse who had cradled me on her saddle almost since birth. Grandpa Floyd stared down mostly, his eyes hidden behind the round brim of his Sunday Stetson.

I heard Monica and Michelle start to giggle; I opened my eyes and saw Monica shaking down petals onto Michelle like a blizzard on Berthoud Pass.

"You bitch," Michelle began.

But suddenly all three of us froze. We heard the door of the middle school close, and then a few footsteps on the cement of the nearby sidewalk. I tried to melt into the mulch and flowers. Through the stems of the Russian sage and the purple coneflower, bee balm and brown-eyed Susan beyond, I could just make out the terrifying form of two square-toed riding boots.

Peppered amidst the middle-aged and aging Sisters of Perpetual Adoration who taught us—some who wore habits and some who did not—were a few middle-aged and younger men, not Religious. Mr. Flynn was the funny one who wore high top keds and taught physics—literally, rocket science. Mr. Marzetti was the sexy one who commuted down from the mountains, who, it was rumored, kept horses and had his classes reading *Bury My Heart at Wounded Knee*.

Unfortunately, he was married. He was new to the school the year before, tough and demanding. Being both sexy and off-limits, that first year we had all decided to hate him, and to hate his wife even more. But over time, he became our secret favorite. However, he was still demanding and tough, and he hadn't seemed to get the memo that St. Clare's was progressive and that Colorado was laid back.

Mr. Marzetti definitely wore boots with a buckle and square toes, and I was absolutely sure he was planted on the nearby sidewalk with his boot toes pointed straight at us. We didn't say a word. We didn't think of breathing. We hoped the burning grass-ash wouldn't burn down to our fingertips. I heard the faintest of respiratory sounds. Could he actually be sniffing the air? Mr. Marzetti was a New York transplant to Colorado, with long hair and a beard.

Holy shit.

He probably knew the smell of pot. Hadn't all New Yorkers his age gone to Woodstock and smoked weed? I clenched my eyes tightly. I'd mainly accepted but never solidified any ideas about God. If there was a God, I thought He/She was doing a pretty lousy job of late, otherwise in that moment I might have prayed. I thought I faintly heard Monica mouthing the words to the Hail Mary.

Finally, the boots spun on their heels and walked back to the school. When we heard the door shut, we breathed and snuffed out our joints in the dirt. Like three Jack-in-the-Boxes, one by one we each popped our heads up above the weave of coneflower and sage to scan for safety. But then, one by one, like young deer each of us was exquisitely paralyzed. Mary Mother of God, there Marzetti stood. He had tricked us. Arms folded. Back against the school doors. He stared us each straight in the eye. Shook his head. And maybe smirked? I almost thought that he and the statue of Clare were exchanging knowing glances. Did the Blessed Clare wink? Had she mystically given us away? We were going to catch hell.

Michelle, being the one with the Ziploc of pot in her lilac colored army jacket, was simply sent home. This was far from her first offense. So, despite the forgiving ways of the good Sisters, they called her father with the news that the Academy just wasn't working for Michelle. Randall sent one of his male assistants in a copper Mercedes Benz to the circle drive to scoop her up. For good.

Monica and I were relative innocents. Besides, we buried our joint bits before wading out of the perennials and denied partaking. Michelle had whispered that we could. She knew her number was up and was willing to take the fall. The nuns accepted this portrayal.

But Marzetti was another story. Didn't buy it for a minute. He had already had his one-on-one with Monica. Now it was my turn. We faced off, in silence, for a long time. A long Denver afternoon. Sunshine pelted through the window, slashing my teacher's dark beard and folded arms. Wordless. It was way worse than being lectured. I tried to look impish as his dark eyes bore holes into my green ones. But I had a headache. Did pot leave a hangover? I never could outlast his silence, even as pissed to the fingertips and ear lobes as I felt. Finally, I couldn't take it and threw a verbal slap.

"They call it the Inquisition, don't they?" I said. "I think it is a Catholic thing." Although the Mass was almost identical to Episcopal worship and we seldom went, every now and then I pulled out my Church of England identity if it served my purpose.

My teacher didn't consider this worthy of a response.

Finally he took a pace or two forward. "What's happened? Last year you were a smart ass, but a happy smart ass, a fun-loving smart ass. Brigid, you're sad and angry. It's obvious. And being a smart ass, that is not going to end well. Why are you upset?"

His skin was more olive, and his eyes more almond. But in

stance and countenance he greatly resembled the braves on the cover of *Bury My Heart at Wounded Knee*. A copy sat on my desk.

"Pot is not the answer," Marzetti continued. He let that sit awhile. "Whatever it is, smoking won't take the sting away. Not for long." He addressed this subject like he knew something about it.

The outside door was cracked and the Colorado air moved between us. I looked out the window, toward the teal blue Rockies in their snow caps, but I pictured the farm. Wind-tossed green fields. Sun-baked beige fields waiting for harvest. Grandpa Floyd moving through them. I remembered dancing with the wheat in spring when I was little. The taste of time that was tied to the sun. I was there: the Brenchley half-section. Dad never wanted any part of it. In fact, that was the worst part of all. Selling the farm was pulling Dad and Grandpa Floyd apart. Increased tension between them. Dad was to have half the land now; Jennie had already signed over her half to him. He wanted the whole thing sold to the highest bidder, an investor who was buying up large tracts. Corporate farming. Grandpa Floyd wanted the whole parcel to go to a family who would live on it and farm it. Whatever they could pay.

The truth was, I wanted to be that family. But I was only thirteen. Dad never wanted any part of farm life. But me...

"You can tell me," he said. "What has you so angry?"

Tell him? A hippie-transplant from New York? Even in Colorado, Kansas wasn't cool.

Not in 1975.

More silence. In the silence, I felt my anger and sadness building, like thunderheads. "Sure. I'm pissed," I finally uttered. "We have this farm. Well, we did have one. But my grandfather had two heart attacks and had to sell it. He looks like a ghost, wandering around this little town all bored. Now, we can never go back. Sure, I'll survive. Stupid farm. I'll live. But my grandfather..."

It embarrassed me to the core. But when what I had been pushing down was named, my chest heaved up, like it was going somewhere. I angrily wiped at hot tears.

Grandpa Barney was sick. Now Grandpa Floyd and the land... When I finally looked up, my tough teacher from New York had wet cheeks. He told me I could go.

Monica and I were not suspended, but we were expected to do some healthy service.

"Mr. Marzetti is sure that working in the gardens with me is just what you need," Sister Julian said, from atop her green wellies.

She situated me behind a wheelbarrow of smelly, close-to-ready compost. Part of a cabbage and a banana peel were reaching out for help. The nun and I stood in Julian's outdoor workshop behind the convent: three-bin composter, worm casting barrel, solar panels waiting for installation.

"He said something about the land," Julian continued. She looked at me knowingly. "Quirky, for me, there isn't much sanity without weather and tilth and plants."

I was not accustomed to hard work. My hands and forearms already ached.

"Sister Julian, this is a heavy load."

"Not half as heavy as the load you will bear if the headmistress and Mr. Marzetti learn that you've refused."

With that, the eco-nun turned on her heels, shovel in hand, and headed west, beyond the tennis courts. Facing toward the afternoon sun and the periwinkle strip of the Front Range, I followed Julian and thought of the farm—some pain, but some comfort. The organic matter I pushed was pungent but healing. The nomadic pile of compost listing before me smelled even more like the farm than Randall and Michelle's Columbian gold.

15

JOB'S TEARS

Tradescantia is a genus of 75 species of herbaceous perennial wildflowers in the family Commelinaceae, native to the New World from southern Canada to northern Argentina. Some people call this plant Job's tears, many call it spiderwort. These weakly erect, scrambling plants are commonly found in clumps in wooded areas. Most flower only in the morning. We planted it in the deep hollows of the rain garden—its eight-foot-long roots soak up run-off.

–Note from Dean Brigid Brenchley's Prairie Journal

Friday Daytime

I start my day as I have been with "Morning Prayer" in the prairie. There is more foxtail to eradicate amidst the sage and switchgrass and, though calmed and buoyed up by Phil, I can't help but still fume a little about Max as I pull out the shimmering, almost invincible weeds.

Maury Zeller pulls up in his restored Mustang and lets off his wife Artemis, our Altar Guild chairperson. Stepping out, Artemis is wearing peekaboo heels and she moves with determination toward Roosevelt's back entrance. Behind where the organ swells and rumbles, the Altar Guild sacristy awaits. Roosevelt and Artemis are the only ones with keys to that particular door; even Merlin and I don't have them. In a church, you can practically chart who has power by who has what keys. Artemis works at the Iowa State Capital and has slipped over to polish candelabra for an evening wedding. She is prayerful and one of the most hard-working people I know. She has taught me a lot about creating sacred space—even through small, silent actions, like the unfolding or re-folding of an altar linen. But Artemis can have a prickly personality, and she swears like a sailor.

"Don't you have work to do?" Artemis says to me, half serious, half joking.

She thinks I spend an awful lot of time looking dreamily about, or gardening. On the other hand, a strong feminist, she has seen me tenaciously push my way through male power-dynamics at St. Aidan's. Artemis already looks a little grouchy as Maury disappears and one of her heels gets wedged in an open corner of a permeable paver.

"Damn permeable bricks!" She awkwardly yanks her foot free and glowers at me. "Did it have to be hippie paving?! Little assholes, right there between every brick, I swear."

"Hard day on The Hill, Artemis?" I ask.

She doesn't bother with a response, but goes in to work out her mood on the altar brass. Right as the door shuts with a bang, I get a call from Henry on my cell phone.

He sounds shaken. Asks if I will meet Pearl and him. My calendar is open for lunch, so I get in my car and head back over I-275 to the bend in the Des Moines River and that part of the city known as the North Side. The highway loop is so elevated, I can't evaluate the state of the river. The rain starts up again, but lightly. Henry says they'll meet me at the bakery. The Marshland Bakery two times in one week!

The bakery is a Des Moines institution. I am one of those people who is always dashing around five to fifteen minutes late, so am surprised that I arrive before Henry and Pearl. I survey the spot for them but to no avail and settle into a booth. The place is famous for old-school, sugary sweets hearkening back to when Swedes and Norwegians traded jovial barbs across the oil black coffee. For the moment, the rain stops and sun shines into the diner-like space, illuminating sugar-cinnamon and broken pieces of cookie lodged between orange vinyl seat cushions. There is a table of older men with newspapers kibitzing, probably since their first morning apple fritter. The Scandinavians are gone from the area except those tethered to the nearby Lutheran College, and the neighborhood is increasingly populated with people from Viet Nam, Laos, and Sudan. A beautiful Asian mother is buying treats for her toddlers who press hands and noses to the display glass, much the way Nicholas did four days ago when we came for the cream puffs.

I breathe. Working downtown, and living in the quasi-gentrified old suburbs, it is a relief to be somewhere more straightforward. I realize the energy it takes to try to be upscale, professional, or hip all the time. The Marshland Bakery is real.

I am thinking this as Henry and Pearl walk in. They sit down and try to smile. But they look very worried.

"Can I buy you a donut? Or, they have chicken noodle soup today," I say. "A bowl of that? You treated last time, let me get lunch."

They timidly agree, and before long, steaming broth is placed before us, teeming with chicken, veggies, and homemade noodles. So steaming hot, the glass windows fog up around us.

Henry removes the oxygen tube from his nose, draping it over the top of Fido. But while Pearl and I dig in, he mainly just fishes around with his spoon in his soup. Henry doesn't look well. Just days ago, he seemed nearly acrobatic, balanced on his stool juggling light bulbs and Nicholas. Today he looks older. Even his anchor tattoo seems faded. The change hits my consciousness hard. As an assistant priest on Chicago's North Shore, I had what my boss called a curmudgeon ministry. The old, Great War era guys liked me—I think I often reminded them of their daughters or granddaughters. Some of the ones at Henry's age would be active and fit as a fiddle one day, and the next day their health would plummet. Especially a gentleman in the parish also with emphysema. In fact, I realize, it was sort of the way it went with my Grandpa Floyd.

Be close to Henry, I pray as he begins to tell me why he called.

"Dean Brigid," he says, "We need to ask a favor of you and the church."

Her hands showing signs of arthritis, Pearl unfurls a piece of paper. She is petite, but there is a leathery tenacity about her, perhaps from hefting bags of dry cleaning for thirty years. What she unfolds is a notice from the county supervisor.

"They came door-to-door with these yesterday," Pearl says and hands it to me.

- Prepare Yourself for Flood Hazard
- Place all valuables on the second floor of your home or in a safe location not in the path of the potential flood.
- Secure items that have potential to float away, such as gas tanks.
- Know your local evacuation routes and location of emergency shelter sites.
- Be protected not only with homeowner's or renter's insurance, but flood insurance as well.
- Plan to recover. Have policy numbers on your person at all times, plus the name and numbers of professional restoration companies so you can remove floodwaters from your home should a flood occur. The water can quickly cause damaging mold growth if untreated.

I look up at them both and nod, "What can we do?"

"Our house is a ranch, just one floor," Henry says. "It's been a good house. Raised all our kids there. Big for one level."

"Hank built it himself with my brother Stan's help almost forty years ago," Pearl proudly tells me.

"Store everything in the basement. Last flood," Henry continues, "completely ruined. Can you keep some of our things at St. Aidan's?"

"Of course," I say.

"I used to be a scoffer," Henry takes the notice and stares down at it, "of climate change. The boys at the plant, we'd mock the notion over beers." Henry shakes his head. He lays aside the paper, studying the mound of egg noodles surrounded by liquid in his dish like it could soon be his house. "Once. But twice? The church already helped us rebuild last flood. Now this."

"We'd have the kids keep our stuff," Pearl adds, slightly biting her lip, "but they're three blocks away, and in the path of the water, too."

"What about insurance?" I ask, though the COAD meetings have prepared me for her answer.

"Homeowners," Pearl says, "but nobody gives flood insurance to people in a flood plain. Never have, never will."

"We don't have many valuables."

"So, are the officials telling you to move?"

"No. Just to be prepared. For the worst."

We finish our soup (except for Henry) and console ourselves by eating a Napoleon each. Chocolate and Bavarian cream are hard to beat as comfort foods.

Then I try to work off these calories by loading Pearl and Henry's belongings into my hatchback: A vinyl suitcase of papers, Pearl's pearls, and their grandkids' track ribbons. A Hoover. A blender. A toaster, an electric drill and drill bits. Some framed family photos. A color TV.

Last, Henry carefully brings me two books carefully wrapped in a linen towel; on the towel is an English teapot outlined in blue embroidery. His sailor tattoo and this whipstitch teapot bundle somehow together symbolize the gentle masculine man who is Henry.

"Mother's Bible and her Church of England Prayerbook. 1662, her favorite. Keep these in your office? They were her anchor. I imagine she's eternally surprised they're mine now too!"

Loading up their treasures, my conscience is tweaked about my own materialism. I picture the artwork hanging in my house and my substantial but dwindling plethora of possessions.

CATHLEEN BASCOM

Probably by necessity, Henry and Pearl live light.

"Public work crews from the city are trying to reinforce the levee. You can see it on your way back downtown," Henry tells me as the last things are secured.

"Let's go look," I say, "Why not?"

I follow Henry and Pearl's small station wagon around some back streets, then through the parking lot of the Marsh-Rose High School. At the very end a vista opens up where Des Moines' first amusement park once stretched, now long gone. It increases our worry to see that the National Guard has now joined the city workers. Dump trucks are pouring out gravel and sand. Some crews are forming it into a make-shift levee, almost eight feet high. Others are attempting to cover the mounds with plastic, and then secure that with sandbags at the base. All of this is happening behind the permanent Marshland Levee. The same one that was compromised in 1993.

The same levee? Same people? Same houses? *Lord, it seems so wrong!*

Henry and Pearl and I lean on our vehicles and watch. The rain begins to spit on us again as I absorb my parishioners' dread. Wordless communion and worry is all we have to share.

We part and I don't look back. I just drive. Driving, I am driven, deep inside... to pray. Or maybe...even to drink. With my mood upon leaving the levee, I am tempted to drive home to the bungalow and start in on the merlot. Better yet, an uncorked Sonoma Zinfandel? But, I recall Phil's caution that escaping into alcohol only makes life's headaches worse. I see his handsome face and caring eyes lit by the restaurant table candles. And then, as the rain starts to pelt down, Merlin calls.

"*The Des Moines Register's* Pasha Kurtz has confirmed his best interview time is three o'clock this afternoon."

I have to smile remembering my middle of the night prayer to be protected from alcoholism. In my experience, the Divine is loving but very tricky!

118

I stroll into Merlin's office, my rain coat and umbrella making puddles near his desk.

Merlin was able to coax some preliminary information from the reporter. "Says he has been following the prairie since its inception. Did see the television feature. *The Register* wants to do a series about the history of the cathedral's land. Initial interview would focus on, Why? Why did the cathedral install the prairie project in the first place?"

"That's helpful. Daunting, but helpful. Can you grab St. Aidan's 150-Year Anniversary for me from the library?"

"Henry and Pearl?" Merlin asks. Perhaps he reads the concern on my face.

"The Marshland Levee is so precarious that they got instructions to be ready to evacuate. Both tied up in knots. Henry didn't look well."

"Not again," Merlin drops his head.

We both grow quiet.

I'm about to move on when I realize my friend Merlin looks as worn out as I feel. "What's got your goat?"

"Ivan's absolutely unglued: the river has jumped its banks near the Center... with the gala scheduled for tomorrow night! He was up all night with angst, so, I was, too."

The rain. The river again. Getting everyone down. The gala is for a long-needed renovation of the Botanic Gardens because of damage from the last flood. Kindly, they are giving ten percent to the cathedral's prairie.

"Why don't you go home?" I suggest.

"Purgatory at home. Purgatory here. Best if I just keep busy."

"I'll be hiding in the chancel until the reporter comes," I say.

When Merlin is in one of these moods, it's best to give him a wide berth. And God has seemed to ordain that I take my many worries into the sanctuary instead of into a bottle.

I am surrounded by lilies, twisting vines, burgeoning blossoms. They burst forth—not in chlorophyll—but in stained-glass, stenciled paint, and marble. In the chancel, I sit at the dean's *prie-dieu*. My right fingers massage the rose and thistle carved in the smooth oak arms. The original grain pokes through on the ridges, the valleys in the wood are cold—all carved by some compassionate craftsman for the long chain of deans who have prayed, sung, and worried in this space.

I have gained steam in my conviction that the prairie should be saved, but I ask God:

Really, what is most holy to you? The building and its worship? Or the prairie?

Slabs of stained-light tumble onto the stone interior— emerald, azure, burgundy. They sooth me. The Aesthetic Movement expressed a tie to nature in balanced, abstracted forms. These windows exhibit Victorian craftsmanship not so different than the interior of The Broadmoor. But I trust these images and messages.

I become mesmerized by the Meservey Window. Less abstract than many, it features realistic swallows and stained-glass grain. With the play of afternoon sunlight, the swallows seem to move, alighting on the bending stocks.

I try to prepare myself, ruminating on the reporter's questions.

Why did we put in the prairie?

Somehow a goldfinch from the shrub outside the window finds a gap in the stone and flits inside to alight at the base of the window! Draws my gaze to the words in serif on the burgundy glass:

Consider the Lilies.

The window is pretty straightforward. It articulates the central reason we put in prairie. We did it for the beauty of the threatened plant species and our conviction that they are of value. Jesus teaches us that the non-human order offers us guidance and blessing. I can tell the reporter that fact.

Of course, I would like to believe that all of our motives were pure and God-centered.

But being honest, I know that in our project there was plenty of worldly ambition involved, too. The old ugly parking lot— with its spaces rented for decades to secretaries, accountants, and waiters—brought some needed income. Cathedral members like income. But a lot of them value beauty even more. It isn't always spiritual: sometimes God as the Source or End of the beauty gets forgotten all together!

Okay, I confess, *we did it for worldly beauty, too.*

My confession makes me aware that St. Aidan's leaders and members, in a fickle fashion, may prove equally energized by the beauty and buzz of a boutique hotel!

Suddenly, my eyes drop from across the nave where I have been watching the window's light.

The figure of Jesus on the elm of our crucifix firmly and rather inexplicably draws every fiber of my being. It reels in my thoughts and pins my spirit to its suffering form. Jesus emerges almost as part of the tree. The limbs of the cross have muscles like wound rope, and they ripple, ripple, radiating outward from the Christ figure's straining ribs. Not a lot of evidence there that Jesus was a comfortable aesthete.

Jesus' pained form makes me think of Henry and Pearl. I am safe. My bungalow sits even above the cathedral, above High Street. What if I were them? Having to move all my keepsakes? To sleep in a shelter, wondering if my children and grandchildren are safe?

Those who are suffering? Are holiest to you?

The cathedral bells chime three o'clock. I have a newspaper interview.

The news reporter Pasha Kurtz is a complete contrast to the television reporter. He is a few minutes late, and there's a lull in the rain, so I am seated on a bench in the garden for a quick breath of fresh air. Pasha rides in on his bicycle, his long thin legs gracefully circuiting the bike pedals, and as the tires bump over the path's permeable pavers, tufts of his long dark hair waft up and down. He is very young. I am impressed as he glides to a stop and dismounts in one motion. He looks at me with pistachio-colored eyes.

"Dean Brenchley? Shall we do our interview outside? I appreciate this garden," he begins.

Suddenly, we know the meaning of a cloud-burst! Quickly, we pull Pasha's bike into the narthex and park it inside. Merlin brings us some Earl Grey and we settle into soft chairs in a side room.

Very new-school-old-school, the main visible tools of Pasha's trade are a small moleskin notebook and a Bic pen. But reporter Kurtz has definitely done his homework.

"So how much is the Hotel Savant willing to pay for the land?"

Kyrie eleison, I stare at him, internally aghast, *Lord have mercy.* Out of the mouth of babes.

So it's confirmed; any illusions I've retained about this offer being known only to a small circle vanishes.

Pasha responds to my look of chagrin with a gentle sincerity beyond his years and foreign to his trade.

"The Hotel Savant gave *The Register* the lead," he continues. "I interviewed their representatives yesterday."

"The cathedral is just beginning to review their proposal." I begin cautiously, my mind back-peddling. "In fact, leaders have not even gathered to discuss it. The vote is definitely out as to whether we will consider selling any part of this historic parcel."

"Dean Brenchley, I covered the city council meeting when they approved your prairie restoration efforts. I heard the mayor's strong support, as well as that of the DNR. I think the native green space is important. Visionary. Especially in light of the chronic flooding in Iowa."

I sigh, relaxing a little bit.

"On the other hand," Pasha continues, "the developers claim that The Hotel Savant will bring at least two hundred new jobs downtown. That has to be a consideration."

"Our cathedral has always tried to serve and support our citizens, as we feel we are spiritually led." I respond carefully, without fibbing, sounding rather vague like a politician.

"Of course," Pasha confides, "the developers would like the newspaper to help incite community support, turn up the heat a bit! I imagine that is why Fox came over. The Hotel is in desperate need of more parking, city requirement, and your lot is one of few options. But watching the prairie emerge and now bracing for the river to crest, I wonder what the true common good is? My editor is also interested in exploring that question."

In my mind, I see the river, and the sandbagging crews. I see the bags under Henry's eyes, and I see the elm-like cross and Jesus wound together. The common good?

"So, Pasha, what exactly are you proposing?"

"A series of features in *The Sunday Register*, about the long story of St. Aidan's land, the development of the conservation project, how prairie relates to flooding, and, yes, the offer from The Hotel Savant too. A kind of window into the history of our city. I think there is a much larger story to tell here. Especially in light of the flood threat."

I try to take in this surprising reporter. Perhaps a new breed? "Pasha, are you from around here?"

"Kansas City. My parents teach religion at the University of Kansas. I guess it's why I was open to having this beat at the paper. My father is Jewish and my mother's background is Tengriism; she's Mongolian. It makes for some lively lectures."

When Pasha opens his moleskin, my spirit moves from the *Kyrie* to a *Gloria.* He folds down its cover. This journalist could not be more different than Aaron Vandermann.

"Pasha, I think I would like to do this series of articles with you."

He readies his pen and we dive in.

16

SNOWFIELDS

The China and Teacup Bowls. What grows here is foot after foot of powder. Sometimes, size isn't everything. The Tea Cup Bowl is one of the smaller back bowls, but it's loaded with cliff drops and steep shots. Bang a right off Chair 17 and follow signs to Genghis Khan. Ski there and contemplate Melville's "Whiteness of the Whale."

–Note from Dean Brigid Brenchley's Prairie Journal

Vail, Colorado, February 1978

At age sixteen, I came to ski Vail's Back Bowls alone.

I had first learned to ski alongside my father Bruce when I was seven and he was forty. Sometimes Grandpa Barney and Grandma Helen were there in tweed hat and fur coat with Mom to offer hot cocoa and jocularity to the those of us trying to learn this awkward if exhilarating sport. My sisters rented skis, too, but mainly flirted with the boys who pulled off their hats and goggles. At first, skiing was a family affair, full of the warmth of childhood.

But much had changed by the time I first skied the Back Bowls.

The night before skiing I was upstairs but overheard my parents talking.

"Mother is beside herself with worry," I heard Mom say. "Though Dad's a fighter, says he may want to go up to Mayo Clinic. "

"Mayo. Why Mayo?" Dad's voice rises.

"They've removed how many feet of his intestines? The doctors are running out of ideas."

Unfortunately, in the morning light the front side of Vail Mountain was crawling with people. I had to ride the long chair lift to the summit with a middle-aged man who said he was a ski chaplain. I rolled my eyes. He seemed kind enough, despite the ice connecting his runny nose to his mustached lip. He tried to make small talk at first. But as I rebuffed his attempts, we fell into silence, watching large snowflakes fall, and the occasional clumps of snow knocked off by skiers on the lift ahead of us.

Under one hundred and twenty pounds? I pictured Grandpa Barney now emaciated. I weigh over a hundred and twenty pounds, I thought. In fact, I was gaining weight. Sometimes, I vented my new anger and anxiety by binging on brownies or mocha chip ice cream. I loathed my new body with its rounding breasts and middle. My body was as out of my control as my family and my world. The farm was gone. No longer in overalls, Grandpa Floyd wandered the town of Norton like a bored boy in church clothes. Worse yet, Dad and Floyd's relationship hadn't improved. Floyd went ahead and sold his half of the farm to a family with five children, who gave a ridiculously low sum but who wanted to live on the place. It was all they could afford and it was all Floyd wanted: someone to live on and farm the land. Dad finally sold the quarter section that Jennie had signed over to him to the corporate farmer. Dad told me that money from the profits would allow me to go to any college I wanted. So I felt implicated, too, especially because I was setting my sights on Northwestern in Chicago. Grandpa Floyd only endured six months "in town." He died from a blood clot suddenly, a complication of earlier bypass surgery. Like I'd told Mr. Marzetti, I knew that without the land he'd let go.

Riding at a steep angle on the cold swinging bench, I tasted guilt—like a metallic taste on my tongue. And now, the bitter pill to try to swallow was Grandpa Barney's seemingly fatal illness.

"Less than a hundred and twenty…"

I felt sleet in my eyes. Somehow Floyd and Barney were pillars supporting my sense of self. Pillars even of reality.

"Are you okay?" The ski chaplain asked, his pert eyes filled with genuine concern.

Damn it. I want to be alone, and I am trapped with this guy. "My grandfather's wasting away. He may not make it."

"Sorry. What's his name?" The man asked from under the frozen mustache.

"Bar… Barney… Byron"

"Dearest God, enfold Byron in your love, your Light," he said to the invisible Beyond.

I was pissed. God? I had let go of that "opiate of the masses" the minute I read some high school Marx. In my mind, No One was minding the store.

"Don't believe. Not that," I muttered. Relieved, I saw the lift ramp just ahead.

"This love you feel for your grandfather. His for you. It has a source, you know."

Our skis hit the wooden planks and we were forced to stand. The man swerved left and I very intentionally went right. I sped away from him toward the Teacup Bowl as fast as I could. At sixteen, I knew I could literally leave him in the dust.

Like Annie Dillard at my age, I had had "small experience of the evil, hopelessness, pain, starvation, and terror that the world spreads about. I had barely seen people's malice and greed." At sixteen, I was simply losing those who had shown me love. I was losing the places that had brought me a sense of well-being. It pissed me off. Unreasonable rage perhaps. I was nonetheless enraged and driven by the losses.

I leapt into the whiteness, making my knees like mattress springs, the way my Swiss ski instructor taught. I plunged into whiteness, trying to purge myself in snow and speed. Only my own motion, audible through my headband, whipping away pain, I pointed downward. The whiteness of the powder engulfed my shins and the bottom of my poles, the skis riding through it like outriggers pushing through ocean waves. The steep incline placed whiteness on every side of me. The mountain was like a theatrical backdrop. Inches behind my back and head, and on every side: Colorado snowfields. Twelve thousand feet. The mountain reigned. I was a dot. An ant, on its massive shoulders. I could be flicked away, demolished at any turn. Swallowed by the whiteness.

Yet, damn it, even the whiteness evoked an image of my skeleton-like grandfather. For he was also wrapped in the chaotic white of hospital walls, tubes, and robes.

Into my parka, zipped to my nose, I screamed, "Screw this... life." I stabbed my poles, trying to puncture the flesh of the mountain, "Just shit! Flush it. Everything. Screw life!"

As if in response, the earth literally gave way under my skis. The springs that were my legs suddenly straightened like sticks. Nothing to hold me. What in deep winter are snowy draws in the Teacup Bowl, in late season become cliffs. I had inadvertently found one. I knew nothing about jumping, but luckily my intense emotions and sudden terror made me draw into a kind of fetal position. I think my released grief actually propelled me further through the thin mountain air. So, my skis did land and then my rear, like a shot-put, smashed through the snow's crust. The velocity and deep snow ripped the poles out of my hands, strewing them up mountain. The wind inside me splintered like a broken mirror. Finally the thick powder stopped my skidding form.

When I opened my eyes, for what seemed a long time, I merely gazed. The sky was blue, but large snowflakes, combined crystals like you see form on your dash before the wipers sweep them away, drifted down like feathers. My body hurt; in fact, my whole left side had grazed a fallen tree limb. But like my breath, my rage had also shattered. For the first time in a long time, I was open. I knew a sense of Being. Looking upward, eyes following one floating form of crystals, then the next, I simply

Was. For what seemed many eternal moments. Somehow, into the openness came Wonder. I became aware as I had been as a child at Elk Falls that the granite peaks and the snow were not of human-making.

"This love has a source." That frozen-mustache-guy's words were inside me.

I lay on a threshold. But it was the Creator who seemed to cross over, to seek me. Not the other way around.

Source of the mountains. Source of me...

In that moment my spirit uttered its first real prayer.

I don't even know if I believe you exist!

In my experience the Divine has a sense of humor. Also seems to enjoy the vernacular. A voice-not-a-voice. I experienced an articulation of the whole Creation without and within me.

You must believe in me if you are talking to me, you dummy.

It hit me like a ton of snow falling off a pine. *Mysterium tremendum* and beatitude delivered through a Valley Girl phrase.

The love that had been crumbling, fading, slipping away, seemed suddenly to fill me. Flood me. I welcomed it.

Years later I would read of C.S. Lewis' experience and grin in recognition. The buttoned up, bombastic Oxford don—it happened to him on a double-decker bus. He wrote that he "felt as if (he) were a man of snow at long last beginning to melt." Not real snow, Lewis nonetheless experienced on an English bus going up Headington Hill in Oxford, what I experienced lodged in a snow drift above Vail.

How long I lay in this state I can't say.

"There, down there."

Then I heard the swish and swoosh of skilled parallel skiing. Two ski patrol crested the hill just above me. A little of their spray hit my face as they stopped and got out of their skis.

"You okay? Don't move yet."

"Bashed up, but fine," referring mainly to the beatitude inside, "I think," I said, but the minute I said it I realized that my exterior body was shivering from shock and cold.

"We are going to give you a ride to the lodge."

"How'd you know to look for me?"

"Gus, the ski chaplain... wanted us to check the China Bowls."

One gathered my equipment from round about and then together they lifted me onto the sled they pulled.

My scraped side screamed, raw, where their arms cradled my ribs. "Ouch."

But in the end nothing was broken. I didn't even have a concussion to explain my spiritual experience. All that broke was my raging grief.

17

PRAIRIE SMOKE

Geum triflorum or prairie smoke. The most distinguishing feature of prairie smoke is not the globular flowers, but the fruiting heads which follow. As the flower fades and the seeds begin to form, the styles form upright, feathery gray tails which collectively resemble a plume or feather duster. Widely scattered throughout the prairie and visible from Pleasant Street, the reddish pink flowers blend well with the color of the cathedral's granite.

–Note from Dean Brigid Brenchley's Prairie Journal

Friday Night

As we both increasingly lean toward keeping the prairie and refusing the hotel's offer, Phil and I know we have a lot of strategizing to do before the board meeting next Tuesday. We also realize that we need to start to let the wider parish know and need to listen to them, as threatening as that may be to our own opinion. With our furor over Max's power play and getting to know one another better, we simply didn't get much business done over dinner yesterday. So we decide to meet again this evening. Because he has a dinner wrap-up with his clients from the finished case that will end at an unpredictable hour in my vicinity, I propose that I make coffee and he bring dessert and we have a working session at my bungalow. I am to further research the flood mitigation impact and garner statements of support from conservation and government leaders, and he is trying to research the original gift of the land and legal ramifications. We are both too invested in the project before us to do anything stupid right now, but I am beginning to think Phil may like spending time with me as much as I like spending time with him!

So, I tidy the living room and clear the dining room table as a work space. I begin chronicling the various data and statements made about the prairie. Handy that Merlin and I had already begun this process in preparation for the Pasha Kurtz interview.

Phil calls, "Sorry this dinner has been dragging on. Too late?"

"Not at all."

"Terrific. Do you like cheesecake?"

He arrives with cheesecake, Perrier, and limes.

"Strange. I am a bit blocked on locating the original deed and title," Phil reports, quickly getting down to business, "but I have been able to review the codes in relation to benefactors' desires."

I show him my flowing list of statements by public figures supporting the prairie, so we can cull the best and build our argument. Phil and I work into the night.

In fact, we have both nodded off in the Ward wingback chairs, with the Perrier bottle, spent limes, two plates of mostly finished cheesecake and my clerical collar on the lampstand near us, when the PDT special siren ringtone goes off. It's 11:52 p.m.

I open my eyes, reach for the phone, and knock over a bottle. Nice: just Perrier. Even nicer: a kind, handsome man across from me.

"What the hell is that?" Phil mumbles. I hit the speaker-button.

Ssssch...ssch...sssssch static...then, "PDT Security. We are reporting an alarm at St. Aidan's Cathedral. 755 High Street. This is a fire alarm." Then, not a computerized voice but a human voice gets on the line. "This is Agnes, at PDT Security. We have a fire alarm at your church. The appropriate authorities have already been notified. Will you respond? Again, this is not an entry alert but a fire alarm."

I freeze. *Dearest God.*

Since pastoring my first historic church, a Carpenter-Gothic gem, I have fretted I would receive such a call. As a young priest, I would lie awake nights worrying that fire might take the church—especially with all the twelve-step meetings we hosted and attendant addict-saving cigarettes. Over time the anxiety lessened. Now I am in shock. No tossing and turning delusion. This call is real.

Phil helps me absorb it, nodding and pointing his chin toward the phone. I come out of my fog, "Yes. Of course, I will respond."

Phil grabs his jacket and I slip into shoes. Forget the collar. We drive pell-mell through the sycamore boulevards toward downtown.

When we arrive we see that the fire is not all-encompassing. It is fiercest near Center Street, well away from the building. Parking and drawing closer, human forms can be picked out, moving with fire-hoses putting out the flames. The firemen are concentrated in a wall guarding the cathedral building when Phil and I pull up. We rush toward them.

A fire official, not in boots and coat, intercepts us.

"I am the dean." I tell him, "and this is my church."

"I'm chairman of the church's board," Phil adds.

"Glad we reached you. The fire is contained. The church is safe."

I cross myself, *Gloria in excelsis. Thank you! Thank you.*

"The grounds on the other hand," the fire fighter continues. "Fire still intense down at that north end."

"What caused it? Do you know?" Phil asks him.

A BMW screeches up and Max Chase, with evidence of silk pajamas poking out from his raincoat, races through the dripping grasses and smoke. He faces the historic cathedral, his eyes frantically searching its form for signs of fire.

He turns to the fireman, ignoring us. "What is the status of the cathedral?"

The fireman assures Max, as he did us, that the cathedral proper is safe. "Maybe some smoke residue, odor.... But the blaze is pretty far away. It was saved in part by all the recent rain. Building's untouched."

Only then does Max turn to us. "I still get the security alerts too. The Chases always have."

Suddenly, I see my new love-interest in a new light. The masculinity that partly attracts me to Phil is a visible force; he looks like he might actually haul off and punch Max Chase. I have been so much in shock, I myself nearly forgot Max's threat, but now I realize Phil thinks Max set the blaze.

"Max, you tyrannical bastard. Arson? You'd sink this low!"

Max looks shaken. His Warhol hair is afloat like a young chick's. Did he forget his own threat, too? Or is he an extremely studied actor?

"Morrow, are you serious? I might threaten, as a way to chasten the dean. I would never. Our family has poured our lives, and hundreds of thousands into this church."

To chasten the dean? A pacifist, I nonetheless almost want Phil to punch him! I am not sure what to believe. Does Max protest too much? He looks more like Dick Cavett, but sounds more like Nixon. Showing up all concerned. Is he concerned, or is it the perfect alibi?

Phil moves toward him.

Then, through an arch in the thick, prairie-side smoke, Merlin steps, in bedroom slippers.

I put my hand on Phil's arm and point.

What in the world does he have in his arms?

Merlin moves our direction and carefully gives his bundle to a nearby fireman.

"Medics!" the man calls.

Delilah. Lord have mercy. It's Delilah.

"Nip in the bud. Butt." Delilah is mumbling. She looks up at us in recognition and points her chin at Max. "Foxtails. Lit up!" Cough. Cough. Choke. She gets agitated as the paramedics lay her on a gurney, "Oww!" Cough. Cough. The three men roll her toward an awaiting ambulance.

"Sleeping in the horsetails. These were in her hand," Merlin says and shows us a charred pack of Camels.

"Any of you family?" A medic asks. We all nod.

"The closest she has," I say.

"You and Merlin go with Delilah," Phil gestures with his head toward the ambulance. "Max and I'll stay 'til the fire's completely out. Call in the insurance claim."

A relief. A comfort... a companion...

But my comfort quickly vanishes as both Pasha Kurtz and Aaron Vandermann stride through the haze. Bic pen in hand. Fox camera crew close behind. News travels fast in a small city.

"Dean Brigid, what's happened?" Pasha asks.

"Get the blaze and the firemen first," Aaron yells to his cameraman.

18
INDIAN GRASS

Sorghastrum nutans or Indian grass has flowering stems to seven feet tall. The seed matures from September to frost and the flower heads are chestnut or copper colored. As forage for animals, Indian grass is nutritious both green and as hay.

–Note from Dean Brigid Brenchley's Prairie Journal

Denver, 1980

I had been such a snarky agnostic, who could I tell that I might have met God? The Monday after my Vail ski crash my high school's zany creative writing teacher, Mr. Steinberg, was busy balancing his chair on top of his desk. In appearance our teacher looked like Woody Allen stretched long. Next, he crawled up on the desk, stacking an array of books, some fruit, and a mop. He was creating a woman figure for us to describe, to teach us about metaphor.

Reverse metaphor he called it: like how can a persimmon also be a nose?

Having left St. Clare's for public high school now, Mr.
Marzetti, Monica, and Sister Julian were not at hand to talk to
about this God encounter. So there was really only one candidate
for my revelation, an equally snarky but believing Catholic friend
named Erin Kelly who sat directly behind me in creative writing
class. Her verbal repartee was exquisite, and her college-aged
sister had set her up with a fake ID—which gave her heroic high
school status. But still, Erin made no secret that her religion was
a big part of her life. Somehow for me her worldliness gave her
spirituality credibility. I felt that Erin was someone I could trust
with my new openness to the Divine.

Earlier, as part of a class assignment, Erin and I had
whimsically written of "Metaphysical Experience." So, watching
Mr. Steinberg with chalk clouds on his tweed jacket and reddish
beard, I scrawled on paper:

> Kells, I had a metaphysical experience at Vail. For real.
> Think I might believe in God after all. Quirky

She wrote back:

> Meta! With a capital M. Excellent. Can't wait to hear
> about it. p.s. I hope this metaphoric goddess doesn't
> fling Steinberg onto the floor as a sacrifice. She looks
> fierce.

It was through Erin that I spent over a year as an "exploring
Catholic." Erin's Catholics were more ethnically and
economically diverse than people at the Episcopal church my
family erratically attended. Mainly they were enviro-hippies—
with head-scarves and hiking boots—who believed in Jesus and
Transubstantiation. Erin's Sacred Heart youth group folded a
hodge-podge together in a fashion rare in those status-conscious
air-brushed-suburbs of the seventies. Most importantly, Erin
and these others corroborated my experience of Divine Love.
Some of them had experienced similar things and adored my
conversion-through-snow-jump story. For us, the Rockies were
the backdrop of our faith.

One day, while driving up to the mountains for a camping

retreat, Erin and I discovered there actually was a Church of the Metaphysical in Denver. We simply liked the phrase! We swore we'd attend someday. But we never got quite that far out of our Catholic and Episcopal worlds, and before we knew it we were off to college.

Evanston, Illinois 1980-81

If there is anyone to credit or blame for my becoming an Episcopal priest it would be Peter Caspian. By the time I arrived as an American literature major at Northwestern University, I was starting to have some questions about the Roman Catholic Church—or at least my place in it. Even in those liberal days of Vatican II, I became aware that most of Sacred Heart's Colorado Catholics were faced with either conforming to the dogma of the Church or pretending to do so. Intellectually it made me uneasy. It also didn't feel totally honest. I figured the Divine knew what I really believed and no acting otherwise or saying rote phrases would fool God.

On one of our Catholic rock rappelling weekends, the last thing we did was pray about our future spiritual lives at our respective colleges. When I arrived home, I had a letter waiting for me. It was from Peter Caspian. The envelope was of textured wheat-flecked paper and it had a rounded Celtic cross in its corner.

Canterbury House, Northwestern University, 2212 Sheridan Road, Evanston, Illinois.

It was a letter welcoming me to the community of Episcopal students at Northwestern and inviting me to an open house.

I had no idea how this guy even got my name!

Weird timing. Are you in this? I reverently asked God.

With some ambivalence, I brought Peter Caspian's letter with me to college in my luggage. Before I even got that steamer trunk up the stairs of my brick Evanston three-story, "Father Peter" rode up on his burnt-orange Vespa. With preppy tortoise shell glasses (flecks of orange in them matched the bike), shoulder-length hair, and a smile broad like his shoulders, Peter Caspian was nothing like any priest l had ever met.

Wispy, ancient Father Boone at my parents' church still used "thee" and "thou" in daily speech! Peter Caspian spoke a lively vernacular. Right off the bat, Peter dubbed me "Brench" for Brenchley—that is until he overheard one of my sisters call me Quirky. Filled with glee, he called me Quirky from then on, transplanting to Chicagoland the nickname l would have been happy to leave in Denver. Later, when he felt sure l was called to be one of the Episcopal Church's early women priests, he would call me Bishop Quirky.

"I've known a lot of quirky bishops," he'd say. "But never a Bishop Quirky!" With Peter and two college males schlepping my luggage, l said yes, l'd attend the Canterbury open house. lt included Sunday evening worship. l saw through the ploy, but figured what the hell, l could give their worship a whirl.

The Eucharist at the Canterbury House had an informal mystic vibe like Roman Catholic Mass (though at Sacred Heart they had never encouraged me because l wasn't "really Catholic"). More importantly, Peter Caspian's sermons were poetic and political, full of relevant wisdom.

He was a master of metaphor and illustration. He described transcendent, spiritual mysteries in images from nature. Peter said the link between the Divine and the natural world was a well-wrought Anglican literary and homiletical tradition: Julian of Norwich, George Herbert, the lesser-known Augustus Hare. This link, he argued, was firmly rooted in Jesus' own parables. l was hooked.

The Canterbury House was a forest-green, Stick-style with peach and yellow accents. Peter's wife Margay was a painter and textile artist and the house was as colorful and interesting inside as out. The Caspian family (who resided on the top floor) and a handful of Northwestern students lived together, holding everything in common much like the first followers of Jesus— sort of spiritual socialism. This was radical stuff to imbibe for a suburban girl. They fed homeless people at the door, handing out peanut butter sandwiches, and they fed dinner to anyone who came to worship on Sunday, sometimes a hundred or more. These people were actually acting on the sayings of Jesus that I was reading for the first time! By my sophomore year, I had moved in.

Of course, sharing everything in common had its downside. About a week or two into my residing there, Peter motioned to me from the doorway of the second floor bathroom. Our house manager David, a kind and witty gay graduate student, was pointing to the underbelly of the toilet. We were all to do chores, and I had been assigned bathrooms that week.

"Quirky," Peter said, "You may need to tighten up your game a little here." He pointed to some mustard yellowish drizzle lines. "Did you clean under there?"

I pulled back about to gag. "What? Under there?! I cleaned the seat... inside the bowl."

Peter laughed. "Don't tell us you've never cleaned a toilet before?"

"We had house cleaners, and we were all sisters. That toilet is disgusting."

"Here you go, honey," David said, and offered me some nice long rubber gloves and the toilet brush. "Uncle David will give you a tour around the finer points of porcelain care."

At least once a month, Northwestern professors would also join us for dinner (and a little sherry or a beer). They would pontificate and lead debates on things like nuclear disarmament, end of life ethics, feminist theology, the Dead Sea scrolls, the poetry of Anglicans like John Donne, Christian pushback against the atrocities of Idi Amin. At this time, I started wondering if maybe I could become a professor. I liked the way they rolled. This high octane spiritual-intellectual milieu was just what I had been missing in the Catholic Church. The freedom to fully engage my mind in this walk with God—not hide any doubts or questions but put them on the table and sort through them in community.

The Kansas Flint Hills and Norton, Summer 1981

Summer after sophomore year, I signed on with a team traveling with the Caspians to Kansas to lead "Creation and Creativity" conferences for high school students. Peter was a devotee of Wendell Berry and Wes Jackson, and our events were sort of like their Land Institute with a sacramental, spiritual twist. We drove from Chicago in the Caspians' old VW bus.

Heading west on I-70, beyond Topeka, Kansas the road steadily rose—ascending one grass covered step, then the next—taking long strides into the vestige of a sea of grass. Only three percent of that ecosystem remaining, we crossed it just south of Manhattan. Here a remnant ribbon of tallgrass prairie stretched in panoramic proportions. The Flint Hills.

For three months, we settled into a lodge that had once been part of a large cattle ranch. It rested down low, in a crevice in the limestone bluffs, in what the locals called gallery forest.

There redbuds, burr and chinquapin oak, ash, and obnoxiously invasive red cedars lived down low closer to streams and run off. Peter and Margay Caspian had two little girls: a three-year-old and an eleven-month-old. With the baby on one of our backs, and the other running ahead, we would hike up out of the trees on to the flat bluff-tops. We walked land that had been sporadically grazed but, due to the shelves of recalcitrant limestone underneath, had never been plowed. Grass and attending wild flower species spread out right where they had existed for at least five hundred years.

So, that September, for the first time, I waded into grasses that reached above my head.

The flora of this inland sea came upon us in waves. At shin level, sideoats grama and daisy fleabane—like shasta daisies in miniature—were our wading pools. Knee-to-hip-high, waves of wine-tipped little bluestem and a parade of flowers like bergamot, liatris, beebalm, and goldenrod lapped around us. The seed head feathers of Indian grass greeted us shoulder high or higher, like the shimmering crests of waves. The Caspians' little daughter in the backpack, her hair a similar hue, would grab the brass-colored plumes in her small fleshy hands, holding them aloft as we walked. 1 became a devotee of tall grass prairie in the Flint Hills.

But being in all that open country, 1 also felt the loss of the farm. The wind often came from the west, from the higher plains near Norton. The wind felt and smelled like it had on the farm: like sun, and grass, and dust, and cattle, and wheat. Jenny had died about a year after Floyd. The grainy wind touched grief and guilt 1 still carried.

One evening, on a hike in those hills, 1 unburdened myself to Peter. 1 told him about the rift between my dad and grandfather.

"I'm going to pricey Northwestern on sacrificed Brenchley land," 1 told him.

At first, Peter laughed, "You were only a kid! You can't hold yourself responsible."

But then he saw 1 was truly pained, truly felt tainted. Nighthawks were swooping over the Indian grass and bluestem harvesting bugs, and 1 could tell Peter went into silent prayer. He entered a kind of outdoor confessional. Finally he tapped words from the Episcopal prayer book:

"May Almighty God in mercy receive your confession and sorrow and of faith, strengthen you in all goodness, and by the power of the Holy Spirit keep you in eternal life."

He made a sign of the cross on my forehead as the sun was reduced to an orange sliver and the nighthawks plummeted. 1 closed my eyes and felt a dark heaviness dissipate on the breeze across those flinty hills.

"*Forgive me, a sinner too,*" Peter said, and then he paused. "Hey, why don't you go there? Don't you need to get to Denver before the term starts anyway? How long since you've been back to the farm?"

1 shook my head.

"Haven't," 1 finally said, "not since they sliced it up."

"Ahhhh," Peter's eyes sparkled with a spiritual idea. "Well, Quirks, in confession the confessor gets to make suggestions of actions that might help heal. This is mine: why not make a pilgrimage to the farm? See what God reveals to you there?"

The car I drove in those early college years was a treasure bequeathed to me from Grandma Jennie: her beloved chrome-rich 1964 Plymouth Fury complete with push-button transmission and teal paint the color of her favorite Fiesta Ware. It idled precariously in busy Chicago intersections but otherwise was coveted by fellow Northwestern students for its eccentric, shiny glory.

So, after a visit with my family in Denver, I drove the Fury on old Hwy 36 across a vastly uninhabited stretch of eastern Colorado. That landscape was more barren and mystical than any monk's hut on the Irish Sea could ever be: nothing in sight except sky and blonde grain, blonde pasture-land, and blonde mixed prairie grasses. Even the cattle were rare. But to me, the Creator seemed to be everywhere. Once, some pronghorn bounded in front of the car. In four hours, I saw three red tail hawks, but only one pick-up truck. If I had broken down, who knows what I would have done!

Finally, near the Kansas border, a town materialized: St. Francis, with a café that still had delicious pie. Into Kansas, more towns came: Bird City, Atwood, and Oberlin. The farm crisis was at hand and they all looked like they had seen better days. I checked into a motel in Norton, making the Brenchley farm my priority for the morning.

Another Brenchley heritage gift, passed on to me the year Floyd died, was a spiral-bound *Atlas of Norton County, Kansas*, compiled in 1972 around the time of my fondest farm memories. As the warm Kansas sun moved into the sky, I balanced a coffee and laid the open atlas on the upholstered car seat. The diagram made my route pretty clear. Leaving Norton, East on Hwy 36 and turning north on Rural Route 3, I couldn't miss it. There, staring up at me, were two outlined shapes of land straddling section 7 and 8 of Emmett Township. The two pieces bore my grandparents' names: Floyd J. Brenchley and Jennie R. Brenchley. The two pieces were on each side of the road.

I was stunned by how instantly and completely I recognized the lay of the land. A certain swoop of the gravel road; a draw to the right where cattle munched on knee high grasses; the clump of cottonwood trees that were the sentinels of the farmstead. I pulled easily into the drive. The familiarity was palpable. It was like the landscape of my childhood somehow lived back in my psyche, no, back in my body, in my cells. The pony-like rhythm of the Great Plains wind, the sound of a meadowlark, cows conversing down the lane. The smell of hot grain. The smell of dust. Clean dust. Memory made incarnate again.

But my heart fell when I got out of the car, for the farmstead was a shell of its former self. Jennie had passed away only two years before, but they had left the farm seven years before she died, and those years had taken quite a toll. The family who bought from Floyd still farmed the land, but in order to make ends meet they had quickly realized they had to move to town near jobs for the wife and teenagers. The barn still held hay and farm equipment. It was tidy enough and just needed a little paint. But the house was empty and entropy had won. What were once Jennie's mowed lawn and kitchen garden were overgrown with tall weeds. The earth was rejecting the sidewalk and slabs of the old concrete were tossed up like a navy pier, with the once-pristine farmhouse at its end like an old, windswept boat.

I saw a swallow exit a hole in the roof and I couldn't bear to peek inside. My sense of loss came from deep-down, as if from my own subterranean aquifer. My chest heaved and I cried. The dwelling that housed all those rural memories of my childhood was gone.

I walked to the road to check out the sections of land. Heat and the whirring of hidden insects were my only company.

The Jennie-Dad section, now owned by a corporate farmer, hosted a center pivot irrigator showering water across rows of corn. I knew from a paper that I had just done for an environmental studies class at Northwestern that recent farmers were pumping as much as 1,600 gallons of water a minute onto fields in the Great Plains. The aquifer, the one that took centuries to create, was already diminished by 242 feet. In the decade since my grandparents actually farmed, there had been bumper crops not only of wheat, milo, and soy beans, but of the fat-farmers-high-paying crop: corn. I stood and watched the seemingly benign, even benevolent, water as it showered down on the crops. Grandpa Floyd had been right to scratch his chin and wonder.

I moved further down the road to what was once Floyd's section. I was shocked to see the wheat gone. But in its place, a herd of cattle waded there. Grass-fed beef? Mainly Marcel Marceau-faced Herefords, with a few Black Angus thrown in. The cows and I gazed at one another—many of them chewing. I could picture Floyd calling them into the coral for the night. I sensed he was there in a way. Silently watching, like he did when he watched me dance with the winter wheat.

19

SWAMP AGRIMONY

Agrimonia parviflora or swamp agrimony is a plant found in wet woodland patches and ditches, oak-hickory forests, and margins of calcareous marshes. Tiny leaflets are interspersed between adjacent pairs of large leaflets. In Wisconsin, this is a Special Concern plant. At the cathedral these grow in our bio-swales, mingling with the Job's tears and swamp milkweed.

–Note from Dean Brigid Brenchley's Prairie Journal

Saturday Lunchtime

So today inside an unharmed church on a city block of charred plants and ash, the parish pretty much comes unglued. The place is packed, so packed that we have to assemble in the cathedral's nave.

"No Max. Nor Madge," I whisper this observation to Phil.

We sit together up near the large eagle-shaped lectern with its feather-scales of oak, as members of the cathedral file in. Our roles as dean and board chair place us in tandem naturally.

"I noticed." Phil adds, "Max is most at work when he's most invisible. He's surely sent his proxies. Though, I must say he was civil, even helpful, working through the insurance. Of course it's a perfect alibi."

"Hmmm. Delilah or Max? Now there's a pair to draw to."

"Or Delilah and Max. Did you see how she looked at him while they were loading her in the ambulance?"

The assembled parish members look restive and the cathedral bells ring the appointed hour. So I don't reply. To me the crowd's mood evokes *Les Misérables*. But the bell stops tolling and Phil courageously steps up to the microphoned eagle. He welcomes everyone and calls the meeting to order.

"Undoubtedly, you all have questions and concerns, and Dean Brenchley and I are here to field those. We know how much each of you cares about St. Aidan's."

Then I step up beside him. "Despite being a little smoky, the building is fine everyone. Let us take a moment of silence and for that grace let's thank God deeply."

As I am bowing my head, for a second I glance toward the north where the fire occurred just outside the Meservey window. I can't believe it, but I spy three goldfinches that have slipped inside through a gap in the leaded glass. I close my eyes, uttering my own prayer to God,

Lord, you are the vine, we are the branches. You have to keep us connected. You must be both the source of love and of justice here. You must root us in you. Please.

I allow space for others to utter their prayers. When I open my eyes and raise my head, the birds are still there at the window. Distracting, right when I need to be a focused leader.

"Why don't we just start with your questions," I say as I scan their faces.

"We raised five hundred thousand dollars for this goddamn greenspace," Artemis says. She has never been a big fan of the prairie. "What now? Did the fire ruin the plantings?"

Marianna, since the cathedral building is not compromised, looks a little like the Cheshire cat. She got her prairie burn! She rises to her feet.

"Great question. But the news is good. On American prairies, fires were commonplace, part of a natural cycle," she explains. "The grass species will actually get a boost. Now, the red twigged dogwoods, they'll suffer. Might need insurance funds to replace those. The flowering forbs will show a little shock, but overall, for the prairie, the fire was a positive."

"Well, it looks like hell. Literally," says Manford Reynolds, a banker and one of the members Max says will leave if we don't accept the hotel deal.

"It's sure to raise liability concerns with the downtown business community, many of whom already found the space unkempt," says Mona Reynolds, Manford's wife. She is an architect. "I say, it's time to re-think the use of that section of our property." Mona is no slouch. She had a hand in the huge West Des Moines mall that Ivan and Merlin call The Emerald City. She has a following, though most of the older families find her designs a bit garish.

"Dean Brenchley, Mr. Morrow," Manford continues, in an oratorical tone that sounds rehearsed, at least in his head if not in a Chase boardroom, a little the way Max communicates. Is it because they were all packed off to boarding schools at fifteen, I wonder? "Isn't it time you two apprise parishioners about the generous sum of money St. Aidan's has been offered? And for this now-charred bit of land! A proposal you have been holding captive from the rest of us!"

Ouch. Save my soul. Okay, he's right, it is time.

"What? Dean Brigid, after our last dean was cagey if not deceptive, you promised you'd always be open with us!"

"The hotel agents just came a couple of days ago," I assure them.

"We need to look closely at the offer with legal and real estate experts, then with the bishop and chancellor of the diocese, and then confer with the full board of directors," Phil explains.

I've found that public meetings like this often sound like a Colorado stream after winter snow. There is a lot of sound underneath, which is a little mesmerizing and disorienting, a lot

147

of layers of conversation whispering and gurgling as people try to comprehend news.

"How much is the offer?" someone asks.

"Three million, seven hundred twenty thousand dollars," 1 tell them.

The ululation 1 imagined in my daydreams is pretty close to reality. No one strips and starts dancing, but the murmurs definitely leap into some astounded cheers.

"Are you kidding?"

"Take it!"

"Immediately!"

Uh-oh. Marianna looks mad and mortified. She is scanning the room for who will rise and defend our environmental efforts. No one so far. She again jolts to her feet.

"After all our work? The prairie project was fully backed by the board and the parish," she reminds people, raising her voice. "Do you know the pollutants we capture? Do you want to add to the flood crisis all around us? How fickle is that? Well, over my dead body."

Prairie conflagration, now parish conflagration. Sweet Jesus.

"The prairie is just taking off," Jason comes to Marianna's support.

"We have a full schedule of school kids coming for outdoor classrooms," Elena adds.

These three stand together, arms folded, like an A.C. Milano human wall in a soccer shoot out. 1 feel disoriented being cut off from them by my role and the podium. They're my team, my adopted family. 1 want to go stand by them and also fold my arms as others take shots at the land and grasses, not to mention the people of Marshland.

"Worship is what we are about, not gardening," Roosevelt blasts. "The disrepair of this building can't go on. Neglect. It's an affront to God."

A mild-mannered member of the cathedral board, Harold Manse has caught sight of the goldfinches.

"Do my eyes deceive me or are there birds in here? Can't get much more in need of repair than that!" He points to where they have flitted into the Lady Chapel. The whole assembly of forty-plus people turns.

"I knew the Lady Chapel linens were being tainted with strange green drops!" Artemis says and rushes to shoo the birds back outside. I see one finch deftly hide behind the marble Christ Child in Mary's lap, a little the way I behave when Artemis storms my way.

People start shouting a myriad of different opinions at me, at Phil, at one another.

Episcopalians, even in the Midwest, don't tend to be shy about their views, but I have never seen such a church commotion. It's like the trout stream has reached Elk Falls and the community is plummeting over the edge, sure to crash and fracture on the rocks below.

My spirit asks, *Did Max do this? Start it all? Pay Delilah? Give Manford Reynolds a script?*

We've survived a fire, and all they can think about is money! Makes my pastor's heart sink. I thought we'd come so far. I realize that I do care about the whole crazy community, not just the prairie team. My head swims as I scan their faces. Though Manford and Mona Reynolds are pretty pompous, they have the sweetest teenage daughter on the planet who has talked to me about a possible call to the priesthood. I am with Harold Manse many Saturday mornings at Habitat for Humanity building projects. Retired from middle management, he is gifted with a hammer and lathe and adores nothing more than building houses for new families. He helped restore Henry and Pearl's home. Artemis' mother is slipping into dementia, and I have held Artemis in my arms as she wept when her mother no longer recognized who she was. Artemis let me weep in her arms when my parents had to cancel a recent trip to visit me due to lack of money. At St. Aidan's, we do these things: are lives are woven and intertwined.

But now this issue of land or hotel is taking a machete to our bonds. Amidst the clamor, Burton rises.

His tall form and accents of gray demand respect; at St. Aidan's, Burton has substantial street cred. He clears his throat and his visage bestows dismay at the disarray of his life-long faith community. The group quiets and shifts. The public mood is divisive, but also, perhaps, looking for someone to provide a way through.

"The dean and board chair...They have not been covering this offer up. Let's be clear about that," Burton declares in a tone fit for the statehouse—deliberate, authoritative. "The dean has shared it openly with me and has begun to seek input and advice from others, too. I believe she has discussed it with Mr. Chase for instance. Dean Brenchley, am I right?"

I nod. I smile.

Burton is a gem and a political genius! That will show Max for making himself scarce. "As Episcopalians," Burton continues, "our policy is clear: the Cathedral Chapter, the proper name for our board, together with the dean, decides matters of real estate." He turns to me: "Dean Brenchley." Then he turns to Phil: "Chairman Morrow. Are you two bringing this matter formally to the next board meeting? I believe it is Tuesday?"

What I'd like to do with Phil is run off to the Virgin Islands, let him show me his bromeliads, and forget this whole damn mess! Phil and I exchange glances, both well-aware that Burton, the old organizer, with shrewd political finesse, is throwing us a life-preserver.

Dear God, thank you for Burton, I pray and follow his lead.

"Yes, Burton. Everyone, we have told the developers and the agents of the Hotel Savant that no decision will be made until the cathedral board discusses it thoroughly."

Phil adds, "We will be looking over various related documents between now and Tuesday's meeting, and between now and then please feel free to give your thoughts and opinions to me, to Dean Brenchley, to Burton, or any board member. We will take them into consideration."

It isn't until now that I see Henry and Pearl in the pew with the others. Their belongings are now safely in my office. Pearl's often intimidated to speak publicly, but usually Henry would be very much in the mix in any parish discussion. But they've said very little. As much as they love St. Aidan's, 1 imagine the fire—especially since everything is fine —is second in their minds to the flood threat. In fact, Henry's countenance, with the bags under his eyes, seems to silently question why everyone has their panties in a wad. In past meetings, he might have said something to that effect, like: "1 say we be thankful we're not debating inside the burned out shell of a cathedral."

1 am pretty sure that is what he is thinking, but he doesn't say it; he doesn't look like he's feeling himself. At that moment 1 come to my senses. 1 realize we need to be praying for the Joneses and all the vulnerable people in our city. 1 feel overwhelmed by the politics, but 1 can lead us toward prayer.

"1 can't believe anything can burn after all this rain," 1 say and step in toward the eagle microphone, getting us back to the original reason for the meeting. "But the fire chief said that the abundant rain and the rain gardens may actually have saved us. Saved the building. However, the rising river is threatening some neighborhoods. Even some of our parish families. The Jones family for one. Henry and Pearl have said 1 can share that with you."

Henry and Pearl nod as congregation members send compassionate looks their way. In fact, remembering the flood concern has a strange effect upon our communal consciousness. At least momentarily, it dissipates the anger and enmity, like the water from the firemen's hoses dissipated the flames. Or like when the stream clears the falls and spills into a broad, peaceful meadow.

With panache, Phil seizes the lull. "So that concludes our meeting. 1 am most willing to discuss any of these matters individually with anyone, but let's recess to the Parish Hall."

"And anyone who wants to stay and pray," 1 say, "gather with me in the chancel. Having learned of the fire while away at the House of Bishops' meeting, Bishop Farnon sent a note urging us above all to remain constant in prayer."

Most of the congregation leave, some to further vent with Phil. But like a collection of worldly monks, the usual suspects make a small rectangle in the chancel pews that face one another. Before getting into a pew, Merlin stops to confer. We can overhear Artemis in the sacristy swearing a blue-streak as she soaks the bird pooped fine linen.

"How much stress can we bear? A fire, a flood, and a parish battle," I ask, "and in the middle of this, my ninety-year-old grandmother arrives for a visit!"

"You? What about me?" retorts Merlin. "Tonight is the gala! But, alas, a cathedral on fire is a little more important than petit-fours from Chocolaterie Vie."

I take my place at the dean's *prie-dieu*. Pearl, Henry, and Nick, who again has his favorite truck, slide into the pew directly across from me. Henry and Pearl look weighed with worry, but luckily their grandson is a bright distraction. Nicholas disappears except for a few tufts of hair sticking straight up as he runs his truck back and forth along the pew seat.

Hummmm, mmmmm.

Harold Manse, whom I can imagine will be our most torn board member, comes and sits near me. That calms me a little, considering the fact that Manford and Mona Reynolds, on their huffy way out of the meeting, confirmed that if we reject the hotel offer they will join the suburban parish in West Des Moines, where pragmatic people pray. On top of the Chases, the Reynoldses pulled pledge could be catastrophic to the budget.

Artemis clip-clops in from the sacristy in her heels and plunks down behind Merlin. I can tell she is miffed, but I give her credit for being present nonetheless. Marianna, Burton, and Maxine come in together and ascend the few steps into the chancel. Maxine steadies Burton slightly so he doesn't slip on the marble. They sit next to Henry and Pearl and ask solemnly about evacuation plans.

It's a small band. But when you've survived a fire you've got to take time to give thanks.

The report is that even Delilah is okay. Simon visited her

this morning. We can't see him, but Roosevelt the organist soon manifests he's stayed, too, wrapping us in a gentle version of the *Jubilate*. Surely it voices his deep gratitude that the fire didn't make flaming pillars of our French Canadian contre violon organ pipes.

When I picture those pipes wrapped in flames, I wonder again if Max would be warped enough to pay Delilah to set a fire. But I quell that thought, and instead open my Book of Common Prayer to the old form of the Prayers of the People and try to turn all of it over to the Divine:

Let us pray for the Church and for the World.

20

BIG QUAKING GRASS

Briza maxima or big quaking grass is not native to the United States. It has a large number of common names, including big quaking grass, great quaking grass, greater quaking grass, large quaking grass, blowfly grass, rattlesnake grass, shelly grass, shell grass, and rattle grass. The seeds and leaves are edible.

–Note from Dean Brigid Brenchley's Prairie Journal

Evanston, 1983

The priesthood thing got serious when Grandpa Barney died.

I had finished my junior year at Northwestern imbibing large quantities of modern literature. Virginia Woolf and William Faulkner captured the shifting light of the mind; Graham Greene and Herman Hesse plumbed the human soul; Willa Cather painted my native landscapes. I was heady on it. Not to mention the occasional course in art history and religion.

So that I might survive the Chicago winters in January and February, Grandma Helen actually let me borrow her coat.

"Denver's so much more temperate," she declared when I opened a sizeable Christmas package.

I was the only quasi-Christian Socialist walking around Evanston in a full-length mink! Toasty, I would leave New Testament Greek class and walk the eastern shore of Lake Michigan. With its far shore nowhere in sight, I called this body of water our θlwọợa: a Greek word for "small sea." In winter, this Sea of Michigan would heave huge blocks of ice into Cubist sculptural forms. On weekends, I would take the Evanston Express to the Loop to check out the real Cubists and to lose myself in the artwork of the Art Institute. For me, all of it pointed to the Divine. *Imago Dei.* Great art surely revealed that humans are in the image of God.

But what still spoke of the creativity of God most exquisitely? More than even the best artists? The tallgrass prairie. The Flint Hills. Despite a hundred degrees and eighty-five percent humidity, I went back every summer.

The Flint Hills, 1983

The summer when I was a college junior, Peter and I and two high school boys were in a meadow excavating a small pond. We had spent the day with Wes Jackson's Land Institute scientists learning about their test acres of a species of perennial wheat called Kernza. Margay and the Caspian girls were trying to bake biscuits with the experimental Kernza flour, while the four of us were digging. Or, rather, trying to dig. There had been a recent abundance of grasshoppers near the lodge, munching the petals off the prairie forbs. The purple coneflower looked more like pin cushions than flowers. The two teens were Eagle Scouts who had attended one of our recent Creation and Creativity Conferences and their idea was to reintroduce prairie chickens or guinea fowl to eat the grasshoppers. But the birds needed more water.

Digging, we came, literally, face-to-face with the root system of the prairie.

"Try to yank that big bluestem," one boy, Eric, said after we had dug around it. I lifted. Not a budge.

Eric dug some more. His buddy Sam dug more, too.

"You are going to have to really get those trowels deep," Peter directed.

As I knelt next to the big bluestem, I saw shimmering silver bell-shaped seed heads, quaking in the breeze. I had never noticed this grass before.

I cupped the beautiful drooping plant. "Peter, what's this?"

He stooped and eyeballed the plant. "Big quaking grass, I think, lovely but not native. You want to get that out of here. Somewhat invasive. In fact, everybody circle around."

He dug briefly around the stand of big quaking grass, its flowers moving with each push of the shovel.

"Okay, Quirky," Peter said, "yank. Pull hard."

After the intransigent bluestem, I bent and put my muscles into it. But the short-rooted, non-native plant came out easily and went flying backward, taking me with it.

"You are so mean," I said from the ground nearby, the plant cradled in my arms.

"I'm sorry Quirky," he said laughing, "but I wanted to make a point: natives versus non-natives."

Peter used the trowel to hack down through the prairie sod. Finally, the three of us managed to pull the clump of big bluestem from the earth. The fibrous roots were tangled and dense and full of moist soil.

"You know, two-thirds of the prairie ecosystem exists below ground." Peter told us. "When the first European farmers made room for crops, people said they could hear the ripping out of prairie from miles away."

We laid down the big bluestem and stretched its roots out on the ground. Sam, the tallest of us, being over six feet tall, lay down next to it. The grass shafts were almost as long as him. The roots added more feet. Now that's one extensive plant!

"Those roots are how these plants survive the drought, the wind, the cold."

"Peter," I said, staring at those roots, "I see God in that, more than anything I know, except maybe the Eucharist. Is it orthodox?"

I'm sure he was tempted to affirm my strangeness. But instead Peter shook his head, "Very orthodox. Incarnational. Irenaeus believed that when Jesus 'took on flesh,' all of creation was restored, as was intended in paradise. The Anglican mystics tend to follow that logic."

"Oops, there's some more quaking grass," I said, and this time took a hand trowel to gently lift it out. The seed heads rattled, and up-close their shape reminded me of the bells devotees shook when I once visited the Krishna-consciousness temple in Denver. "Better do our part for paradise."

As the high school boys took the wheelbarrow downhill to gather limestone, Peter turned to me and his tone got serious.

"So, Brigid, you've decided to forego applying to Law School? Is that definite?"

"I think so." This was a prickly subject. "Law School would help my family. My dad is getting older, and could use some legal advice at the firm to buttress his insurance knowledge. But...I think being an attorney might just suck my will to live!"

Peter hesitated a moment. "I think I should tell you... Some of the college chaplains at the last conference told me they thought you ought to become a priest."

What I experienced was like the movement of air in the center of my being, along with a kind of focus in my mind. It was unlike anything I'd experienced before... though it was like it sprung from my experience at the Teacup Bowl. I think it was what we sometimes term a calling.

I quickly stood up from where I was still kneeling.

"What?!" I gazed at Peter with incredulity.

My family's main form of Sunday worship was champagne brunch, and I had never even set eyes on a woman priest!

The wind of the plains? The Holy Spirit? I felt like I had swallowed a Hoover vacuum.

The notion had seriously never crossed my mind before. It

was either the worst or best idea I had ever heard. It sent me into a panic.

I wonder if it was really as immediate as I remember, but it seemed as if right then, the minute after Peter uttered those words, Margay appeared over the ridge with the two Caspian girls, Kernza flour on their hands and clothes. Upset.

"We got a call," Margay said, "from Brigid's family. Quirky, they had sad news. Your grandfather has died."

I needed to fly home.

Denver 1983

Grandpa Barney had lingered longer than any of us could have hoped for. Mayo Clinic had given him five extra years of life. A waning, compromised life. Not much strength to play golf or to trout fish, but more time with Grandma Helen and more time with us. He retained his great sense of humor and laugh. He never lost his laugh or the twinkle in his eyes.With the news, all of his twelve rather grown grandchildren flew in to Denver to encircle Grandma Helen and our parents. At one time or another, each one of us had reeled in a rainbow trout with Grandpa at our side.

With years to write it up, Barney's final wishes were simple, clear, and in his own hand:

1. If warm enough, a day for all to fish at Elk Falls
2. An Irish wake with drinks and music
3. (For Marilyn's sake) a brief memorial service in the church

If Father Boone was still alive, he would have led the service, "thees" and "thous" included. But he had died about a year before Grandpa Barney. My parents' Episcopal church had a new priest who barely knew our family—this happens with Christmas/ Easter Episcopalians.

This priest was willing to preside, but asked, "Is there someone in the family who can share about Byron's life?"

I had absolutely not told anyone about Peter's crazy idea that I should become a priest. However, the extended family knew I loved to write and that I was on a kind of spiritual quest. So, not long after my arrival in Denver, my mother and father came to me.

"Brigid," they said, "Helen is definitely not up to it, and both of us think if we try to give the eulogy we'll break down. Your uncles, ditto. So we wondered. You were so close to him, would you write something that the new priest could read at the funeral?"

I knew instantly I wanted to write about my grandfather! It was a little tricky considering he was not really a practicing Christian. But, while we were digging out the big quaking grass, Peter had given me the thread of an idea I could preach with sincerity in my grandfather's honor: the Incarnation and taking our place in Paradise. I experienced that in Barney. Especially at the lake. I could speak about that quality, that reality.

I knew that Peter preached from a format that fused academic outline with beat poetry; I had seen his notes in the pulpit. I emulated what I'd seen him compose.

> Jesus said, *I came that you may have life, and have it abundantly.*
>
> Our grandfather, Byron Robert Ward
> Had an urban, rather poor, childhood.
> Though middle-class and educated, owner of a General Store,
> Barney's father suffered from severe depression.
> Not good for business.
>
> Even as a boy, Barney helped raise money.
> At the turn of the century...
> On the cold Kansas City streets
> He sold newspapers and parked cars
>
> He had a buoyant personality,
> But, life was not particularly abundant for Barney.

But then he met Helen.
Absolutely fell for her!
And also all her parlor-singing Irish American family.
They were the ones who dubbed him "Barney."

When Helen and Barney were young,
nearly two hundred clubs and speakeasies were open all
night in KC!
Think *The Great Gatsby* and Charlie Bird Parker.
Barney did the Charleston with the love of his life.

And boy did they live!

Then he got hired by *The Kansas City Star.*
He became a newspaper reporter and started a family.
Life was improving exponentially.

But it was when he first set foot in Colorado
that our grandfather discovered trout fishing.
In black and white home movies we have from 1931:
Barney's wearing a tie and khaki jodhpurs. And he pulls
a trout from the lake
And he is overflowing with life.

He would tell us
that it was in the Rockies,
in those trout streams and lakes
that a new kind of Life imbued him.

After all the news beats and the concrete
He found communion with the water
And the mountain grasses:
The mutton grass,
The squirrel tail,
The fish scale sedge.

He found communion with the animals of Elk Falls
The V-waking beaver

The standing elk
And above all the TROUT,
With their bellies of watercolor sunsets.

Byron learned to think like the trout.
Hunt bugs like them.
Relish the glistening rain.

Barney, the older gentleman,
as we knew him in our childhoods, was fluid, moving
with life. Abundant Life.
We all saw it!

Grandpa communed
With the One he came to call The Fashioner,
Fashioner of the peaks,
of the flies,
of the fish.

Communion!

Today
We proclaim
And celebrate
That this Communion
is stronger
than death.

AMEN.

It was extremely simple, but I was nonetheless pleased with
what I had written for the priest to deliver. I figured my dad and
uncles could flesh out the fishing bits, and the priest could refine
the theology.

But then came the kicker.

Hours later I was descended upon by a large cadre of my
family. "Quirks, it's perfect," my sister Bev said.

"Captures him to a T," Cousin Barney, named for him, added.

"Now we wonder," said my mother, "could you deliver it at

the service? Do you think you could manage? Father Jacobs is comfortable with that. He thinks it's a commendable sermon for a college student."

"You want to write and used to want to be an actress," Bonnie said.

"A real ham," Barbara added. "If anyone can do it, you can."

Oh my goodness.

The Holy Spirit's Hoover vacuum filled me again, though they couldn't tell. Full force. High level. Me preaching? After Peter bringing up the priesthood? A big, big quaking came upon me.

"Byron will smile if you do it," Grandma Helen said, despite her grief-stricken, Limoges-like face.

My dear Grandma Helen, after fifty-eight years of marriage standing there without him, in shock in her mink. Our mink. What else could I do?

So I stood in the pulpit, knees hidden but truly shaking, and the priesthood thing got serious.

But it also got fun.

I looked out across a wonderful, eccentric assemblage of family and friends. Grandma Helen sitting straight because she was so galvanized by loss. My father's curl of blonde, graying now like frost on wheat. My mother managing somehow to beam and weep all at once.

At first, I felt a moist stranglehold in my throat as I fixated on the gap in the pew next to my grandmother where my grandfather should be. I imagined him reeling in a trout. The goldenrod colored golf sweater. I saw it all. And he wasn't there.

God, I don't think I can do this.

But then, something filled my ears like a flowing, mountain brook: the remembered sound of Barney's voice telling a story. I suddenly felt Barney's Irish storytelling gifts coursing through me. So, I just opened my mouth. I started to read the Beat outline I'd written, with Grandpa Barney's lilting rhythm. It was fun. Like he had fun.

I would read a line, pause, look out into the faces of family and friends and see an expression of recognition. Suddenly, it transcended Grandpa. It was like the Love that had filled me on the ski slope at the Teacup Bowl came bubbling out—what St. Paul describes as an endless fountain. It wasn't meant just for me! This Love was for all of humanity, and right there a section of humanity sat. A section dear to my heart. An imperfect bunch, but worthy of love.

This preaching I found had a rhythm, just like skiing. Oratory moved. Moving from the page to the people, extemporizing occasionally, it was, verbally, like slalom skiing. Go there. Straight. Okay. It was a rush. A meaningful rush. The rhythm of Grandpa's storytelling, too. Finally, I sat down.

Those present seemed to appreciate Barney's eulogy. After the service, many shook my hand and said my words evoked the man.

I had skied my first sermon.

But, I still didn't utter a word to my family about the possibility of seminary.

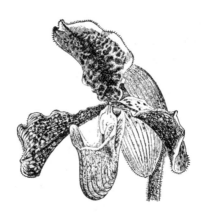

21

WHITE LADY'S SLIPPER

Cypripedium candidum or small white lady slipper is less than one inch in height. There is usually a single flower at the top of the stem, the white slipper, actually a modified petal. A member of the orchid family, it has been eliminated from many places where it formerly grew. Rare, but it does still appear in moist prairies and fens. We could not find a nursery who could supply this lovely prairie orchid, so there are none in our prairie.

–Note from Dean Brigid Brenchley's Prairie Journal

Saturday Afternoon and Evening

After the meeting about the fire, Maxine Graham insisted I let her accompany to pick up Grandma Helen from the airport. Maxine and my grandmother greatly enjoy each other.

"You know," Maxine says persuasively, "that our car is so much easier for your grandmother to get in and out of than that tiny, foreign thing you drive. And with a wheelchair and luggage, you really need an extra hand!"

"You're right, Maxine," I replied. "Sure. If it's not a burden, it would be a help. Thanks for thinking about us!"

"I do. You know how it is with your grandmother and me. For one we love the same music: can't get enough of Cole Porter or Ella Fitzgerald. I am so glad Helen felt strong enough to make this journey. Besides, Burton and Phil are trying to do some research regarding this cathedral land situation."

So, Maxine packs me into her roomy Lincoln and we roll on over to the airport.

Maxine and I are biding time in Terminal B. The rain has started up again, hanging down like bedsheets, and Grandma's plane from Denver is slightly delayed. It is actually circling and I am worried about her stamina, when Merlin calls.

"Word came from the Red Cross. They are urging people in Marshland and near the Fairground to evacuate. Have you had any phone calls from the Joneses?"

"No," I reply, double-checking my missed messages.

"Henry and Pearl," I tell Maxine who is wondering. "They're evacuating Marshland."

"Dear Lord..." she replies. "We just saw them an hour ago!"

"It's voluntary at this point," Merlin continues, "but strongly encouraged."

Now, I am extremely concerned for Henry and Pearl. With Grandma's delay, I try to reach them by phone. No answer. I call their son Richard, Nicholas' father. Also no answer.

As I stare at the gray liquid sky, I call Merlin back to see if he has made contact.

"Cathedral Church of St. Aidan," Merlin answers.

"It's Brigid. Any luck getting through to the Joneses?"

"No. I've tried repeatedly, in between requests to get into the cathedral's vault. Do you know what that is all about?"

"I don't. Phil said something about the deed."

"Phil Morrow, Max Chase, Mona Reynolds, and Burton Taylor Smith all suddenly have great interest in records in the vault. Documents related to the land purchase, I presume. I do have the combination. But with the gala just hours away, and the rain coming down like lions and greyhounds, trying to keep Ivan from blowing his circuits is all I can manage. I've got to get over to the Botanical Center. So, I put the parishioners off until Monday. Besides, as the dean, you should get in there first and see what you find."

"OK. Give our best wishes to Ivan. Tell him Maxine and I are both really looking forward to tonight. With all this craziness at the cathedral, we need an escape!"

I hang up with Merlin, my stomach in a knot about Henry and Pearl and the evacuation, and Maxine turns to me in what seems a self-conscious fashion. "Brigid, do you know who originally gave the land the prairie is on?"

"No...."

"I believe it was my ancestors. It was their land: Willowbend Farm... There are family stories about it all. But Burton is seeing if he can prove some of them to the board on Tuesday—that is if they have relevance to your decision."

I look at Maxine, astonished. I never knew.

I would ask more, but Grandma's plane lands at gate B-7. So Maxine and I head to the arrival area.

With a steward pushing her wheelchair, my grandmother waves animatedly and Maxine and I rush to her with a couple of roses.

My sisters have tried to prepare me: her skin drapes from her bones and her frame swims in her clothes. Still, her hair has a lovely wave, and her eyes sparkle with fun. I give her an extra hug, aware that each trip is possibly her last.

"I made it!" she declares, clasping one of my hands and one of Maxine's. "Your sisters doubted the wisdom. But here I am. After a nap and before the gala, you must tell me everything about your life."

Maxine raises an eyebrow and laughs.

"Well, now," I tell Grandma, "This week that may be as good as *Doctor Zhivago!* You have no idea."

The steward helps me get Grandma's bags while Maxine goes for the Lincoln.

Seated in one of her old Ward chairs with the embroidered arms, drinking tea from her old rose chintz teacup, Grandma is full of life even if weary. Part of it is simply her face. Helen has an open face with large eyes and mouth. She is one of those women whose thoughts and emotions pass visibly across her countenance like clouds and sun on a windy day. She finds delight in many things, and that is often the sentiment animating her countenance. It is hard not to like someone who visibly seems enthralled in delight with your very being. At least this is the way it feels as her youngest grandchild.

Maxine stands dripping on the front mat.

"Maxine, you absolutely can't stay for just one cup of tea?" Grandma Helen asks her. "It's orange pekoe I brought from Denver."

"I really need to rest if we're attending this crazy party tonight. You should too, I'd think."

"Will they have live jazz?" Grandma asks.

"We can only hope," Maxine says and laughs. "Say, Brigid, how are you two getting to the gala? Should Burton and I swing by?"

"No. Phil has offered to pick us up," I reply.

"Who is Phil?" Grandma asks.

"You met him last year," I tell her.

"The attorney who, if my eyes don't deceive me..." Maxine gives a knowing look to Grandma, "is beginning to take a shine to your granddaughter."

I feel myself turn rosy around the cheeks and ears.

Guess we are not hiding this as well as I thought. Oh my.

Grandma's large animated features now light up like Lake Michigan on the Fourth of July.

"Ah-ha. Phil. Is it Phillip? I've always loved the name Phillip. Well, like Maxine, I'd better go straight away and take that nap. Whatever else has been going on..."

"Oh, only a four million dollar real estate deal and a cathedral fire last night...not to mention a flood alert."

"A fire? A flood? And four million dollars?" Grandma looks incredulous.

"You heard her right!" Maxine confirms. "We're all so exhausted, one drink tonight and we'll fall down drunk..."

"Still, none of it can be as important as telling me all about Phil," Grandma says to me and winks.

Maxine lets herself out, and I trundle Grandma off to rest in the guestroom. I hear her snoring within minutes. Then I try again to reach Henry and Pearl and their kids. But to no avail. I should get my sermon for tomorrow firmed up, but I take a much needed catnap in my chair instead.

As we approach the Botanic Garden, the flooding river has inundated the main entrance and made it impassable.

Should I even be here?

I see the lit geo dome reflected in standing water.

Where are Henry and Pearl right now? Are they safe?

Tonight all the extravagance seems like a waste of time and money. Another year, I would not have come. But with a percentage being shared with the cathedral, I am between a rock and a hard spot. Moreover, it's a high point for Ivan, not to mention Grandma Helen—she has been looking forward to the gala for months.

"Battle axes in Givenchy. That's my prediction," she says after we wind our way through the detour and finally pull up in the circle drive behind a small queue of other cars, some of them limousines. She is both delighted and snarky: very Myrna Loy.

The dome resembles a glass ornament with a jungle scene inside, and condensation adds to the mystique. Small talk and laughter cross the percussive sound of the rain as we open the car door. Phil spies us and steps out to help. Together, juggling umbrellas, we maneuver Grandma into the wheelchair and I go park the car.

When I get back and step into the geo dome, Phil and my grandmother are admiring the softly moving waterways.

"Ivan has outdone himself there," Phil observes.

Floating candles, each with an orchid attached like a sidecar, illumine the water. My grandmother's delight is already secured—she has adored orchids for over fifty years. We could probably just go home.

She is telling Phil all about it. "Our son Jack took Byron and me to the Big Island, and we saw bamboo orchids growing straight from the lava rock."

How many orchids does Grandma have left?

"Helen. Did Brigid share that my passion is bromeliads?" Phil replies. Standing with these two fills me with gratitude.

"If we are talking about obsessions, do you two know there are such things as prairie orchids?" I ask. "Last year I was hiking in a wetland area and suddenly came across one called a small white lady slipper. It was so exotic looking, it stunned me."

We move toward the bar near the waterfall and the shrimp and hors d'oeuvre near the koi pond. I steel myself. Almost certainly, I will have to run a gauntlet of small talk with parishioners who may be frosty if not hostile about the fire or the hotel offer or both. I scan the crowd and heave a sigh of relief: I see neither the Chases nor the Reynoldses nor Bishop Farnon and his wife—yet. Who knows? Maybe like the flycatchers and finches flitting high in the palm leaves near the foggy octagons of glass, I can just skirt them all night.

On the other hand, because ten percent is going to the cathedral's project, most of the Prairie Team is here. Jason strolls up with his date and that lifts my spirits. He's got on a red cummerbund and she has a nose ring—and Pasha Kurtz is with them.

"So your feature made the *Sunday Register*," Pasha tells me. He has gel in his hair and looks more his true age. "Of course, with the fire and the flood, we had real news!"

"You didn't tell me it was Pasha doing the feature!" Jason exclaims.

"I didn't know you knew Pasha," I reply.

The three young people look at me like that's ridiculous.

We spot Marianna and her husband Carl, who do not look in their element. Until now, I have never seen Marianna in a dress! Never heard her yell until yesterday, never seen her in a dress until today. Fortunately she and Carl arrived early and Ivan quickly hooked them up with Dave Stone of the Des Moines Waterworks. He's initiated a legal suit against counties upstream whose practices are costing the city large sums to purify our drinking water. In Dave Stone, the only other man there not in a tux, Carl and Marianna have found a life-buoy to navigate the waters of the gala.

Burton and Maxine come up arm-in-arm. He's stubbornly refused to bring his cane and needs Maxine to steady him, despite her stilettos. I can't wear them at forty and have no idea how Maxine manages at eighty.

"Well, it's a string ensemble," Maxine tells Grandma. "No Cole Porter tonight."

Burton gives my shoulder a squeeze, communicating that church politics will never jeopardize our relationship. Then he draws back and looks me square in the eyes.

"Been praying," he says, and his eyes glisten. "Interesting epiphanies."

"What?" I ask.

"Maxine has a story passed down in her family. Phil and I made a little progress pinning the details down this afternoon, but we need to get into the cathedral vault to confirm."

"Merlin said that this afternoon Max Chase and Mona Reynolds both wanted in the vault, too."

Phil and Burton exchange looks.

"No real surprise," Phil adds.

Dear God, what is in the vault?

"You two have good news, and you are not going to tell me? Tell me!"

Burton explains, "Could be just an old family tale, Maxine's bunch liked to weave tales, exaggerate we might say."

Phil understands that I have every right to know what is going on.

"Let's just get through dinner," he says, "and over coffee I will fill you in completely. Slightly complicated, but if it's true, it could be a game-changer," he winks.

Burton turns to a new subject that lowers his levity. "What of

Henry and Pearl?" Maxine overhears and leans in to listen.

"Don't know," 1 say, and get emotional, "Look at us, tuxes, stilettos, Jason's cummerbund. Merlin and 1 both tried all day to reach them. We don't even know if they're still in their house, if they're okay. It weighs down my spirit like the sandbags all across town."

Burton gives a silent cue, bowing his forehead toward his puff-pastry.

We all observe a silent prayer.

Burton turns to reassure me.

"Listen, if the levee was gone, officials wouldn't ever let this soiree happen. Tomorrow, I'll phone some folks 1 know in Marshland. We'll find them. Now, for an hour or two," Burton concludes, "let's just try to relax and have a good time."

Usually my strong suit. Not tonight. Burton and Maxine move on. They have many old friends at the party.

"Champagne?" Phil hands Grandma Helen and me each a glass.

"Phil," Grandma asks, obviously charmed by him, "1 have to ask, do you happen to be Jewish?"

1 cover my face with my free hand and Phil laughs out loud.

"I'll explain later," 1 say and glower at my grandmother. Maybe my sisters are right—the onset of Parkinson's is affecting her judgment!

Fortunately, Ivan and Merlin make their way over to greet us. Ivan is about ten years older than Merlin and a much shorter man. He has written over thirty garden books, two of them with famous movie actresses. He's clad in a linen jacket, the hue of a jonquil named for him.

Merlin stands, a loving sentinel. Ivan is in his element and gracious.

"Dean Brigid, Grandmother Helen, Philip. Wait until you see the renderings! The screens will come down from the ceiling momentarily. 1 couldn't be more pleased. 1 took leave to place you at the mayor's table. After dinner, a fabulous dance troupe. Dionne Farnon is one of the dancers and fantastic. Of course, 1 put the bishop and Dionne at another table—I never seat people near their superiors. Spoils a good gala."

The lights of the geo dome dim, and screens drop. This seems about as close to the Oscars as I will ever get. The lead architect speaks, and then the mayor, who lauds the flood mitigation and water-filtering characteristics of the plan. He also sensitively updates everyone on the flood. Explains what the city has in place for disaster relief. He even puts in a good word for our cathedral prairie.

"Well, the mayor mentioning St. Aidan's land can't hurt our cause!" Phil whispers. "I'll get a copy of his comments for the board meeting."

When the lights come up, we move toward our table.

"Mr. Morrow. Dean Brenchley." The mayor sees us and gestures us his direction. "Please join us."

Phil and Grandma move his way.

I am thinking about Mayor Burnish—if the flooding tugs at me, I can't imagine his ambivalence about being at such an event with his citizens so vulnerable tonight. I am going to ask him about that...when I am suddenly immobilized. I stop dead in my tracks beneath a royal poinciana in full bloom. I stare down at its petals on the cobblestone path. Flame tree.

Flamboyant. Frozen, orange-red anger flowers inside me. For the mayor's "us" —his table—includes Max and Gwen Chase. I am supposed to convivially dine with a man who has threatened me and who is possibly an arsonist?

Lord, is this some joke? A test? Please!

In height and features Francis Burnish is more equine, but like his city offices on the river there is something about the mayor's manner that always strikes me as lionine. Tame lion, but lion still. People don't cross him much. He gets things accomplished. His policies: wise. He makes untold numbers of people feel noticed and appreciated. In fact, as he pulls out a chair for me, he bestows a look of benevolent concern, I imagine because of the cathedral fire.

"Do you know Mr. and Mrs. Chase?"

"Of course. We attend St. Aidan's," Gwen says. "Max's forbears were founding members 160 years ago. How long have you been there now Dean Brigid? Five years?"

In three sentences Gwen delivers both an arson alibi and a catty dig: cathedral deans are ephemeral, old Des Moines families are perennial.

"Of course, of course, St. Aidan's," The mayor replies. "Max and I were choirboys together in the day. The cathedral stole me briefly from the Presbyterians, until my voice changed. Then they threw me back," he tells me.

"Max," Phil says, shaking hands across the table. Phil is more rested and doesn't quite look like he'll punch him. But anger is still there in his popping jaw muscles. Also, I see that the flame-tree petals inside me are also in Phil's eyes.

"The fire? I was so sorry to learn of it! But, minimal damage? None to the building?" The mayor asks with genuine concern. "Did the fire department respond well?"

We all nod. We are seated on one hand of the mayor, and Max and Gwen on the other.

Luckily, Dave Stone, Carl, and Marianna appear and complete our table, thankfully creating another buffer between me and the Chases.

Nodding at the three who join our table—it seems he had already greeted them earlier—Mayor Burnish continues. "I was so pleased when Marianna told me that, ironically, the fire will only help the plants." He winks at Marianna who gave him a summary of everything.

I know that the mayor has met with SansCorps. I know he is a strong environmentalist, but that he is also committed to the re-development of the city's core. I imagine that he may be as torn as I have been. Phil and I are his constituents, but so are Max and Gwen.

"So, tell me," the mayor is sort of holding court. "What do you all see in the Botanic Center plans? Opinions as we move forward?"

"The design has much to commend it." Max replies. Then he

strategically adds, "The Botanic Center will be able to display and teach about native species, going a step beyond what St. Aidan's members have attempted in their modest way. And it's situated better."

Max is so fast from the starting gate! He immediately fills the mayor's ear with a fit argument for why the cathedral land can now easily be sold!

God, he really is a calculating bastard.

"I don't know, Max," says the mayor, "with the degree of flooding we're witnessing and the price tag to clean our water, I imagine we need as many sites with natives and water mitigating features as we can get."

Touché! When can I sign up for this man's re-election campaign? Phil shoots me a smile.

"Cleaning the water costs the taxpayers money," Phil adds with an edge, knowing the Chases' political leanings. "Just ask Dave Stone."

It's a good thing that Dave and Carl and Marianna and Grandma Helen are so engrossed in Carl's description of a sorghum experiment in Senegal that they are in their own world. If Dave entered the fray with Max, there could be an all-out brawl at table seven.

I absolutely cannot look in Max and Gwen's direction. I stare instead at the table centerpiece: a mini-version of the garden's waterways. A shallow glass bowl in which one burning candle floats and one orchid. Blood-orange petals of the flamboyant also scatter onto the water. My brain keeps rehearsing Max's words: "I would not put my faith in the staying power of grass."

Who knew fire could float on so much water? Makes my spirit and stomach sick. Would Max stoop so low as to have a homeless woman start a blaze? Do we sit with such evil, willing to make a profit at the expense of so many? I fear greed is rending our parish apart.

Lord, did he have Delilah ignite it?

Should I just blurt out our suspicions to the mayor?

Would Delilah be fined, even go to jail, if she did set the blaze?

No one would believe her word against multi-millionaire Max Chase.

Screw you, Max, I think to myself again, still not raising my gaze from the flaming, floating orchid.

To voice it here in public would be political suicide. Even so, I am tempted.

Suddenly, maybe inspired by all those Henry James novels I read as an English Lit major, I deliver the same message in a different way. The sideways approach.

"Mayor Burnish," I ask, and include Phil in my pronoun, "if we were to suspect arson, what would we do? Go to one of the city attorneys? The police?"

Now it's Max's turn to avert his eyes from me for most of the meal!

Francis Burnish ponders my question. "Dean Brigid, if that concern is real, why don't you or Phil call my office on Monday and we can discuss it."

For much of the meal, a chasm opens up, splits the table between me and the Chases; the burning water centerpiece is our only link. For a while I actually enjoy what malice feels like. I despise Gwen and Max, and I try to erase their very existence.

However, my malice doesn't last.

When the basket of hard rolls is passed to me, I inadvertently meet Max's gaze.

Suddenly, the I Am the Vine icon overlays our table. I may have to stop praying with these damn icons if I really want to hate anybody! In images a bit like Giotto's, I see Max and Gwen in the Vine's branches, I see Max and Gwen in Port-au-Prince, I see Max lifting a wall into place for a house for a bereft mother and her children.

Silver shimmering hair, foxlike features, black bow-tie beyond price—it's all the same. But not. I Am the Vine. Like it or not. Now I can't help but see it. Max and me. Both ruthless and stubborn in our own ways. But, unfathomably, both entwined in Christ's branches.

This is no joke.

The Creator remembers prayers that I have already forgotten! The phrase descends into my consciousness as if from the upper reaches of the glass dome—or from the distant recesses of my soul.

An eternity of thoughts fills me as I hold the bread basket. How many times have I broken bread with Max at the communion altar? How often has Max borne a chalice of wine at my side? We may well betray each other yet. We could even pursue a legal battle. In less than four days we will probably come to verbal blows at the board meeting. I have no idea what Max Chase is thinking, but from my side the betrayal will not be tonight.

The words I have so often used to consecrate extra bread at the communion altar rise to mind. I cup a sesame-speckled hard roll:

By your Word and Holy Spirit bless and sanctify this bread also.

"Can I use your pen?" I whisper to Phil.

He slips a cool, heavy pen inscribed with *Philip Morrow* into my palm and I write on my drink napkin: We are the Body of Christ." I tear the blessed hard roll in two, take half and eat it. Then I place the message in the bread basket with the other half.

"Will you pass this directly to Max?" I whisper to Phil.

Basket in hand, Phil reads the message. To my surprise he tears off a piece for himself and reverently eats it. Then with a smoothness only his, he manages to convey the basket deftly past the mayor, without offense, while grabbing Max Chase's full attention.

Max reads the message on the napkin. It seems like forever. His hands actually look smallish and pale as he holds the basket. Then, he does it, he takes bread into his mouth. His face is down. He does not look up, and for the first time ever I see that there is a thinning circle on top in Max's white-gold, not unlike an inverted monk's tonsure.

Some lightness returns, even though Max never returns my gaze. Things lighten even more when the rest of our table rises for a trip to the dessert island. Carl kindly offers to push Grandma Helen there, who loves her sweets. Phil and I are gloriously alone.

"We'll talk about your mystical, forgiving behavior toward Chase in a moment. But first, why does your grandmother care whether I am Jewish?"

"Daniel Goldberg." I may as well go straight to the point. "My last lover. Ancient history. Became a rabbi, which sort of threw a wrench into our romance."

"Ah-ha." This time it is Phil's nose that scrunches, and he laughs.

Then we hear a voice from behind us. "You've survived the fire then?" Bishop James Farnon has walked up to our table with his wife Dionne.

Dear, God. All in one night?

I wonder if the bishop or Dionne sensed our intimacy. Luckily, I think they are both too focused on the cathedral troubles to notice.

Dionne hugs me. "We were so worried when we got the call!"

"How are you two holding up?" James asks. "And the parish?"

Dionne comes from a Harlem stage family. She met James in Romania when the iron curtain was fraying. She studied dance and he studied theology. They fell in love running Bibles to underground Christians. Dionne is dressed in wonderful, gossamer, chartreuse-colored cloth. Her dance costume.

"Do you see that centerpiece?" I say and point. "Pretty much my life! We have dear Henry and Pearl Jones and Richard Jones and their children vulnerable this minute to the flood, maybe at an evacuation center, and I can't find them. Then, the prairie fire. How can grass even burn with all this rain? And, if that is not enough, a hotel offer that is splitting the parish." Then I see the orchid and am thankful I have Phil and my grandmother. "So, a flood, a fire, and parish members at each other's throats, but other than that everything's great."

I am very fond of this bishop and my eruption of pent up stress and emotion prove how I trust him.

"I see," now the bishop's brows knit. "Glad you are not holding anything back."

He stares down toward his fuchsia-colored shirt. He knows

how strongly I have felt God calling us to restore the prairie. But he also knows the economic needs of the cathedral. He knows all too well how such a decision can rend a congregation asunder. Bishop Farnon is a very prayerful man, and now he comes up with a complete surprise.

"The chancellor of the diocese has an interesting notion, a memory he needs to investigate, which may alleviate one of your issues. He wants you to get into the cathedral's vault for land records. Said something about a glebe."

Glebe? It is a strange English ecclesiastical word. I recognize it from church history or maybe my time as a graduate student in England. But for the life of me I can't bring up what it signifies. A glebe? A glebe? I mouth the question to Phil. He nods. He smiles.

Ah, this must be the mysterious thing he and Burton were talking about, too! Maybe even what Maxine began to tell me at the airport.

"Just try to find the original deed and any related vestry minutes and come to the diocesan house on Monday," the bishop directs.

"Bishop, that day we are actually on Mayor Burnish's calendar over the lunch hour," Phil tells us. "I set that meeting during dinner just a few minutes ago."

"Will we wear costumes?" I ask with a giggle, remembering "Lettuce Overcome" and Mayor Giuliani.

"Yes, of course!" Phil replies without missing a beat. "Big and little bluestem."

"I think I have no idea what any of you are talking about," Dionne interjects. "Come on dear, help me collect the dancers. We go on any minute." She tugs at the bishop's arm.

I melt into my chair. How much drama can one dean take? The lights fall and the choreography is enthralling.

However, Grandma Helen falls asleep in her wheelchair, and we seize the opportunity to leave early.

22

HARE'S-TAIL GRASS

Lagurus ovatus or hare's-tail grass is native to the
Mediterranean Basin and nearby regions, and it is
naturalized in Great Britain and scattered locations in the
Americas. It has pale green grassy foliage and oval green
flower heads, turning to a buff color as they ripen, all
summer long. I saw it growing on Dartmoor in Devon.

–Note from Dean Brigid Brenchley's Prairie Journal

Northwestern, The Academic Year 1983-84

The panic over the priesthood did not go away after Grandpa
Barney's funeral.

Back at the Canterbury House for my senior year, I could not
shake my spiritual experience of slalom preaching. It didn't help
that Peter kept stuffing info about women priests in my mail
slot. One was a *New York Times Magazine* article about a woman
who was both an Episcopal priest and a stage director. Peter had
scrawled on the top of the news clipping:

Bishop Quirky, See, you could be both an author and a cleric.

The thing kept me up at night. Literally.

One night I was awake, unable to sleep because my thoughts were spinning like a gymnast on the parallel bars. So I padded down to a common room in the old house. I knelt on bumpy carpet that resembled a topographic map, placing my knees on a raised section that was shaped like the horn of Africa.

Me, a priest? Of anyone, you know my love of worldly things, I said both to God and to myself. *Maybe this is just a phase. Except Peter, I've never even really known a priest! I've never laid eyes on a woman priest.*

With the indentations of river bottoms pressed into my kneecaps, I moved and propped myself against the slightly frayed plaid sofa. Eyes closed, I continued to place my hesitations before God. The room was dark. Eventually I opened my eyes, and sat up. What I saw really made me sit up! The energy from what I perceived entered my eyes, ricocheted around my brain, and straightened my spine.

There on the wall across the room I saw a figure in light: a woman in a robe on her knees. It was a transparent filmy form, the consistency of thin milk. Now I know that the robe she wore is called a chasuble, but then I had no such words or paradigms. Even in my awe, I found it humorous that I could see the stripes of 1960s-wood-paneling through the body of the figure in light.

Eyes incredulous, spirit in shock, I didn't say anything to God. I couldn't.

I stood up and walked toward the window behind me. Surely this thing was a reflection? Probably formed by a streetlight through tree branches outside?

I waved my hand across the window and looked over my shoulder at the figure. No change.

I went and sat back down and gazed again at the outline of this woman in light. For hours? Or seconds? I am not quite sure. Eternal gazing. It was beautiful. She was beautiful. Calming. I rubbed my eyes. Closed them. The form was there whenever I looked.

I pulled the Bible I had brought with me to the sitting room toward me and opened it randomly—the roulette wheel with scripture. The ball landed on words from St. Paul:

Now there are varieties of gifts, but the same Spirit; and there are varieties of service but the same Lord; and there are varieties of working, but it is the same God who inspires them all in everyone. To each is given the manifestation of the Spirit for the common good... For the body does not consist of one member but of many.

Paul's analogy of the body politic seemed to say: *Just be yourself. I'll do the rest.*

I breathed a little easier, and finally went back to bed.

Instead of running to Peter with this experience, I decided to make an appointment with an endowed professor of religion from Yale Divinity who was spending his sabbatical in Evanston. He came to Canterbury House to worship and looked like a thinner, kinder Karl Marx. His specialty was mystical theology, so he seemed just my guy.

"How do we know we are not just crazy?" I asked him after sharing my experience.

"Well, the contemplative tradition has guidelines, three simple questions one can ask."

I nodded.

"One: was it an idea already in your brain? Something you have wanted, this becoming a priest? Something that, on some level, will bring you gain?"

I shook my head emphatically. "The opposite of that!"

"Second: does the decision bring more life or death? Will it bring harm or destruction to yourself or anyone?"

"My father maybe." At this point Dad still held on to hopes that I would leave Northwestern for Law School and then join him in his insurance firm.

"Real harm? Or just surprise or disappointment? Would you be intentionally hurting him out of anger?"

"No."

"Third and last: What do others, like the Canterbury community, think of the revelation? You need to ask them." He chuckled. "You've started with me. And it sounds like Father

Peter has also perhaps discerned this in you. So, from your description of things, I think you may in fact have a calling."

"But I'm so young—spiritually. I don't know anything about the Church. I was agnostic like a second ago!"

"Time? There is always time. God will work in God's time."

So, I did not immediately tell my family, but I did tell Peter and Margay Caspian. Margay, with big and beautiful German-American bones, hugged me hard.

"God keep you." She was a person honest about the rigors and oddities of clergy and clergy-family lives. "It can get really weird," Margay said, "But it's a meaningful life."

Peter was smug and walking on air, "I knew it!"

Then he called the bishop of Chicago.

I was a senior, so my parents were asking: Law School? Signed up for the LSAT yet? So, before seeing the woman in light on the wall, I was enrolled that autumn in constitutional law. It wasn't quite as intense as Harvard and *The Paper Chase* on TV, but nerve-wracking enough. One night, I surveyed the constitutional law book. I held its heftiness out at arms-length. Turned it around. Outside? A boring black cover. Inside? Nice headings in a cool font, but then columns and columns of cerebral clauses that evoked little to no inspiration in me. Blather, think, blather, think, think, think, blather, blather, blather *ad infinitum.* No color. No poetry. No existential questions. I respected our legal system, and I comprehended the huge impact these laws had on society. Yet, I simply could not find myself in that book, inside or out.

Books of literature or spirituality had the opposite effect. I valued many. For instance, Thomas Merton's *Seven Story Mountain* or G.K. Chesterton's limited edition of *St. Francis of Assisi*, with its hand-painted inserts... these carried me to the deepest and highest ruminations. In them I came to understand previously unknown parts of myself, or facets of existence I experienced but had had no words to describe before reading them.

It was not long after Peter's call downtown to Bishop Grishom, that the professor who was guiding my honors thesis in modern literature asked if I was interested in applying for the Exeter exchange scholarship. The scholarship meant master's work in England, at least a year, maybe two. Often a PhD scholarship would follow. My professor thought that my interest in the literary techniques used by twentieth-century prose writers to capture transcendent experience might be fresh for the scholarship committee –different from the usual post-war-God-is-dead modernist proposals. Might just catch the committee's eye, she said.

My spirit sang! Studying in Britain and putting off this decision about the priesthood to boot? Like Alice's rabbit, it was as if this literature professor handed me a small bottle that I might shrink and run away. Besides, I told myself, these studies would only make me a better preacher if that truly was my calling. At the very least, it was a rabbit passage out of the urgency of applying to law schools.

"Not very practical," Dad said on the phone when I described applying for the graduate scholarship instead of studying for the LSAT. I could hear the disappointment in his voice. "How are you going to make a living from reading English mystics? Learning to write like a mystic?"

I didn't have a good response.

I still couldn't bring myself to say to my parents, "Well, English mystics might be relevant because I am actually thinking about becoming a priest." Such a thing would never have crossed their minds, and the prospect of shocking them with that sentence was almost unimaginable. However, I knew the opportunity to travel would translate. After all, the second they got me settled in college, they had set off on a six-week cruise around the Mediterranean. I guess with a seven-year wait since my closest sister left for college, finally empty-nesters, they deserved it.

"I won't make anything. But, it's a full-ride: tuition, room and board, and the scholarship even provides a stipend. Travel money. I'd be in Europe for at least a year, maybe two."

Dad's turn to not have much to say. If I was awarded the

Exeter deal, 1 knew he and Mom would both be thrilled for me and even a little envious.

The unfortunate thing was that the rabbit hole caved in, or like Alice in Wonderland, I grew. Near spring break, I got the disappointing news that I was ranked third in the queue for the Exeter Exchange. By the time I learned, I had missed the LSAT and law school deadlines.

But the vision of the robed woman of light still lived on. So...

I let Peter bundle me onto the train, down to Huron Street to meet with Bishop Grishom, bishop of Chicago.

After I ran a gauntlet of receptionists and secretaries and go-fers in collars, the bishop greeted me in an office banked in glass. Well-spoken, with an aristocratic nose and chin, the svelte man about age sixty wore a lavender cassock robe, its soft nap tinged with violet. I had never talked seriously with a man in a full-length dress before! But he was so astute and centered that the garb soon seemed as natural as the blue cashmere blazers worn by the men zipping past his windows toward the Wrigley Building or the Sears Tower. The bishop was the father of two daughters, and he seemed both bemused and amused by this young woman in a floral skirt, lace leggings, and dangling earrings who thought she was perhaps, reluctantly, being called to be a priest. His interrogation had a sort of fascinated, if not totally earnest, glee about it.

However, he was a serious practitioner of the spiritual exercises of Ignatius of Loyola, so when I gathered the courage to describe both my conversion at the Teacup Bowl and my vision of the woman in light, his tone changed. He listened in a new way. A person of alacrity, he seemed to be filtering our conversation at a new and intricate level of discernment.

"You know it is less than ten years since the first US women were ordained." He wanted to forewarn me, prepare me. "Chicago parishes have yet to call a woman rector, though I've installed a few vicars. You would undoubtedly face some fierce opposition."

I may have looked frightened. Not only was he speaking

a foreign language, using words like rector and vicar, but the whole thing suddenly felt a bit like being in a Fellini film.

"And yet..." Bishop Grishom continued, some ways more in conversation with himself than with me, "...the tides are changing. Kenya, Brazil, Canada," Bishop Grishom moved from warning to supportive coaching, "all have their first women now."

He gazed lovingly at me, as if he gazed into an icon. He stroked his sculpted chin with one hand and cradled his pectoral cross in the other. Finally, he seemed satisfied. "You have my blessing. And you will be in my prayers. You'll need them."

After our interview, he had his assistant ring Peter Caspian. The bishop told Peter he could start filling out the paperwork toward Discernment for Holy Orders.

So that spring break, I told my parents that I might, eventually, go to seminary.

Surprisingly, it was my mother who was thrown by the gender issue.

"A priest? We don't have a single woman priest in Colorado! Will people accept it? You'll have to lead all those men."

Of course, when I told Mom that the revelation came when I was preaching at the funeral of her own father, Grandpa Barney, she softened. She could begin to see it. After all, she was the one who had asked me to do the eulogy.

Grandma Helen thought it was hilarious. "Like Bing Crosby in *The Bells of St. Mary's*? Or Spencer Tracy in *Boys' Town*? You do look good in black." She said in earnest, "You know my mother was quite the woman suffragette in Kansas City, a pioneer in her own right, even held political office. Of course it was in the days of Pendergast and the Irish machine. Always a good Catholic, she'll probably dance a reel in heaven to see a redheaded woman with the surname Quirke amidst all those stodgy men in white collars. But still, Brigid, what of your writing career? Your acting career? You have such stage presence."

My sisters were too busy with their own lives to say much at all. Just another Quirky thing their little sister was up to now.

But with Dad it was painful.

We sat together at a small table at Scott and Zelda's, his favorite pub on South Gaylord Street. There was a lot a father and daughter couldn't really say. If my father believed in God at all, it was in a distant Maker—One who set things in motion and then put it into our hands. Now his most academically-interested, once most-materialistic daughter, his Joseph-and-the-multicolored-dream-coat daughter, possible heir-to-the-business daughter, was telling him that she wanted to give it all to God. Someone or Something that might actually be a figment of her imagination!

A reserved man, of course my father said little of this aloud. But he did order a second scotch and soda, and as we shared Alaskan king crab legs, I knew what he was thinking. We passed culinary tools back and forth in our buttery fingers, splitting the jointed shells like rough porcelain, and our relationship seemed to crack and fissure the more we tried to talk. I was hurt, for he made it clear he wasn't likely to offer any financial support. After all, he'd already sold the back forty, literally, to pay for Northwestern. I knew that he would have gone into debt up to his eyeballs for law school. But for seminary? I wasn't likely to see a dime.

It was one of the hardest lunches of my life.

He didn't really believe in God. I did. What could we say?

But the Divine orchestra leader—who has a sense of humor—was in fine form.

Less than forty-eight hours after I had bitten the bullet and had all these conversations about the priesthood—with the bishop of Chicago, with my mother, with my grandmother, with my sisters, and finally with my father—I received a phone call from the Director of International Programs offering me the Exchange Scholarship to Exeter after all.

"What?" I felt higher-than-high.

"Well," she explained, "you know that you applied for both a Fulbright and the Exeter exchange simultaneously." I knew this. "The young woman who ranked first got a Fulbright." I knew her—she actually worshipped at the Canterbury House and had shared that she was off to Cambridge. What I didn't know was the director's next piece of news: "The person who ranked second..." another acquaintance who struck me as possessing an ego the size of the Grand Canyon, "...applied only for the Fulbright. I think she thought she would receive one. She didn't. It seems she declined the Exeter opportunity." This puffed-up young woman had simply not checked the Exeter box on the application form. "So you are eligible. Are you still interested?"

Was she kidding? I had won the lotto! I had faced the truth that I might in fact be called to become an Episcopal priest. But my postulancy could simply carry on while I was abroad, to be resumed when I returned. If I returned. I could read mystical writers and other literature, continue to write, and be on a kind of extended spiritual retreat, making sure the Divine felt the priesthood thing was really in the cards.

Now, suddenly, like a rabbit I was scampering off to Devon to further my studies.

23

SWAMP MILKWEED

Asclepias incarnata or swamp milkweed is found throughout the tallgrass prairie region in moist soil at the edges of prairie potholes or marshes. It grows to a height of over five feet, with pink blossoms, and a small amount of milky juice exudes from its glabrous stems when broken. In our biocell, these are the giants Unlike us, they adore all this never-ending rain!

–Note from Dean Brigid Brenchley's Prairie Journal

Sunday Morning

By the time we get her home, Grandma Helen has found a second wind. We open the door to the bungalow and get her settled with her feet propped on a small footstool she once needlepointed herself. To my chagrin, she notices the blank wall.

"Quirky, didn't you used to hang the *Wilheim Thomè* just there? The Edelweiss?"

Shit. I stick my head deeper into the coat closet and act busy stashing raincoats as if I can't hear. Luckily, she moves on to more riveting topics.

"The undercurrents and innuendos at our dinner table," Grandma Helen proclaims, "like roulette. Those Chase people flicking the steel ball, you sending it back, the handsome mayor spinning the wheel. What is it all about?"

Grandma demands we interpret all the gala drama for her.

"It's a lot for a young woman to handle," she says and reaches her hand out to enfold mine. Her gaze communicates faith in me, but concern.

"Well, there's some cause for worry all right," I say with a sigh.

I go to make tea and toast for all of us and let Phil launch in about the Hotel Savant and the prairie. He tries to explain to her who wants what outcome. With the open design of the bungalow, I call over additions as the kettle steams.

My grandmother seems to take glee in all the agonizing details.

"Oh, to have the stuff of life again!" she says. "Assisted living is so tepid in comparison. Decisions about what pills you took, whose table to join for dinner, where to stow our walkers."

She takes a break to add milk and sugar to the tea I hand her.

"The threatened prairie plants or the money, now that is a quandary," Grandma Helen confesses like the materialistic naturalist she is, "but I do know you two should grab this moment and live it with all the zest you can! You'll make a good decision, and then be on the other side of it."

Phil smiles, "Helen, I sincerely like your outlook."

Satisfied she now has a true window into my life, and aware there is a handsome man around, Grandma Helen declares she is ready to retire. Phil waits while I help her to the guest room.

"Okay," I confront him upon return, "what is in the vault and what in the world is a glebe?"

"I was hoping maybe you could explain it to me! After all, you're the church rat," Phil replies.

"I guess that is a point."

"It seems the term goes back to the Middle Ages. In England. But was brought with British immigrants here as well. Maxine Taylor Smith has this story passed down through her family. One branch of Maxine's family tree was Scottish Anglicans who had homesteaded large tracts of land around here. Like the Chases, they were founding members of the cathedral."

"She was starting to tell me about all this at the airport, but Grandma's plane landed."

"Well, Maxine says the reason St. Aidan's extra acres weren't sold long ago is that they are legally and politically a sticky wicket: the Taylors donated them to be a glebe."

I still look at Phil blankly. "I vaguely recall the term from my time in Devon, but for the life of me I can't remember what it means."

"Tomorrow, we need to get the deed, or see old records, and verify. But, basically," Phil explains, "it means that the use of the land belongs to the priest. Legally. Brigid, to you."

Dear Lord.

Basking in the wonder of it, trying to absorb this news, our teapot on the lampstand, we again fall asleep in the wingback chairs.

A little before six-thirty a.m., the Marshland Levee breaks.

Merlin and Ivan had never gone to bed what with gala clean up, paying musicians, tallying contributions, re-visiting Ivan's small triumphs. So, they hear the news almost immediately.

By seven o'clock a.m., Merlin calls, in case I haven't heard.

Burton calls a few moments later and we all immediately rush to meet at St. Aidan's, where Simon agrees to lead eight o'clock a.m. worship: Communion in Special Circumstances without a priest. I figure if there were ever special circumstances, a flooding city surely qualifies. Maxine calls the parish prayer tree, and everyone starts praying for the Jones family.

Merlin, Burton, Phil and I climb into Phil's SUV.

Burton rides in the passenger seat because he grew up just west of Marshland and knows all the routes. Merlin and I are in the back. Phil gallops along as if his four-wheel drive Saab was truly all-terrain.

"The levee above the Marshland Neighborhood was breeched at 6:18 this morning," the radio voice announces again. "Travel in that area of the city is highly compromised."

Where the highway crosses the river on 2nd Avenue, heading north from the hill that is downtown, it is very elevated. We look north and see what looks like a bay. Where once urban streets spread, a body of water stretches.

"Dearest Lord," Burton says exhaling.

"Are those boats? Or did I have too much champagne last night?" Phil asks.

We see boats. No joke. Where cars once drove. In one small motorboat, two rescue workers stand. The highway coming the opposite direction is actually closed, and not far from us we see a family with some belongings in a slightly larger craft, taking shelter for a moment under a viaduct. We almost hit someone standing on the highway taking video footage.

Luckily, we do see land ahead where 2nd Avenue exits off toward Henry and Pearl's neighborhood. Second Avenue is a little like a land bridge. We start down the street most direct to their house. But once we turn, we see it looks like a fishing ramp. Completely impassable.

We back the car up. We try the next street and cover our mouths: sewage seems to be bubbling up into the water from somewhere below. The odor and the devastation make us all silent.

Burton points, and Phil finds another drier street and our hopes rise for a block or two. But there we encounter mudflats and downed trees. A dead dog lies amidst soggy twigs with its tongue draping out. In the arid west, where I grew up, people fight wars to gain trickles of water. Now, I see the power of water in a new light. I become aware that floodwater is actually heavy, and that many things ride on its strong moving shoulders like a conveyer belt.

When it dissipates, the floodwaters hurl and drop their baggage pell-mell. Where the water had subsided, clothing, appliances, play equipment, campers, street signs, as well as plant and animal life lay strewn.

I used to read of the primordial flood of Noah's time and imagine some pristine end to the flood—like water draining from a swimming pool. Now and forever, reading those chapters in *Genesis*, I will see and smell the damage left from that deluge.

"Once again," Phil asks, irritable. He's not a man used to being blocked. "Where exactly? Give us the exact address again. Think Burton, there's got to be another way there. "

"Four hundred nine Elm," Merlin replies from the back, next to me. We turned off Siri long ago; she was getting very confused amidst the natural disaster.

The sun is actually finally out, warm, ironically present and beaming down upon the destruction, warming the thick pungent air, adding insult to mortal injury.

We've gone way north and circled back toward Marshland from a new direction. Here the road makes a sharp dip toward the Des Moines River bottoms.

"Down here," Burton points.

Modest frame houses, circa 1950s, have dirty water lines up past their main windows. The water was here but has receded. Some of these house windows are like excrement-and-muck-Band-Aids pasted across the structures' battered faces. People are returning here. On the spits of land edging the water, refuse is piled and strewn everywhere. People walk backwards out of their houses, with soggy mattresses, soiled belongings.

Jesus, your suffering... Be present to them. Somehow.

We see a woman weeping, staring at her house where the roof has caved in. I get choked up as I ride. Merlin is absolutely silent and his face is like marble. I have never seen him undone.

Henry and Pearl. I have no other words.

I realize we are actually near their house. I start to recognize things as Phil aims the car downward, weaving around driftwood and small dunes of mud. My pulse quickens, it reverberates in my neck. My adrenaline soars because I feel a little flutter of hope. Maybe they will have been spared? Maybe, in a minute, we'll be shaking their hands over a near miss? Our road, their road, proceeds. Soggy but accessible. But then.

"Damn it." Burton says.

A fire truck appears stretched across our path. Phil bangs the steering wheel.

A policeman signals Phil to stop the car. The officer and a woman in a FEMA sweatshirt holding a clipboard step up to the window. Phil rolls down the glass and putrid air rushes in, attacking us like a wrestler—verdant, sewage-laden, humidity. I fear I'll vomit. Merlin looks down and breathes into his collar. Yes, I'll always remember this stench when I read of Noah.

"Friends of ours, members of our church, live down this road," Phil explains. He gestures back to me in my clerical collar, as he covers his mouth with a handkerchief.

"Four hundred nine Elm," I manage to say. "We need to check on them."

"Elm and Oak. Both been washed out. Everyone's been evacuated," the officer informs us. "This road is closed. You have to back up. Will take a few days to make it passable."

I think that all of us, not only me, had been compelled forward by visions of finding—hope beyond hope—Pearl and Henry's house in decent shape. Maybe we'd discover their street was just above the water's path... finding them safe... already digging out. Our collective sadness is palpable.

"Try Saint Barnabas AME church," the woman in the FEMA shirt tells us. "You should find them there. They've got food and cots. Most of the residents from Oak and Elm went there."

We back up, park in the Habitat Re-Store lot, and Phil dials the AME shelter. I feel stunned and useless. For a few attempts, the line is busy. Then it rings and he hands the phone to me.

I give to the rescue worker who answers Henry and Pearl's full names and vital statistics. Merlin has brought their birth dates and social security info as we'd been instructed at our COAD meetings.

The experience is indescribable: with the unique intonations of Pearl's voice, relief pours over me; every clenched muscle relaxes. Hearing her familiar sound is like stepping into a warm shower. Then she puts Henry on the line.

"House's hit," he says, wheezing terribly. "Means a lot, you checking on us." But then he sputters into a coughing fit and hands the phone back to Pearl.

"Sorry. Taking its toll. No rest. And he got drenched, trying to help the kids at their place. Odor. Moldy. Hank's lungs can't cope with much more of this."

24

CROSS-LEAVED HEATH

Erica tetralix or cross-leaved heath is native to Western Europe and found in bogs, wet heaths, and damp coniferous woodland. It is a perennial subshrub with small, pink, bell-shaped flowers and leaves in whorls of four (hence the name).

–Note from Dean Brigid Brenchley's Prairie Journal

Exeter, Michaelmas Term, 1985

I probably jogged or rambled past at least one glebe while at Exeter and just didn't know it. I would leave my dorm in South Cote House and head east out of town along a paved path hugging a ridge above the highway, jogging up away from the Fiats, Fords, Mini-Coopers, and lumbering lorries racing in and out of Exeter toward the M-5. Eventually the path descended again at a juncture where a Tudor-era, timbered pub called Scrumpy's was wedged into a fork in the highway. If I could get past the pub and across the crazy intersection, my daily run included a quiet country road with its occasional cottage, rolling

Devon fields, and flocks of sheep. There was a boggy patch too; in the right season it bloomed in a blanket of heath.

Near the end of two miles, winded from the run, I would turn into a small churchyard. A note in typewriter font, in a plastic sheath, attended the door:

Holy Communion 11:15 a.m. first and third Sundays Matthew Tenby, Vicar

Flopped upon a wooden bench, I panted in air alive with notes of grass, primrose, and heath; it tasted like England. I would stretch out my Lycra-covered legs toward the most entertaining thing about this oasis: a handful of sheep and goats. They co-mingled around a shelter just over the churchyard fence. A picnic table was part of their parcel. I particularly enjoyed the antics of the goats. The sheep were cliquish and skittish. I imagined they coveted the hutzpah of the goats that clambered onto the top of the wooden table to eye me, hay protruding from their gums like newsmen's cigars.

My Exeter tutor, Ron Killion, was convinced that the Gospel writers heard Jesus wrong. Ron saw many merits of goats over sheep, and he had a couple of fine poems about it. Watching these particular specimens, I tended to agree with him. In retrospect, the zany, integrated flock could have been part of Matthew Tenby's glebe, a small parcel of land linked to the clergy person caring for the parish.

I first met Ron Killion inside a three-floor high modernistic building at Exeter University. One of Britain's more prestigious red-brick institutions, the university's architects had tastefully mixed and matched twentieth-century structures around historic ones. Descending a stairwell to meet my tutor, thirty feet of windows spilled whatever sparse Devon light could be captured onto colored tiles. Ron Tamplin officed on the lowest level. I tentatively knocked on a shellacked door. I was nervous. So different from our American system: one's tutor was the linchpin to the whole English college experience. Would I like this man? Respect him as a scholar?

Dear God, who exactly will open this?

After I got up the courage to knock a second time, I heard a shuffling. The door cracked open, and a small man peeked out as if he had some qualms about engaging the outside world. He was framed underneath a thick archway of books. I swear there were shelves on all sides, and even above the doorway were shelves crammed with books. He was not much taller than me.

A respected T.S. Eliot and Seamus Heaney scholar, and a poet in his own right, Ron Killion had a kind but mischievous face which immediately evoked Bilbo Baggins. I actually glanced toward his feet—only slightly scuffed sienna-colored shoes. No fur.

Once he discerned who I was, he both smiled and opened the door widely.

"Come in, come in! I say you've had a long trip. Chicago, Denver, I've always wanted to see the Rockies."

Inside, tomes ancient and modern were piled and stacked from floor to ceiling; I had never seen the like of it. It was just before Microsoft and computer files, and stacks of manuscripts and manila folders were strewn across the professor's desk. In fact, they also covered various small tables and stuffed chairs.

"Many summers I teach in Kashmir. The Himalayas fill me with awe. I wonder how the Colorado Rockies compare. Have you been to Kashmir?"

"No. I hope to spend Christmas in the Alps though."

Despite the state of his office, Ron's brain had its own crisp intellectual organization.

During our two- or three-hour sessions, he would weave an intricate web of thought. As he explained religious phenomena or literary techniques, he would lean back or roll around the room in his wheeled desk chair, deftly pulling things from off the shelves or from within piles of folders. Like an English literature Jester, Ron knew intimately his floor-to-ceiling collection and would juggle the contents for me with pert eyes and swift moving hands. After every visit, I left like a camel or circus elephant, books in my packs or balanced with my trunk. I finally learned to bring an empty carry-on suitcase with me to tutorials.

I learned that Ron "took me on" because of my interest in the literary portrayal of mystical experience. Ron's mother was a lapsed Roman Catholic and his father a lapsed Church of Ireland Anglican. Like me, God had surprised Ron by "crossing the threshold" while he was a student at Oxford. He chose the Catholic path, and every now and then he would probe whether I was sure I wanted to remain an Anglican. But he was also a feminist and was totally fascinated by my prospects of priesthood.

However, straightaway he confessed that he didn't care for one of my primary authors. "Can't say I liked Lewis much, personally speaking. A lively lecturer, but otherwise? As an under-graduate I found him dogmatic, bombastic, even a bit cruel," Ron said. The Inklings were aging dons when he was a student. "But, I so admired my own tutor, Hugo Dyson. Brilliant man of letters, and he loved Lewis like a brother. So I figured old Clive Staples must have a redeemed side. Maybe he just had a liver-condition. That group threw back their share of pints at The Bird and Baby after all."

Ron pulled a photo from his desk: Killion as a young man next to a solid-built, jovial Oxford don, who I assumed was Dyson, both in academic regalia.

"Now G.K. Chesterton, one of your other interests, Chesterton I highly esteem." I didn't say it but thought Ron probably also liked the fact that Chesterton left Anglicanism to become a Roman Catholic. "I think Chesterton is underestimated by most modernists. Here," he handed me his autobiography, "after you have read everything Lewis ever wrote."

Read everything Lewis ever wrote...did I hear right?

"Did you just say, read everything that Lewis wrote?" I asked. The British system was showing its true colors now.

His gray eyes bore into me, much more Gandalf than Bilbo.

"Of course. How can you begin to think you can write a thesis about Lewis, say anything illuminating, otherwise. That's just your starting block. Then, do move on to his influences. Read George MacDonald and read Chesterton: note his use of paradox and light imagery. In fact, read Chesterton and Lewis in tandem," Ron said, swirling around to grab *Man Alive* and a Father Brown mystery from a nearby shelf. "Yes, yes, light imagery *is* something Lewis gleaned from Chesterton. Abounds in the children's books. Paradox and strokes of light."

The two pillars of my studies at Exeter were these tutorials with Ron Killion and the "Mods" Seminar. The Modern Literature Seminar was an assembly of eleven students from around the globe—three Brits, Australia, Algeria, Germany, Holland, Japan, and three of us Yanks—meeting with three Exeter professors for three hours at a time.

One of the other American students was Daniel Goldberg. With open intelligent eyes and dark curls, Daniel was one of the quieter members of our course. Daniel mainly listened intently. Yet, when he did finally speak, his literary assessments were crafted like sonnets and were full of insight.

Sharing a pot of tea after class and comparing our American interpretations of *The Times* and *The Guardian*, I quickly fell for him. A week or two later at an Indian restaurant off-campus, forks deep into a lamb vindaloo that turned our ears red, we confessed our God-interests. He was a Reform Jew, and I, an Episcopalian. These realities were cards we held close to our chests in Mods, not wanting to be intellectually ostracized. But on the weekends, Danny kept Sabbath and studied Torah, and I visited one Church of England parish after another. In Devon, I could feast as if at a spiritual smorgasbord: Evangelical Anglicans preached at the bottom of the hill at eight a.m.; Broad Church Social Justice folks protested apartheid at eleven o'clock; the canons and choir did evensong at the cathedral at five p.m. with cream tea on the cathedral close following.

Unfortunately, I also soon learned first-hand that many Anglicans in Devon were unfriendly to the idea of women being ordained. When they learned of my possible calling they would say, "Lovely, lovely," the way the Southern English do, and then avoid me like the plague. I began dating a young sexy Jewish man, which complicated the matter. So, I went to worship regularly, but increasingly kept to myself my continued prayers about whether to become a priest.

Together Danny and I joined Exeter's Out Of Doors Society (fondly called OODS). Fitting in neatly between his Friday night Sabbath and my Sunday morning Eucharist, on Saturdays we would climb onto a tour bus with other students. We likely passed more than one glebe as we hiked Dorset, Devon, and Cornwall. The driver would leave our group in some English seaside town or country village, and we would weave our way along sea cliffs or ramble across moors and heaths. Unlike hiking the Rockies, there was always a ploughman's lunch mid-point and a pint of hard cider at the trail's end. Ambling together, there was an ease to this growing relationship with Daniel. We could share our intellectual ideas, talk about our families, laugh about our foibles.

Daniel and I explored our intellectual notions, our religions, and we also explored each other. As our love interest solidified, we would finish off our Saturday jaunts in my dorm room. Along with my American drip coffee maker (that was a novelty to the Brits), my particular room was coveted for its placement directly above the furnace for the entire South Cote House. In a land of infamously chilly interiors, I was given a Swedish sauna of a living space. Danny and I would leave grass- and heather-marked wellies with our dripping mackintoshes at the door, and practice our young adult skills of removing heavy wool sweaters, turtlenecks, and lace. We would peel down to his skin the color and texture of carob and mine of willow bark.

Our love affair definitely put decision-making about seminary on the back burner. But I wasn't the only one keeping things under wrap.

Julia Jones, the middle-aged Welsh student in our seminar, and I were in a pub after class one day, when she said animatedly, "Good Lord, Brigid, how come you never mentioned that Daniel wants to be a rabbi?"

I almost drowned in hard cider. "What?" Had I heard her right? "Because I didn't know he wants to be a rabbi!"

"Surely you've told him you think about becoming an Episcopal priest?"

The look on my face must have spoken volumes. I thought my forty-year-old friend was literally going to fall on the floor in hysterics.

"All we've told each other is that 'we contemplate further studies.'"

Julia wiped her eyes. "Well, I guess one only strips so far at twenty-three."

25

THE GLEBE

In Church tradition, a *glebe* is land, in addition to or including the rectory or parsonage, which was assigned to support the priest. The word glebe itself is from Middle English, originally from the Latin, gleba or glaeba, meaning clod, land, or soil. Wide-spread in Europe, glebes exist but are rare in the US and Canada.

–Note from Dean Brigid Brenchley's Prairie Journal

Sunday Morning Continued

Once we've located Henry and Pearl and their family, know they're safe, we head to the cathedral for the ten o'clock Eucharist. Just in time, I fall in behind the cross and the choir, almost pulled by them into the sanctuary to lead worship.

With the opening acclamation and collect, my voice echoes between the Neo-gothic stone walls. My own words boomerang back at me. It all feels very out of body what with sleep deprivation, stress, and the shock of the flood. Still, I have to lead. And preach? Exhausted: body, mind and spirit, alb and chasuble askew. In a moment, I am supposed to climb into the pulpit.

Not too much about Christianity makes sense when one stops to really consider it. Of course, that might be said of all of the major religions of the world. If you're looking for things to make logical sense, there must surely be a better path. But life often doesn't make sense.

I have studied the basics of various other religions and respect devotees of many beliefs. But, I stick with Christianity because it fits and brings meaning to my experience of life. It has pieces that connect with pieces of real existences, both complex and messy.

Listening to the choir's ethereal *Gloria in Excelsis*, I realize that the sermon I so carefully crafted is inadequate and frivolous in light of all that has transpired. In it, I had dodged naming the elephants in the room. But I am on a threshold and momentarily must bear some word to a congregation divided by sale and fire, and to a city besieged by flood water. Let's face it, I think, the elephants have pretty much stampeded. I have little to lose from being honest in the pulpit.

As the sopranos sing Powell's *"have mer..r..r..cy on us,"* their voices bathe me, but I also hear another sound: the colony of goldfinches outside the Meservey Window and wings inside! I look and see that the lone infiltrator goldfinch from our tumultuous post-fire meeting is trying to join its fellows on the other side of the stained-glass swallows. Finally, it finds its escape through a gap between glass and lead near the words CONSIDER THE LILIES, and I know what I am going to do! I know the sermon I must preach. I will preach our windows and what I have been reading. I will face the turmoil we are in and preach what's written in my heart.

I ascend the pulpit steps, now enthused to break open this Word with the faithful friends in the pews. Even the grouchy ones. The worried ones.

I push off down the homiletical ski hill:

Dear friends,

Where do we stand? ...
Upon an ashen acreage.

Where do we stand? ....
In uncertainty and disagreement with one another.

Where do we stand? ....
With neighborhoods and people inundated and
displaced by floodwaters

We stand, O God, full of questions.

Since last Sunday,
Over only seven days,
Our parish has known fire.
Our parish has known division over stewardship of our
land.
Our parish has known floods!

And so it is right, today, that we ask questions about
things of the Earth.

Walt Whitman asked this question in his epic poem:
What is the grass?

It may seem nothing but poetic musings.
We might think that,
We might let it go at that,
Except for the fact that Jesus, our Lord, said:
Consider the lilies of the field... Consider the birds of
the air.

(From the stone pulpit, I point at these two phrases in the
windows. The ones the goldfinch lured me toward. People in the
pews turn to see and I allow silence for their gazing.)

Jesus urged his followers
Not to worry
And believe me, as poor subjects of the Roman Empire,
They had plenty to worry about...

He told them
to look to the Earth

for wisdom,
for a greater understanding of God.

Walt Whitman considered the flora:

A child said "what is the grass?" fetching it to me with full hands...
I guess it must be the flag of my disposition, out of hopeful green stuff woven. Or I guess it is the handkerchief of the Lord,
A scented gift and remembrance designedly dropt,
Bearing the owner's name someway in the corners, that we may see and remark, and say "Whose?"

The poet-writer of the twenty-fourth Psalm would answer boldly, what Whitman only implies:

The earth is the Lord's.

The basic revelation bestowed when we consider the lilies...
When we consider the birds, even flitting inside our church...

Whose?
Whose is the grass?
The water?
Whose the city blocks?
Whose this house of worship?

Whose are we?

Former Archbishop of Canterbury, Rowan Williams, while asserting that if humanity annihilates ourselves, the earth, even without us, will still be beloved of God, writes that our deepest identity is wrapped up with earth-care.

So, it is little wonder that the current decisions about

our land
are important and complex!

For so it has been from the beginning.

Humanity and the Earth
were created by God for our mutual fulfillment;
Without each other, we are not ourselves!

This relationship with the earth, with the water, with
the grass, with the birds, is not secondary, but primary.
In it, we reveal who we truly are!

So, in these worrisome days immediately before us,
let us devote ourselves to prayer.

Let us, deeply,
Consider the lilies of the field.
Consider the birds of the air.

And in our faithful consideration
May God reveal to us what we are to do.

AMEN

Once I leave the pulpit, the rest of the worship service is a bit
of a blur.

We are all shells of ourselves as Simon and Merlin and I move
down to the cathedral's undercroft toward the vault. They look
equally wan. Though, with my white cliffs-of-Dover complexion,
probably not as wan as I look. Burton is too spent to be with us
at all; in fact, he went home before receiving communion. Henry
and Pearl's loss weighs heavily on him.

However, when we were about to leave Marshland, Burton
switched places with Merlin and got in the back of Phil's car. He
told me at length everything he knew from Maxine:

We are to search for documents related to her ancestor Angus Taylor. "Angus Taylor, giver of the glebe. Look for records of him," Burton told me.

The basement undercroft is cold. No matter what the time of year, it carries a chill. Which is strange because in the north corner room of the lower level our huge old furnace is housed. Going into the furnace room you encounter a pot-bellied torso of iron with many appendages. It's like some Hindu god, fierce and jolly, with fire in its belly. But all its benevolent heat goes up. Roosevelt, as organist, is its most devoted shaman— checking the furnace-god's health and happiness, calling for repairmen, incurring unauthorized charges as needed. All because Roosevelt's beloved organ has a symbiotic relationship with the furnace. If the temperature in the cathedral's sanctuary either plummets or sky-rockets, the quality of the organ music goes with it. Like Hindu mysteries, I do not totally understand the dynamics. Another mystery to me is why all the heat goes up, little of it comes sideways, leaving the undercroft as a kind of cold, murky underworld.

Its appointments are also now slightly depressing. When my parents visited Romania soon after the Cold War, it struck them as a place of lost grandeur, like a man in a thread-bare tuxedo. St. Aidan's undercroft has a similar aura. The carpet was once a swirling, rich floral pattern, but is now worn and faded. Inside the raised *fleur-de-lis* designs, decades of *hors d'oeuvres* and Shrove Tuesday pancakes flour the once-vivid burgundy. The ceiling is supported by hand-stenciled pillars that once looked down on the gayest of coffee hours and parties, when St. Aidan's membership was over a thousand—real warm bodies, not just names scrawled in the parish register.

Those pillars looked down upon *grande dames* who perched, drinking coffee in pearls, and who still drove themselves to church; younger women in Jackie-O dresses who were torn about how liberated to become; men smoking Salems and discussing their careers and Des Moines politics; and an army of children conceived to "In the Mood" or "All Shook Up," who would race through the undercroft in knee-socks and plaid jackets to devour whole silver trays of sugar cookies.

St. Aidan's still has after-worship coffee hour and less formal parties, but these take place upstairs in a parlor more fitted to our current size. Now, it is the serious eating and the rollicking laughter of the Agape Café that the undercroft pillars watch over.

"It's freezing down here," I complain, as I grope the walls for light switches.

"But do you notice something?" Simon asks. He easily flips on the lights, for of course he uses them every noon, and bends down and pushes a thin hand into the carpet. "Miraculous! Dry. Completely dry. Ever since the prairie went in."

It is crucial that Simon is along on this quest. The vault has a tricky, stubborn combination, and he is one of the few who can pop it. As can Artemis. She keeps our jeweled communion set in the vault as well as the sterling candelabra and chalices. Merlin, although he only has luck with the combo about half the time, is also invaluable because he knows his way around the historic parish records inside the vault. Simon takes off his jacket, rolls up his sleeves, and eyes the large antiquated lock when Phil traipses down the back staircase.

He has a box of bagels and cream cheese in hand and a couple of Sunday *Des Moines Registers* under his arm.

"Before we dive in to the vault," Phil says, "you may want to read this."

Phil unfolds a paper for me. Across the top is an aerial shot of Marshland: the high school looks like an aircraft carrier and the houses like boats in a bay.

Underneath it? A picture of me in the prairie! "The front page?"

Oh no.

"Well?" I ask him, searching his face for his assessment.

"It is a very positive piece. You, St. Aidan's, the prairie project... all come off well. Young Kurtz captured the spirit of the thing."

I continue to scan Phil's face. Even his handsome sandpaper features look wan. The words he speaks say good news, but his tone communicates concern.

"But?" Simon asks what we all want to know.

"Placement," Phil points to the main piece on the flood. "The top story is scathing: asks how the Marshland Levee could be vulnerable again. Implicates the mayor, city manager, and head of the waterworks. Implies they allowed the levee to remain weak as a kind of escape-valve for assets downtown. The feature on our prairie, while unspoken, reads like a further indictment: we are modeling water practices the city should have been investing in. No, Pasha and the editors don't pull many punches."

Together, Merlin, Simon and I read as Phil holds out the story for us: *Where Does the Responsibility Lie When the Marshland Levee Breaks...Again?*

We read and I shake my head. It's all so confusing: good publicity for the prairie and St. Aidan's, finger pointing at our beloved, eco-friendly mayor.

"Remember you and I see Mayor Burnish tomorrow, right after the bishop and the chancellor," Phil chuckles. "It should be an interesting day!"

Merlin, totally shattered by fatigue and uncharacteristically showing his age, starts in on the bagels and cream cheese.

"Comfort food," he says and points at the paper, "but there is a further comfort. Look at how gorgeous the asters and goldenrod are in that photo."

I am glad to see that the feature still includes a list of species and the anecdote about the thirty swimming pools of water.

"We'll probably get a lot of visitors from the article," Simon adds. "Now, let's get this safe open."

He moves again to the huge steel door of our bank-like vault. We wipe the cream cheese from our lips and fingers and follow.

"That's strange," Simon says, "it's already on the last number." Without touching the dial, he pulls the shiny handle and the thick door easily opens.

"Psychedelic tie and bitch with the silver," says a voice from inside. I jump, and Merlin looks like one of his comic theatrical roles.

It's Delilah! Recovered, sitting in the vault, with only a bruise on her head.

"Delilah, how are you feeling?" I ask, delighted to see her on her feet.

Usually we'd be furious to find her in the vault, but we are too tired to ask how in the world she got there. After the scare of the fire and the hospital, watching her chow down on shrimp, I realize how much spice she adds to our parish circle.

"In a flash, would I go back. Best sleep. Good, good sleep. Sheets. Except those ladies in white poking me, stabbing me every minute! Sinful."

Delilah's rhetoric reveals she's fairly back to normal.

"Psychedelic tie...bitch... here first thing. Beat you to it. Barely light. My father always said a pastor should rise with the dawn, before the sheep go astray."

"Max." Phil utters what we all know 'psychedelic tie' probably means.

"Papers," Delilah supplies the answer to our next question. "Spider fingers grabbing papers. Not the church lady, she just grabbed a big old goblet."

"And Artemis," Merlin supplies. "I noticed we used the best silver set for Communion. She keeps it in the vault."

"God damn it. Max almost certainly has the deed." Phil sounds discouraged and his jaw starts that popping again. "The bishop told us expressly to get it."

Merlin speaks up, "The deed perhaps. But, I doubt Chase got all the records. If there was a glebe bestowed, it will come up in vestry minutes."

"And, I'll scour the treasurers' reports," adds Simon. "Probably traces of its revenue there."

"And public records," says Phil, consoling himself with a new idea. "It's a pain, but I can request them while we're at city hall tomorrow."

Delilah spies the bagels and cream cheese and exits the vault as the rest of us go in, Phil looking for legal documents; Merlin, vestry minutes; Simon, treasurers' reports. I station myself at a large plastic bin of antique photos and newspaper clippings. Someone has arranged the tub in reverse chronology. I pull the waxy sheets forward.

The earliest artifacts are two tintype photos of St. Aidan's first building, before we became a cathedral. It was a wooden, Carpenter Gothic church structure, down close to the river. According to the notes hand-scrawled on the photos, lightning struck the steeple motivating the congregation to re-build up on High Street.

Flip.

Next: a yellowed newspaper clipping, written in a Victorian voice, not unlike Dickens' *Pickwick Papers,* all about Bishop Lee (a huge man) designating St. Aidan's Church to be the new diocese of Iowa's cathedral.

Flip.

Next: a grainy but large professional photo is paper-clipped to an article in the *Des Moines Register.* Dated 1870:

"Founder Contributes Stone for Episcopal Cathedral"

I focus my eyes on the cloth-like newsprint under the headline.

This photo mesmerizes me.

In one corner, a wagon is pulled by a team of black mules with long ears that poke out in odd directions. The wagon's wooden belly sags because beautiful red granite and blonde limestone are piled high in its bed. Stone to build a worship space for God.

Who is the donor?

"Look everyone," I say, "Phineas Chase. Max's great grandfather."

Phineas Chase stands where the cathedral will go. The brim of his hat is round. He wears a slightly wrinkled linen coat and vest. Phineas has the same short stature and white hair as Max, although he is more square in the shoulders and sports a handlebar mustache.

"Don't tell me," Phil says, "is that a white bowtie?! In what, 1869?"

"The best local granite," Merlin quips.

Then however, driven by their own individual missions, my three companions quickly turn back to searching their files.

But I am totally entranced by the photo. There is a gravitas to the moment it captures: this man with a mustache stands on the threshold of a century and a half of worship. My heart softens toward Max, the calculating bastard, who just came and stole the church's deed. With his great grandfather and all that rough-hewn rock, I appreciate the Chase gift.

But... Then... Behind the man, behind the wagon full of stone, my eyes are thrilled by something else! Marianna is right: Phineas Chase and his team swim in it. Our land. It was grass, grass, grass. The other inheritance. There, stretching unbroken to the horizon, are waist-high prairie grasses.

It is Merlin who breaks the silence and my reverie.

"*Coup de Foudre!*" He always speaks cabaret French when he is really happy. He pulls the hefty tome that he has been perusing up to his nose and squints through his reading glasses. "Proverbial pay dirt," he continues and reads: "Tuesday, seventh of February the year of our Lord 1882. Received by the parish: the estate of Angus P. Taylor leaves the south five acres of Willowbend Farm— that is of Monroe Township, sections 46,47—to the Cathedral Church of St. Aidan and its Dean Timothy Weeks. It is given to be, in perpetuity, a glebe for this and future clerics' welfare and use."

Phil bursts out, "Angus Taylor. Maxine's family. She was right! Let me see that. *In perpetuity?* Does it really say in perpetuity?" Merlin hands him the dusty volume.

"Brilliant work, Merlin." Phil looks up at us and beams. "Absolutely clear: it looks like we've got ourselves—or rather, Brigid, you've got yourself—a glebe."

I smile. I think.

"Glebe? Glebe!" Delilah stands in the vault's doorway, cream cheese on her lips like white 1960s lipstick. She bellows it like a Welsh poem, "Glebe, what the Paradisio? Where's the tobacco? The cotton? How's a pastor to live on grass? Bring in cattle maybe. Now us, in Kentucky, our church had a real glebe."

26

SHOOTING STAR

Dodecatheon meadia or shooting star has a most unusual flower that rises from the earth on a foot-long stalk. Part of the primrose family, shooting star is an ephemeral. It is closely related to garden cyclamen and in America it is sometimes called cowslip.

–Note from Dean Brigid Brenchley's Prairie Journal

Exeter, Trinity Term, 1986

Daniel was more realistic than I was about the possible merging of our vocations. I clung to romantic, sit-com notions. I could picture us—me in my collar and him in his yarmulke—kissing in the doorway of a Kansas City house with him off to the synagogue and me to a parish church.

He kindly listened, "I wish it, too. But Brigid, it would prove harder than you imagine. For one, there is my mother! She would love you as a person, but be totally against me marrying a Gentile. She'd make our lives miserable. And oh," he smirked at me, "while good for television, Reform Jewish men don't usually wear yarmulkes. Long-term is going to be hard for us. But we have the present..."

So, we simply kept our romance going in a kind of sacred present, as if we would never leave England. Still, with the Daniel-rabbi-wrinkle, I gently resumed my own spiritual and vocational pursuits with new energy. Then, they came upon me in full force.

"Well, if you're sure I can't lure you back to Rome, are certain of your loyalty to the established English Church," my tutor Ron Killion teased me, "then you must meet Matthew Tenby. Old friend. Good sort."

Ron urged me to go hear Tenby speak at a meeting of the Anglican Student Society. The Rev. Canon Tenby was a rural dean, which meant he oversaw many small parishes and had "other duties as assigned" by the bishop. I remembered: he tends the little parish with the goats! That made me more open to Ron's suggestion. It turned out that Tenby was coming to speak about the Dead Sea Scrolls, a topic which intrigued both Danny and me.

The University's chapel filled with students—Wellies (aristocrats) and giggling young women, mainly. It smelled like wet hair, wet woolen scarves, and sherry. One of the stiff upper lip students announced that the group would be continuing its exploration of the topic of Women's Ordination all term. Then he introduced the speaker.

Matthew Tenby was as short as Ron Killion—perhaps it was part of their affinity—and even wispier. But he had a beguiling, forceful rhetorical style, a voice that seemed impossibly large for his frame. From Bristol, there was a broadness to his speech and a rollicking, intoxicating rhythm, like Alfred P. Doolittle's voice in *My Fair Lady,* but pouring forth from a much smaller man.

Before diving in about the Qumran community and the scrolls, Canon Tenby wanted to get his two cents in on the conversations announced.

"About women's ordination?" he began,

Oh great. I looked over at Daniel.

"I want you to know that I am one hundred percent," the Canon continued, "undeniably, unequivocally, adamantly, decidedly, and irrevocably—"

Impressed by his waterfall of rhyming adverbs that captured the attention of all in the room, I nonetheless steeled myself.

Daniel gently cupped my hand, while looking straight ahead.

"In support of the ordination of women!" Canon Tenby proclaimed.

What a shock. After all the Devonian, ecclesiastical nay-sayers! Danny looked over at me, eyes smiling beneath his black ringlets. So, of course Daniel and I spoke to Canon Tenby after his presentation. Having visited the Dead Sea, Daniel had numerous ideas to discuss about Qumran. I gathered up the courage to tell Matthew Tenby that I was discerning a possible call to the priesthood.

In him, my calling found its shelter in the tumultuous English ordination storm.

The diocese of Exeter had a Ministry Training School, which was one of Matthew's other "duties as assigned" by the bishop. I had no idea really what it was, but Tenby invited me to tag along. One weekend a month, leaders from these tiny parishes—town and country—who were testing a vocation in the Church came together for education

The venue was a bed-and-breakfast that rattled near the busy Exeter train station. Its proprietor was a silver-haired jolly man who took no other guests and turned the place over to the diocese for training weekends. He lavished hospitality on us. Around seven a.m., he appeared in the hallway outside our bedrooms with a cart of coffee, tea, rolls, and the daily news. Around ten p.m., after our last session, he would roll up his sleeves and step behind a wet-bar in the parlor. In between, we feasted on lessons about the Gospel writers or German theologians like Bultmann or Schleiermacher.

I was quite surprised on Sunday morning when, down near the wet bar at a make-shift altar, the proprietor appeared again. He was a deacon, now all clothed in robes and sash! He lived out his calling to connect the Church and the World through Bed-and-Breakfast. I loved it.

It was on those weekends that I first met English women who felt called like me, women I sensed would make grace-filled, gifted priests. They had experienced things similar to my woman-in-light-in-robes experience, but, unlike me they had little hope of actually becoming priests. At that point, the only order open to women in Britain was to become a deaconess—no consecrating the sacrament, no preaching, no parish oversight.

Getting to know these women gave me gratitude for my opportunity back home and made me want to help things change.

That spring, the Anglican Student Society decided they should end the term-long conversation with a formal debate. Tenby and a spikey Anglo-Catholic Canon from the cathedral were to put forth the first arguments. Matthew Tenby tried to talk me into being his second:

"I swear, Brigid, all you have to do is tell your Quirky story," he chuckled at his own double-entendre. "I swear, you tell that and be brave, and the Spirit will do the rest."

Who would I be up against? Who was the second for the "No" side? A woman professor named Alice Moorman! A sixty-eight-year-old Full Professor of History. She was built like Winston Churchill and made Margaret Thatcher seem like a sweetie pie. Moreover, she had given a rousing speech at the British National Synod in opposition to the ordination of women. I've always found it ironic that women who enjoy speaking to thousands want to deny other women the right to preach.

When I learned who my opponent was to be, as well as some details about her, the thought of facing her in oratorical battle made me as terrified as I had ever been in my life.

I sat in my sauna-like dorm room freaking out over the decision. At this point, I had the backbone to tell Matthew to find another, more qualified, second. I was about to call him and pull out of the debate, when I prayed and opened my Bible.

And I tell you, everyone who acknowledges me before others, the

Son of Man will acknowledge... do not worry about how you are to defend yourselves or what you are to say, for the Holy Spirit will teach you at that very hour what you are to say. Luke 12:8, 11-12

Would 1 ever learn not to play Bible-roulette?! Now 1 was stuck.

"You do have a great story," Daniel reassured me.

With the words of my encouraging lover, 1 pictured the women 1 had met at the B&B on the ministry training weekends: called to be priests but destined to be deaconesses, and 1 knew 1 would be doing this for them. It was something Daniel, in his quiet way, understood and was trying to tell me. 1 had little to lose back home in the States, with male clerics telling me to get ordained. The Church of England needed these women. The faithful of the goat parish could have Holy Communion and preaching every Sunday if the English Church would just open up to the women leaders in their midst.

Oddly, the debate was held at the Roman Catholic Newman Center, maybe because they had a large hall and an attached pub.

The place was packed! 1 thought 1 might faint. Ron Killion gave me a Bilbo-like wink from the crowd. Daniel was out there, his dark eyes a little nervous.

Matthew Tenby's presentation of the arguments was flawless. But 1 was so anxious. 1 kept trying to rehearse in my brain the concepts he had laid out, but it was like 1 had cotton in my ears and frontal lobe.

Eventually, it was my turn behind the podium. 1 looked out at a couple of hundred people where 1 had expected only the students of the Society and a handful of others. But there sat church members, priests in collars, professors too. My legs started to shake. 1 felt like a bobble-head on some dashboard trying to shake the panic from my system. Matthew kept nodding as if to say, "Go on, you can do it."

1 was momentarily frozen.

Well, just make it about you. And the training school women...

Graciously, suddenly, 1 realized it was like being in the pulpit at Grandpa Barney's funeral. 1 was atop the hill, once again, for another great rhetorical slalom. This time it was a charity race, for all those women in Britain thwarted in their calls to be priests.

Suddenly, throwing all notes aside, I knew I would tell them about Peter Caspian and the college chaplains who told him I should be a priest. I would tell them about being invited to preach at Grandpa Barney's funeral just twenty-four hours later, *and* about my experience of the robed-woman-in-light. I threw in a last mogul jump describing the wonderful women I'd met in Devon with stories similar to mine. I told them how there was no Communion at the goat church, but how there might be. I ended with St. Paul's words about the Body of Christ—no part is superior, all are needed for the work of the Gospel.

God had woven the narrative of my life. I just shared it. In effect, I was simply a living example of the arguments Matthew Tenby had just laid out so well for them: First, God uses everyone, "slave and free, Jew and Gentile, male and female." Second, and more importantly, Jesus himself chose a woman, Mary Magdalene, to spread the news of his Resurrection to the men no less. They could take it or leave it. I simply skied my "Quirky story" for those gathered, and after the erudite theological and ecclesiastical arguments of the other three, the crowd turned festive and mesmerized by this tale told in the American vernacular.

By a narrow margin, we won the debate.

In the pub afterward, Matthew Tenby was ecstatic. He was buying everyone a pint.

Especially me. Two for me.

To our amazement Professor Moorman, holding a snifter of port, started our way like a battleship.

"Gird your loins," Matthew whispered as she approached.

"Young woman," she said, staring straight into my face. She even sounded like Winston Churchill. "I do not endorse your ideas for one minute. But by God, and I think I mean that literally, you've got guts."

27

PRAIRIE PHLOX PHOS HILARON

Phlox pilosa or prairie phlox has a wide variety of flower colors, from nearly white to shades of light and dark purple and pink, with a slight fragrance. The lower leaves tend to turn yellow and drop off the stem when the plant becomes stressed out. The shape of any phlox is a good example of how it has evolved with the needs of the butterfly visitor in mind. We have it scattered in the midst of the butterfly milkweed and that area thrives in waves of purple and white first, and then in explosions of the vivid orange of the milkweed.

–Note from Dean Brigid Brenchley's Prairie Journal

Monday

The Diocesan House is tucked in an oasis of old-world homes not far from downtown. The bishop's offices are in a Tudor Revival house, next to the home of the president of Drake University. Inside, the only access to Bishop Farnon is a narrow, winding, stone staircase. I have no idea how it accommodates the geriatric saints that now make up most of his diocese. Bishop Farnon has asked that I come a half hour before Phil—hopefully not to query me about our relationship. If Maxine can see our unfolding affection, the bishop may perceive it too. With all the other tumult, the last thing the bishop will want is a sex scandal at the cathedral.

When I arrive, Bishop Farnon is finishing his morning prayers. Whereas some executives have a wet bar or putting green as part of their suite, this one has a chapel. As he emerges to greet me, his look is beatific. Such a change in countenance from the gala! In Judeo-Christian tradition those who meet with God sometimes carry a shine on their faces—the "shekinah" of Moses and Jesus. Above his fuchsia shirt the bishop glows. We settle in chairs in an alcove of windows nestled high in the branches of the oak and sycamore trees that hug the property. It's an upper solarium, but feels a bit like an ecclesiastical treehouse.

"Before Phil and the chancellor arrive," the bishop begins, "I want to know where your heart and spirit are on this whole matter of the sale. Where have your prayers been leading you?"

I breathe deeply, "Well, I have been asking: What is holy?" He nods affirmation.

"It has been like a tug of war of holiness—two holy possibilities in conflict."

"What are the two?"

"Restoring the disappearing prairie. You know I find God's fingerprints are all over these beautiful grasses and flowers. I don't think God wants the memory of them erased. The loss of prairie is one factor in all this unrelenting flooding, and as we're seeing in Marshland, it's poorer people who are suffering. The Jones family was evacuated, and their house was possibly submerged."

"I am so sorry. Yes...the devastation is so extensive. We must stand with those who are suffering. What is the other holy aspect?"

"Cathedral worship. You know that we just can't keep up with the building repair, can't get in front of that financially. The community inside is as beautiful and vulnerable as the prairie plants."

The bishop's shine does not dissipate; it actually seems to gain luster as he listens. "Holiness you say? Uncanny. Well, a God-incident I imagine. This morning I pulled this from my shelf for you."

He places in my hands Thomas Merton's *Life and Holiness*.

"Maybe my nudge was the Spirit; maybe it will help your sorting and sifting." The bishop gives me an encouraging look. "I applaud your quest for God's pleasure. Don't give up."

So, he is not going to tell me what to do.

"Hello?" Phil peeks his head in. "Bishop," he shakes Bishop Farnon's hand, "I hope I am not interrupting?"

"Not at all, we were just wrapping up," the bishop says and he moves us back toward his office. "Chancellor Charles should be joining us any minute."

On the bishop's desk we see the Sunday *Des Moines Register* unfolded.

With obvious enjoyment he asks, "Interesting set of news articles yesterday. Will the Honorable Francis chew you up and spit you out? Said you are meeting with him this noon, didn't you?"

Phil and I both wince.

"The mayor put a call through here bright and early this morning actually," the bishop continues, "asking what I knew of the newspaper story." He lowers the boom of his gaze on me. "You know, it would be nice to let your superior know when major news-ops are in the works. What is it, three or four stories in less than a week? We'll have to start paying celebrity royalties if you keep it up."

"I haven't been seeking these things out, I can assure you."

"I'm not reprimanding. The article—on the prairie and the cathedral—is actually a fine portrayal of your convictions. And I assume you didn't know about the controversial story on the levee?"

"I absolutely did not. I was floored. Felt a bit betrayed really."

"Well, all that's Mayor Burnish's headache. My jurisdiction is this glebe business. And the two of you."

Uh, oh.

Luckily, before we can find out what the bishop means by 'the two of you,' the legal counsel for the diocese, Thomas Charles, walks in. He is a small man, nearly eighty, who is so refined he reminds me of bone china. A calming smile, Iowa gentleness, but a mind like a steel trap.

He and Phil talk in legalese for a bit while the bishop and I listen in.

Then Chancellor Charles turns to me. "Dean Brigid, there are two things at work here. When the cathedral was being built, the Chase family gave the land for the church building and for a deanery for the priest to live in next door to it."

"I know about that," I tell the chancellor. "The parish sold the deanery and built the Sunday School wing there." Instead of a deanery they give each priest an interest-free loan to help buy a house. It's how I was able to purchase my bungalow.

"Everyone at the cathedral knows that piece. Lives large in St. Aidan's legend," Phil adds, "as well as the Chase family legend."

"However," Chancellor Charles continues, "after the Civil War, it seems another party, a Mr. Taylor, owned a tract of land immediately to the north of the cathedral. Part of a farm. He left it in his will to be a glebe."

"We had them in Britain," Bishop Farnon interjects. "They go back to the medieval period, and continued into the modern era. Most clergy received a tithe, but the priest was often also given a glebe. The produce of that land belonged to him."

"Or her, in this instance," the kind chancellor says with a smile. "I will confess it is difficult to translate today. As a young law clerk, I assisted attorneys from the cathedral when the land was turned to rental parking. Dean Brookes of that time, later Bishop Brookes, thus received all the profit as part his salary. Made some members grumble, especially Max Chase, Sr."

Aha. That is why I had to sign off on that pay-cut when we put in the prairie!

"However, while the legalities around a glebe are archaic," Phil adds, "the original intentions of a benefactor are paramount and are still water-tight in a court of law today."

"Now, the way the gift reads," the chancellor continues, "neither the dean nor the cathedral leaders can sell it without the other's consent. Furthermore—though this would probably be battled in court—as I read it, if both the cathedral board and you did decide to sell to the Hotel Savant, the profit from the land sale would rightly go to the priest."

The men all pause and with some amazement and amusement look at me like a newly minted millionaire—but one who will likely choose green grass over the stack of greenback dollars.

"Of course," the chancellor adds, "if this did occur, you could choose in turn to give substantially to the cathedral."

"I've been in prayer over the grace of this nineteenth-century gift all morning," the bishop chimes in. "Brigid, the cathedral parish, in its humanness, may be hurtling toward entropy and division. But due to Mr. Taylor's particular generosity, you must all work together!" Bishop James Farnon has that *shekinah* glow all over again.

With that, we take leave of the bishop and chancellor, and head to the mayor.

In the past, my imagining that the parallel wings of the mayor's office look like the outstretched paws of a stone lion had just been a bit of whimsy. Now, as Phil and I walk between those paws to the front entrance, the idea evokes trepidation.

"Brigid," Phil stops mid-stride, "I forgot our costumes. Should I run back for them?"

He grins. I laugh, imagining us dressed as big and little bluestem, and the levity definitely helps as we ascend the marble stairs.

"The mayor is expecting you," his receptionist says.

"I imagine he is," Phil mutters under his breath.

Mayor Burnish is at his desk surveying a document, his reading glasses down on his nose. He looks over his specs at us and his jaw muscles work a little, the way Phil's do when he wants to punch Max. Displeased lion. But, a gentleman and a man of protocol nonetheless, he stands, walks around the desk, and shakes our hands. Then he leads us to a semi-circle of leather chairs.

"Always lovely to read these articles before worship Sunday morning. Gives me a number of things to pray about," Francis Burnish says and centers one eye on me.

"Mayor..." I begin.

"Dean Brenchley," he interrupts, "I very much want to hear what you have to say. Quite handy Phil set this meeting up Saturday night." He squares his other eye on Phil. "So did you know that your feature would run in tandem with the critique of our office?"

Right then, Pasha Kurtz appears in the doorway. He looks both younger and older at the same time—half third-grade boy, half old man. I think it is the way his brows are aloft in frozen semi-circles above his avocado eyes. However, in those eyes I also see youthful indignation. The kind of look Phil probably wore when he pulled off his lettuce head in Giuliani's office.

"Come in, come in, Reporter Kurtz." Mayor Burnish motions him to an awaiting chair. "I think you all know one another. So, now, Dean Brigid do you want to continue?"

As Pasha sits near me, I am miffed. "Pasha, you didn't utter a word that you intended to dredge up—pardon the pun— controversies about the Marshland Levee in connection to our prairie project."

And I thought he was so transparent.

"That is not completely true," Pasha sounds loaded for bear. "Brigid, I said we wanted to gain a window onto the history of our city, a window into its larger issues. Well, a breached levee and a flood came pouring through that window last night!" Pasha turns to the mayor. "Mayor Burnish, admit it: the delay on the Marshland levee repair—of seventeen years—is unconscionable!

The people of Marshland deserve an explanation."

I realize he is right.

Yes, Lord. Pearl and Henry do.

My plan is to go straight over to see them when we finish with the mayor. I can only imagine what conditions are like at the shelter. I picture Henry trying to sleep on a cot, with Fido *phsst -clicking* away next to him. My mind is distracted by the thought, so I am not listening well as Pasha continues.

"People of Marshland wait for greedy politicians to make good on promises. They are like sitting ducks, their struggling neighborhood a convenient escape valve for protecting downtown assets." I almost think I hear him slide from "assets" into "assholes" under his breath.

The mayor is visibly irritated. But instead of erupting, he picks up carefully assembled packets from the coffee table around which our chairs are circled. He holds one up so we can all see. "Anyone recognize this place?" he asks.

The cover is a glossy shot of a city block in Marshland, which I think I've seen just around the corner from Pearl and Henry's house.

"I said, do any of you recognize this place?" The mayor asks, a little like a headmaster.

We all nod, though Pasha looks like he might spit.

Right then, Dave Stone, the head of the water works, appears, his large bear-like form filling the office doorway.

"Marshland Goddammit!" He answers the mayor's query with perfect timing.

Oh my.

"Sorry I'm late," Dave says to the mayor, as he moves like a hungry grizzly toward Pasha, "You lousy little shit. What are you doing, running a story like this without a comment from the city?"

"Stone, you're a hypocrite," Pasha actually rises to his feet. "It's been seventeen years! For seventeen years the people in the Marshland area have had lies and empty promises from officials. Their houses have been destroyed, mold-ridden, twice."

"Seventeen years? Seventeen years? Tell me about it!" Dave throws his arms about like he wants to strangle someone. "From where I sit, those seventeen years are like seventeen-hundred!"

Phil and I raise eyebrows and exchange a relieved glance—at least we are not the eye of this storm. We are now more observers.

"Pasha. DAvenue Sit down," the Lion speaks and it is clear he wants the floor. He waits in silence to assure that he has our rapt attention. He holds up the glossy packet again. In the silence, we can all read the title: *2011 Marshland Area Re-Development Plan.* The mayor continues. "Brigid, Phil, do the people of St. Aidan's Cathedral—who helped with reconstruction there last time—have the best interests of the residents of Marshland at heart?"

I nod. "Mayor, one of our parish families has been deluged, lost their home, twice," I say. "They are in an emergency shelter now." I want him to know.

His countenance registers this news, but he continues, "Reporter Kurtz, do you and the *Des Moines Register* have the best interests of the residents of Marshland at heart?" Pasha nods.

The mayor raises his voice in a manner that is at once fed up but almost jovial. This is a man who must enjoy politics.

"The director of the waterworks and I are understandably exasperated," he roars, "that you seem to assume that Des Moines city officials do *not* have the best interests of the residents of Marshland at heart!"

"Seventeen years of doing nothing does not look like interest, Mr. Burnish," Pasha retorts. I picture young communists standing up to the czar or westernized leaders in China. Pasha is no coward, that's for sure. I think Phil is maybe silently egging him on, memories of Green Guerilla days and all.

Finally, seasoned attorney Phil enters the mix. "Mayor Burnish, you now know that Dean Brenchley wasn't made aware of the final scope of *The Register's* coverage. Our cathedral is extremely grateful for the support you have offered, especially in regard to our prairie project." Pasha is muttering something like middle-aged-sell-out under his breath, before Phil adds, "But, the reporter is right to inquire: what has taken seventeen years? Has the city government done due diligence?"

At this point the mayor sends around the packets: a copy of the *2011 Marshland Area Redevelopment Plan* for each of us.

"Read it," the mayor says. "Now."

A little like chastened school children, we bow our heads over the document. It is a full and impressive plan. It carefully recounts the 1993 and 2008 flood history. The salient detail? The city of Des Moines first petitioned the Army Corps of Engineers to study and repair the Marshland Levee in 1997!

Pasha is staring at his black Converse high-tops and I think I detect a rose complexion rising to his ears.

"A very complicated process completed and filed in 1997, you lousy little shit," Dave Stone says. "We have been busting our political butts to get that levee repaired—through the federal and state red-tape—since fucking 1997."

The mayor's expression tells Dave to tone it down, to lose the expletives.

One by one, we each finish perusing the plan and look up. Not only is it a plan to fix the levee, it is a plan that honors the Marshland Neighborhood. The Vision Statement reads:

- The Marshland Neighborhood is a great place to live because it is a close-knit, diverse community.
- The Marshland Neighborhood is a great place to work with easy access to downtown and beyond.
- The Marshland Neighborhood is a great place to play because the most innovative part of this plan is to create a beautiful bike trail and linked green space on the repaired levee.

"Well the money is finally approved in Washington, and the contractor chosen," Dave Stone tells us. "Construction begins next spring. I just couldn't be sorrier that this flood beat us to the punch. My heart aches for all those people we had to evacuate."

My cell phone rings.

"Excuse me," I say, seeing that the number matches the number of the emergency shelter.

I step outside the mayor's office into the hallway.

When I step back in, I am crestfallen. I look at Phil. "It was Richard Jones. Henry has been rushed to St. Mary's Hospital."

Henry is lying face up, eyes slightly open, in the bed when I edge open the door. Though holding tight to Henry's hand, Pearl is asleep with her mouth open in the chair next to him. It's obvious the Jones clan has been here—playing cards, poker chips, and a box of mostly eaten donuts from the Marshland Bakery scatter the area. The only sound is of the oxygen.

Click, phsst... click, phsst—plays its lullaby. Hospital oxygen now—water-pocked and cord wrapped on top, like a retired Star Wars droid, Fido rests near the bed by Henry's slippers.

I walk into Henry's field of vision. It takes effort for him to apprehend me. "In from church? Or the bars?" He whispers. A sense of humor still.

"The mayor's office actually."

A crucifix hangs above the bed.

Phsst, I see the ribs of Christ in the ivory.

Click. Henry struggles to breathe and the small-blue-daisy cloth of his hospital gown is indented by his rib cage.

Pearl wakes up and clasps my hand in hers. Her hand is both smooth and nobbled like a late summer squash.

I slowly pull from my pocket a palm-sized vessel, its bronze stamped with a Lamb of God. Inside, there is saturated cotton. I place my thumb in and press to cover it with balm blessed by the bishop. I make the sign of the cross with the clove-scented oil across Henry's liver spotted forehead.

"You are the light of the world."

Henry's chest continues to heAvenue But his eyes gently close and his face softens toward a smile. He understands my code. The pallor of his skin is strangely beautiful.

Then, Pearl sobs into my shoulder. Her weeping mirrors the pattern of Henry's breathing.

For better, for worse, they braid their suffering into one strong rope. One flesh.

My tears fall onto her dyed, thinning hair. Finally, Pearl gently kisses Henry's forehead, and she moves to get his mother's *Prayer Book,* the antique one I kept safe from the flood waters. But I couldn't keep them safe.

"Hank loves this prayer," she says, turning the onion skin pages to the *Phos Hilaron,* Christianity's most ancient hymn of light. Hunched over the old volume, Pearl and I pray together:

O gracious Light,

Pure brightness of the everliving Father in heaven, O Jesus Christ, holy and blessed!

Now as we come to the setting of the sun, And our eyes behold the vesper light,

We sing your praises O God: Father, Son, and Holy Spirit.

You are worthy at all times to be praised by happy voices, O Son of God, O Giver of life,

And to be glorified through all the worlds.

I stay with Pearl until Henry's breathing goes silent.

28

DUST TO SAN DAMIANO DUST

Rosmarius officinalis or rosemary is a woody perennial herb with fragrant, evergreen, needle-like leaves and white, pink, purple, or blue flowers, native to the Mediterranean region. During ancient times, rosemary was universally used as a symbol of remembrance.

–Note from Dean Brigid Brenchley's Prairie Journal

Via Cantico delle Creature, Near Assisi, September 1986

The dust powdered my feet through my sandals, like wading in sun-burnt talcum. It soothed the blisters rising under the metal clasps at my ankles. The only dusty, deserted roads I'd ever known were Jefferson's yeoman farmer grids, stretched straight as rulers across the Kansas plains. So this soft, sienna-colored substance that I trod from Santa Maria degli Angeli to San Damiano seemed surrealistic, ribboning through aromatic vineyards, olive groves, and poppies. The nuns hosting me in the valley near the sputtering train station warned that it was a substantial walk for a warm September day. But they finally conceded that a twenty-three-year-old, freckled American on a spiritual quest should manage it. My devotion, my questions, would carry me.

After the women's ordination debate at Exeter, I had cloistered myself in my sauna-like dorm room and poured myself into my thesis. Finally, I emerged. With the dollar strong and a thesis draft done, I lit upon the idea of going to Italy. When I heard rumors that Daniel was at a Kibbutz near Tel Aviv and then received my "Dear Brigid" letter, it sealed my plans. My spirit needed a pilgrimage—train miles and footsteps—to sort through both lost love and priestly call.

Ron Killion said I absolutely deserved a break and knew of a Franciscan Order with houses in both Florence and Assisi. I penned a letter of inquiry in Italian, he edited it, and the reply came: I was welcome for an extended retreat.

So, I arrived from Florence, got settled in a room at the convent on the outskirts of Santa Maria degli Angeli, and found myself seated around a jovial table of habited and un-habited nuns and young women exploring vocation—about fifteen women in all. The women, eating bread, cheese, olives, and stuffed grape leaves, drinking bottled water and wine, were conversing in Italian, Spanish, and French simultaneously. Most seemed fluent in all three languages. I was simply a visitor, a traveler in their midst, interested in the Franciscan way. Then, I was hit by lightning, spiritual lightning.

Allesandra, a recent Al Italia stewardess, was my guide and appointed interpreter. But she was also the interpreter for an old German nun just back from the organization's work in Senegal. Allesandra was also the most animated story-teller of all, so she forgot the English translation half the time, and I just let the tides of foreign phrases wash over me. Allesandra told wild stories as fact. And the others regaled her.

C'est vrai?.

E vero. E vero!

But in all the frivolity there was a lull (maybe they realized they were hungry), and in the lull the Mother Superior gazed at me. She was the most petite person at the table, dressed in a white short-skirted habit, striped with sky-blue near her face. With great intention, she asked me something in French. When I simply stared back at her slate eyes and whittled features, she cocked her head. It was a gesture uncannily like a plover bird who had alit near me on the beach soon before I left Devon. Both nun and bird seemed to search my very existence. Some of the other nuns looked slightly uncomfortable; others warmly smiled, as if this had happened to them before. I chewed and swallowed the best bread I'd ever tasted.

I shrugged my shoulders. "*No parlo Francese,*" I tried. I barely parlo-d Italiano.

The nun spoke with the same intentionality, this time to Allesandra, who then turned to me.

"Mother wants to know if you are going to become an Anglican priest?"

I had a great, great grandmother—Grandpa Floyd's grandmother—who actually died from lightning while homesteading near Strawberry, Kansas. I had always wondered what it was like: a bolt; a reverberating sizzle; the inability to speak; falling down dead in the dust.

This question, about whether or not to become a priest, was precisely why I had come. *Solamente.* But I had never mentioned the possibility in my letter to the nuns, nor verbally to anyone in Italy. I knew right then and there that nuns who really pray are scary.

The silence of the gathered women clearly signified that if Mother Superior asked you a question, you responded.

I met her well-traveled, seabird stare and said, "I don't know. Maybe. I am here trying to find out if God still likes the idea."

Allesandra translated; Mother nodded, and the group cheered. It seemed I had crossed a line. Maybe from tourist to genuine pilgrim.

Dear God... How did she know that?

The fact that Americans become Episcopal priests and the English Anglican priests was beside the point. *How did she know that?*

Spiritual lightning. Tingling up my body, toes to scalp. I might have run outside to throw up, but felt drawn instead to eat more bread. They had some English cheddar there, too, just for me. The bread had a chewy crust that stroked my palette and dissolved because of the pockets of air hand-kneaded in.

I found myself laughing as Allesandra spun into another story. Now she was standing up and acting things out. Something about a businessman on a plane to Rome. I laughed, tore off bread, shaved some cheddar to go on top, and laughed some more. Unlike the uptight prigs and adamant feminists of the Exeter Anglican Student Society, the nuns of Santa Maria degli Angeli seemed to receive my openness to the priesthood without political tension and as a genuine exploration of a calling. Catholics even. I was astounded and lightened.

When we left the table, the confab of nuns in the kitchen carefully drew me a map of back roads safe for my hike to San Damiano, and I went to bed early. The Mother Superior had not asked me to join their order, as the sexy Milanese man on the couchette train had warned she would. But in sleep's haze her face and question were staring at me intently.

How did she know? I asked again in my dream.

Then the plover alit in my dream just as I was on the threshold of sleep. It tilted its head quizzically, opened its beak, but spoke in Allesandra's voice:

"Mother wants to know if you are going to be an Anglican priest?" I slept.

The grapevines tied to posts cast shadows in the elegant early sun. Wearing a sundress and toting a cloth backpack, which the nuns had stocked with provisions, and with a cover-up for my shoulders upon entering holy sites, I sat with Allesandra on a rough-hewn bench. She was to see me off on my day's journey. Allesandra had generously given me a smooth, curved, wooden cross the size of my palm to hold as I walked. She was teaching me Franciscan wisdom.

"Poverty and joy," I said, and shook my head. "I don't know."

Allesandra was picking up handfuls of the sienna colored dust and letting it fall through her hand like a sieve. "Poverty-*and*-Joy!" she said with gusto. "San Francesco was adamant: if there is no joy, the poverty must go! But he found that poverty led him into joy. It was his poverty that exposed him to the elements, to Brother Sun, and Sister Moon, poverty that threw him outside to preach to the birds and converse with the wolf at Gubbio."

"Poverty-and-Joy?" I repeated. I didn't say it, but I couldn't imagine any idea less American.

Allesandra clenched the earth in her hands in a spirited gesture. "All these connections... they brought the *Poverello* joy! Yes, Poverty-and-Joy—not one without the other—but *insieme*, together. Above all, of course, Francis said poverty brought him close to our Lord. You can ponder it your whole life."

I nodded at that. We rose and Allesandra pointed me down the right path.

A breeze licked the back of my knees like a dog anxious to walk and I tripped across the valley. For some reason, I had expected all of Italy to be urban, like Rome with its classical architecture, or like Florence with Gucci and honking Vespas. I hadn't foreseen Umbria's agricultural hills and plains. I don't know where I thought all the pasta and wine originated! As I left Santa Maria degli Angeli, there were pedestrians and a few youth on bikes.

But as I moved into the valley, the only other people I saw were workers out in the fields, tending grapes and checking grain with lined, leathered hands like those of Grandpa Floyd. I soaked it all in. I didn't think. I didn't pray. Just wordless gratitude. Even the anticipation of reaching San Damiano, where Francis heard Jesus say, "*Va, Francesco, repara mi chiesa*" and where St. Clare spent years in prayer, was formless, imageless gratitude.

It wasn't until I started the incline, perhaps somewhere on the *Via Cantico delle Creature*, and the blister on my left foot started to scrape with pain, that I was reminded why I'd come.

"Mother wants to know if you are going to become an Anglican priest?"

How am I even here? I asked God and myself incredulously. I am the descendant of real estate agents, wheat farmers, and an insurance executive. Not a priestly sort of lineage. Of course, I recognized that my family was not so different from Francis' merchant bunch. Despite my woman-in-light vision and steps toward postulancy before leaving the States, like the formaggio, toasted bread, and apricots in my backpack, I had continued to carry three different ideas of my identity around Europe for nearly two years now. I needed resolution.

A sign post marked the way. *3 K a San Damiano.* 3 K. Handy. A funny English nun from Dorset, who wore brown muslin and drove a tractor, once taught me visual prayer: picture things (she did this while she plowed) and then offer them up to God. 3 K. Okay, I decided, I would hike and picture my possible lives one kilometer at a time. In prayer at the summit, at San Damiano, surely God would bring clarity.

The first kilometer. I see a full lecture hall at Exeter University with trendy (some snarky) bright students. Scholars and Wellies. I see myself at age forty throw open the doors, my hair in ringlets, earrings dangling. In an animated style, chewing on the end of reading glasses, I unlock for the students the hidden mysteries of Henry James' pronouns. Especially his societally charged italicized pronouns. Or, I highlight for them the paradoxical phrases in G.K. Chesterton's mysteries. Professor Brigid Brenchley, PhD. I tried to lift this image to God. But it seemed flimsy. Pronouns are not much to dedicate a life to! This option I released easily. Open-handed.

The second kilometer. I am in a fishbowl conference room, dressed in a pinstripe suit and pearls. The Rockies are framed in the west window. I have a sumptuous brown leather valise which I unzip, and I pull out actuarial tables for the others seated at the table—all men in ties.

This is my father's insurance company. I imagine myself

recently back from law school. Yet, seeing the rows of figures and myself computing insurance quotes makes my temples throb. Immediately the vision transforms itself into a scene after the meeting.

I am with one of the handsome men from the conference room at a restaurant on S. Gaylord St.—Dad's old favorite, Scott and Zelda's. His tie is loosened and my pearl earrings rest on the tablecloth. A waiter uncorks a bottle of wine and another brings us steaming Alaskan king crab legs. We are planning our trip to Maui for the national insurance convention. In this career choice, the work isn't for the work itself, it is for the money. The money for crab legs dripping with lemon butter, French wine, and Hawaiian outrigger canoes. For the lifestyle most upper-middle-class people crave.

I try to lift this picture to God: but with my blatantly materialistic motives, the picture sours. It's distasteful in my throat. Brigid Brenchley, Esq. CEO. It's almost bitter in my mind, and yet, it is hard to let go. I still clench this vision in my mind like a fist.

The third kilometer. I have my auburn hair pulled up and wear a black clerical shirt and collar (hell on a woman's figure). I am in a city neighborhood, holding a prayer service where an old woman has been hit by a motorcycle. Then I am chanting the Lord's Prayer inside a lofty church. Then I am in a hospital room pre-dawn with a lonely, dying man. Reverend Brigid Brenchley. My vision keeps shifting, because in reality it is a life about which I know next to nothing. I have fear. Nonetheless, I lift it, in imagined fragments, to God.

I reached the summit. Just above me were swaying cypress trees and the blonde stone of San Damiano. In 1205 the young Francis hiked this incline himself, drawn to a forgotten oratory, a nearly ruined place of prayer. From its weathered but intricately painted eleventh-century crucifix, he heard Jesus: "Francis, go rebuild my church."

Entering the dim sanctuary, I put on my cover-up and knelt. I gazed at this same crucifix, moved by this particular cross design: human figures, heavenly and earthly, surrounded the gentle portrait of Jesus. Squinting at this cross, I was intrigued to see down near Jesus' feet on one side a primitive poultry-type bird and on the other a small animal, perhaps a cat. I realized that all of creation rides on this twelfth-century cross!

Moved, I prayed. I longed to hear Jesus speak to me. No such luck.

On the road back down the mountain, I was spent and parched. The sun now reverberated off the flaxen dust as off a sheet of metal. The farmers had gone indoors to rest, or eat, or make love as Italians do in the heat of the day. An occasional horsefly was all that breathed. I had not brought enough water. My mouth was as chafed as my feet and my throat was becoming hoarse. I realized that in my two plus decades of life, I had never really known thirst. I felt I might faint.

Poverty. Thirst was poverty. I was a dependent creature. I had unwittingly stumbled into a small taste of Francis' poverty.

I was still standing as I reached the mottled shade of the Santa degli Angeli valley.

There, upon level ground, down in their hairy fibers, my ear cavities filled like cups. A familiar, rhythmic, liquid sound. I took a few strides. I had not even noticed it on my upward journey, but there tucked along the roadside in a mossy wall of stone was gurgling water: a very old fountain and a bench. Was I dreaming? Hallucinating? No, there are public fountains in Umbria even from Roman times. Caution about dysentery thrown to the wind, I drank thankfully and deeply.

Then I sat on the bench, took off my sandals, and burrowed my feet down into the dust. I smelled rosemary. Huge, as it never grows in the hippie gardens of Colorado or Kansas, an ancient shrub framed the bench. Pungent, calming, flowering rosemary. My nostrils filled with its smoky scent. I closed my eyes. I remembered the smoke of Grandpa Barney's campfire and a sizzling trout. The smoky tangy herb wrapped me in its odor, like fresh cut hay did on the farm. It smelled like a prairie burn in the Flint Hills.

I reached my toes down through dust to the solid, cool earth undergirding all. Light and shadow moved across the back of my eyelids. I saw no images, no romanticized TV sitcom versions of who I might become. I just was. I bent over and, as Allesandra had in the early morning, I sifted the sand through my hands. Its softness made me remember the soft snow of the Teacup Bowl.

Poverty? Joy? Being ordained? It was a kind of death to things my culture prized.

Ashes to ashes, dust to dust. I had put it off long enough.

From the earth and the rosemary I gained peace about becoming a priest.

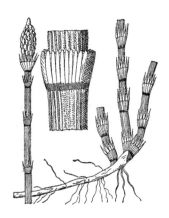

29

HORSETAIL

Equisetum hyemale, or horsetail plant (also known in South Africa as snake grass) is a perennial herb in the fern family. Horsetail has vertical jointed reed-like stalks of medium to dark green. The hollow stems are up to 3 feet in height. It is a native plant found across North America, Europe, and northern Asia. It is primarily found in wetlands, and in riparian zones of rivers and streams where it can withstand seasonal flooding.

–Note from Dean Brigid Brenchley's Prairie Journal

Tuesday Night

Glebe, glebe, glebe. My head is full of the funny word that sounds like Lewis Carroll describing wild turkeys. I am in the chancel at the dean's *prie-dieu.* I want to offer it all to God.

Glebe.
Glebe.
Glebe.

Holy.

Holy.

Holy.

In life, there are decisions we have already made that are still excruciating in the implementation. When I was in elementary school, Grandpa Floyd would come to Denver for the Great Western Stock Show. He loved to watch horses, any place, anytime, and I loved things English, all sorts. So together we would stay late in the main ring where at around eleven p.m. the English jumping occurred. After calf roping and bronc riding and the clowns in barrels, the crowds thinned out. Then small women in fitted jackets on horses with braided manes entered the lofty coliseum. Both the women and the horses knew what they were going to do. They had decided. They were determined. But it didn't make the leap over the barricades easy.

I kneel there under our elm-like crucifix suspended above the altar by invisible wire.

Jesus' ribs and suffering body, like wound rope, ripple and ripple out, melding with the sinews of the tree. Henry's straining to breathe is over. I pray for Pearl and all their family. It happened so fast, so forged with the trauma of the flood.

I realize now that my dualistic thinking has been all wrong. St. Irenaeus teaches that by taking on flesh, the Divine becomes one not just with humanity but with the materiality of the whole creation. With similar vision, the artist who carved our cross has tree and human wedded together. His artist statement reads: "This Crucifix was my study of mycelial networks. Trees may look separate in the forest, but underground the roots are connected and interwoven."

With Henry's death, I now see that it's not the creation *or* the people, the land *or* the cathedral. No, the creation *and* the people suffer together. The creation *and* the people are to be redeemed together.

I have carried into the worship space two things: the Merton book the bishop loaned me and the antique photo of Phineas Chase that I discovered in the vault.

The old photograph rests on my prayer desk. With my thumb I rub the photograph's yellowed, card-stock frame.

God, Max really does look like him.

With the huge offering of stones piled in the wagon nearby him, Phineas Chase's eyes seem rapt with an inward vision of the majestic structure he felt called to erect: the cathedral in which I now pray. A place for people to worship the Creator of these stones. All those stones, earthen bones, erected by humans into a place to honor God. I see why Max cares so passionately. I understand Max's calling, and for one last moment I open myself to taking the money and aligning myself to it.

It too would be a holy choice. I see that truth now.

But my gaze drifts, from the wagon of stone and Phineas Chase, to where they stand.

I breathe deeply. I am filled with awe and gratitude. There is no getting around it: what I am moved by, above all, to my core, are the prairie grasses in the background. Now gone. Now, almost nowhere to be found. My eyes cannot tear themselves from what is all around the man and the mule and the wagon. Chase's well-starched cuffs and his hands disappear altogether. His legs below the knee are invisible. So are the bottoms of the wagon wheels and the legs of the horses. All partly submerged in a sea of grass that is running, running to the horizon, in an undulating line that meets the sky.

What have you got to lose, except earthly memory of these grasses?

My calling. I face this fact. As Merton writes, "to act on what I perceive of the mysterious design of God" is as close to holy as I'm going to get! I carefully place the old photo in my valise on top of the letter from The Hotel Savant and leave the chancel for the cathedral boardroom.

St. Aidan's boardroom is called the "chapter room" because the body elected to oversee a cathedral is really called a chapter. In English Church history, it was a monastic-like assembly who gathered with the bishop. But most days, we just call the group of leaders the board, because it is what our twenty-first-century people understand.

I open the door and am relieved to find I am the first one to arrive. With characteristic turn of the twentieth-century ambience, beside our large octagonal conference table, a sweepingly wide mirror hangs above a claw-footed sideboard. As Merlin once pointed out to me, there is a gilt-framed mirror in every room at St. Aidan's, even the copy machine room!

When leading a meeting or debating a point at this table, it is a curious phenomenon to look up and see oneself in the mirror. Do I look convincing? Terrified? Beautiful? Is that a black smudge of mascara? I can also catch the glimpse of other leaders: a hidden chuckle, a sneer, an expression of gratitude. What will the mirror watch tonight? I wonder. Behind my seat and out the windows you can see the prairie highlighted by the early evening light. I look at it wistfully as people begin to file in.

Soon, the table fills with the cathedral leaders who make up the chapter.

"Well," Phil says, calling the meeting to order, "the obvious, important item on our agenda is the real estate offer from The Hotel Savant. It was delivered to us by agents from SansCorps Development Corporation, a company from Chicago."

I pull out the original letter and hand around copies for each chapter member.

They read what they have heard so much about; living proof is now in their hands. They contemplate. They stare at me. Wow.

Max speaks up. "We have an overwhelming opportunity before us. There is really very little to discuss. Am I right?" He scans the group and tries to capitalize on the awe the letter and offer engender. As usual, he is first out of the starting gate.

"Well, actually," Phil enters in quickly, as he told me he would, "as it turns out this matter is not so much before 'us' as it is before the dean."

"I understand... our dean has holy convictions and romantic ideals about the value of prairie. Yet, Dean Brenchley, any cleric with the parish's best interests at heart, with God in focus, will use this opportunity to assure the future worship in our historic church." Max sounds like he remains unsure about whether we have discovered the details concerning the glebe.

Phil gives him the signal and Merlin passes out copies of the historic vestry minutes and further documentation confirming the glebe that Phil has found in city records. The board members read again.

"Glebe? What in the world is a glebe?' Harold Manse asks. "Is this something that has been hidden?"

Burton snorts in response.

"We are all aware of the glebe," Max starts in a silky but dismissive tone.

"I wasn't," a number of the members say. "What does it mean?"

"Archaic canon law that the attorneys at Chase are convinced will be overruled." Max is very practiced with boardroom fencing, but Phil is quick on his feet, too.

"Max, I think you're wrong. Your attorneys, or we could call them yes-men, are wrong. We can go to court, but Chase Enterprises will lose. In current Iowa law, the intentions of a benefactor are primary, rock solid. The pertinent statutes are included in what Merlin just distributed. The land was given to support and to be used at the discretion of the cleric."

What a Lancelot.

Many clergy hate this part of our job. But I have always rather enjoyed watching the political maneuvering—like debates at King Arthur's round table. I often enter the fray myself and I am very aware that this will be one of those nights. I will not be able to sit, like Guinevere, on the sidelines and watch the men joust.

"We will sue," Max says.

Samuel suddenly manifests that he really has done politics at the symphony. He responds calmly, like he has anticipated this turn. "Max, you know, and we all know, the Hotel Savant will either find another property or go back to Chicago long before a lawsuit is over."

Go Samuel!

A tap sounds at the door. Harold, divided older member of

the board, opens it. It is Jason and Elena.

"Chapter meetings are open to the congregation, right?" Jason says.

He wants to be heard. He looks more suave than ever, skinny-cut jacket and cufflinks. "We heard that the fate of the prairie is on the agenda tonight. We have a petition. We want to present this: over seven hundred names of people from all over downtown and nearby neighborhoods who want it to stay."

"For the beautification of our city. Its environmental impacts. Help mitigate this flooding." Elena's passion is contagious. "Professors at Drake, many of them signed. Also teachers of nearby schools, and leaders of the housing project near us. Prairie contributes to the community."

I take the sheet from them and stare down at the names. Some are scrawled and barely legible, some half-print-half-cursive, some in careful open loops. Each one representing a flesh-and-blood human being on the side of the land, the water, the grasses. We pass the petition around. Jason looks to Phil who gently gestures with his head toward the door. With the petition circulating, Jason and Elena take their leave.

As the door closes, I see Max morphing from Andy Warhol into Iceman. My eyes float down to his bowtie, a swirling paisley of burgundy, magenta and cobalt. I see it in the gilded mirror and it is even more frightening to witness it there! No. No. *Keep me steady.* I make myself look at his face. Livid. Calculating. Obviously he fears he is losing. Losing what his great grandfather bestowed; for him it is like losing his very being. I see it in the mirror.

But his voice sounds like ice, dry ice. "Dean Brenchley, act on behalf of the parish and accept the Hotel Savant's offer. Let go of these environmental delusions."

Delusional or not, my sense of what God values and what I value most deeply, wrought in reflection and prayer, must guide what I do. I am in the horse-ring. I focus.

Unnerved by lack of my verbal response, Max falls into a Max moment made public, totally against his own usual strategic protocol.

"The Chase family will stop our pledge. I have the names of other families who will do the same."

Hearing this threat uttered, Burton is so angry he is about to blow his circuits. I have never seen him so angry. But he is also in a strange way ebullient. He looks as if a door has suddenly opened for him to say something he thought he would carry to his grave.

"Max...just like your father, aren't you? So obsessed with control! You have been running this place behind the scenes for decades. But guess what? This body of believers is not your corporation! And this is a pill you are just going to have to swallow. My wife's grandfather gave that land to the cathedral's dean soon after the Civil War because of the man's proclamation and actions to end slavery. That priest was an abolitionist through-and-through. Old Taylor also gave it because skinflints like your great grandfather wanted to pay the cleric peanuts. Taylor wanted St. Aidan's priests to stand on even ground. And the Taylors gave that land for good, forever!"

Phil adds, "Max, you will note, it does say 'in perpetuity.'"

Unlike herself, Artemis has not uttered a word, has not sworn, not even mumbled disparaging phrases. She has been listening intently. She has been feeling out the temperature of the water, the tides. She is also familiar with politics, state politics.

"Dean Brigid, does this mean you could sell the land to the hotel, and the money would be yours?"

Thus far intimidated to enter the heated discussion, but emboldened by Artemis, a younger woman named Hannah Axle asks, "Brigid, if you sold, could you afford to give some of the profit to the cathedral for building repairs? Maybe create an endowment in honor of your family?"

I love this! The women have come in with a smart and strategic plan, too!

Well, I have now been in my fitted jacket in the arena with my horse for a bit. Strange. Usually I talk and talk at these meetings. But carrying the authority the glebe bestows, I have slowed down and listened. I carry a heavy responsibility. I realize I am a kind of every man/every woman. We each have to make our decisions about when and whether to put the earth first. It's time to move.

"Interestingly," I finally speak and respond to Artemis' question, "perhaps divinely inspired, this glebe situation weds us to one another. Like it or not, one big tangle! This is how the chancellor of the diocese explained it: the land is technically owned by the cathedral, but any profit from it is mine. So the parish can't sell it without my consent. On the other hand, I don't own it to sell it without your consent. *But* if we all consented, and we did sell, then yes, it would seem I would receive the profit."

I still have to jump.

I look into the mirror: Phil, Max, Burton, Merlin, Artemis, and me. We are all reflected there. But behind us, the mirror also captures what is outside the windows: the grasses and flowers. It is like each of us is part of what's blooming in the prairie as well. With Henry's death, I see clearly that his suffering, and all our lives, are woven there with the green stuff.

I reach into my valise and pull out the antique photo.

I turn to Max, whose head is down. The weight of defeat? I can just see that thinning place on top, his only vulnerable point. "Max, I respect, more than I can say, the gift of your ancestors."

He looks up at me, and our gazes meet perhaps for the first time. Genuine. I hand the photo around the table to Max.

"I found this photo down in the vault," I continue. "I believe it is your great grandfather with the granite stones he used to build our cathedral. What an incredible gift and effort!"

Max lowers his head again, engrossed by the image he now cradles in his hands. "But, you see, don't you, where he stands? Everlasting prairie! I get it, that our tiny parcel does not have huge environmental impact. But it is an icon, right downtown. Like Whitman's handkerchief designedly dropped that people might see it, and ask 'Whose?' So memory of those grasses might not be lost!"

I ride.

"Max, seeing Phineas Chase in that photo, he looks like

a person called by God to do what he did. You can see the conviction on his face and in his eyes. I feel sure of that now."

Others glancing at the old photo nod.

"Too true," Burton says with some admiration. I approach the bounce.

"All I can do is the same," I tell them. "Max, I do accept your challenge to do what is best for the parish. But the original understanding of a "parish" was not a building with pews and a choir. No. It was everything in the vicinity of the church: all the people, the animals, the crops and flora, the natural resources. The priest and the people in the pews were to pray for and care for everything around them—with the suffering love of Christ. Henry Jones' death has made this even more clear to me. It's not the cathedral or the prairie, the land or the people. What happens to the grasslands, happens to us."

I jump.

"I'm called to preserve these species and keep our water from flooding and polluting our neighbors who live downstream—whom Jesus loves by the way. In this space and time, it's my calling. I won't consent to the sale."

The Hotel Savant offer was the only business that really mattered.

Being settled by my decision, we all filter out. Only Max remains, head down, countenance inscrutable, gazing at the Phineas photo.

Afterward, alone in the dark of the prairie, Phil's kiss, no words, communicates his esteem.

30

OBEDIENT PLANT

Physostegia virginiana or obedient plant is a member of the mint family. Common throughout the tallgrass region in wet prairies, along streams, and in low marshy areas. The flowers, purple in hue, can be rotated around the stem, and remain where they are placed; thus the common name obedient plant. Fittingly, we planted obedient around the garden bench donated by Bishop James and Dionne Farnon.

–Note from Dean Brigid Brenchley's Prairie Journal

Chicago, December 1989

At my pre-ordination retreat 1 learned that the diocese of Chicago, being rather Anglo-Catholic, retained the old custom of prostration at ordinations.

1 was back from Exeter and went on to seminary. 1 had peace about my decision. With the time away in England, my family –even my father—had also gotten over the shock. In fact, when the time came for my ordination the whole lot of them decided

to make a holiday of it, booking rooms at the Palmer House, for what they teasingly term the "Quirky ceremony." Yes, I knew peace and joy about becoming a priest.

But this prostration thing was a little much.

For three days we were at a semi-silent prayer retreat near Lincoln Park in Chicago. Six of us. All soon to be priests. Unlike my earthy, low-slung Franciscan lodgings near Santa Maria degli Angel, we were staying in a high-rise convent on the Gold Coast. When we prayed, we looked out at yachts bobbing on Lake Michigan to the east, and at a swirl of ethnic restaurants and nightclubs to the west. During free time, I walked north to Lincoln Park Zoo. There I watched the elephants dance.

I was internally probing some last reservations about my vocation, when the smaller, female elephant came over to the rail where I leaned. She nudged me with her trunk, with her snout, her forehead. She had smiling elephant eyelashes. Like a living Ganesh, she was coaxing my last hesitations from me. Remover of obstacles.

That was just before I learned that, during the ceremony, we were to physically lie down before Bishop Grishom. No self-respecting girl from Colorado lies down at the feet of a bishop!

"What happens again?" I asked one of the other seminarians about to be ordained. "It's right after the examination, when the cantor chants the *Veni Creator Spiritus*. While everyone is in prayer for us."

"Is it mandatory?"

"I think the term is obedience. Bishop Grishom believes our bodies carry our prayers and intentions. It's why he still likes kneeling at points in the liturgy. Or standing. Very Anglican."

I was mortified. But what could I do?

My family filled two pews, looking like they wanted their usual popcorn and cokes. This was better than the Cooper Theater and Cinerama!

Bishop Grishom, in his ornate chair, beamed kindly at us because we were willing, moved, to do this crazy thing.

Then, there I was. Flat. Upon beautiful white tiles.

Veni
Creator
Spiritus

Come
Creator
Spirit.

White robes, white marble. White upon white. All I could see. Suddenly, it's the Teacup Bowl in the Rockies all over again. I'm blinded, exploded, on white. Love crosses the threshold. I'm filled with Love. But, love not just for me. Love through me!

31
EVENING PRIMROSE

Oenotherea biennis or evening primrose is found on most Midwest prairies on dry ridges and gravelly or sandy areas, blooming from July through September. In the second year, a stout stem develops that may reach 6 feet tall, though usually closer to four feet. Because the bright yellow flowers open abruptly in late afternoon and last only one day, pollination is mainly accomplished by night-flying moths. New blooms continue to appear until frost.

–Note from Dean Brigid Brenchley's Prairie Journal

Wednesday Evening

Whether it is the fog of gravel I have stirred up, now in my nostrils like talcum powder, or the sun's warmth where I stand sheltered from the breeze in Madge Chase's walled garden, or the pungent scent of her prize rosemary plant, I am not sure. But I taste the version of grace I first knew on pilgrimage in Italy. What a week! But, with the balls of my feet immersed in the gravel, I feel rooted. Whether I will have a splintered congregation...

whether important cathedral families will leave when they learn of my choice... whether I will lose my job as dean... remains to be seen. But I made a decision. I found my voice. And now I know a priestly variety of peace.

Of course, I have visited Madge's country estate a number of times since Marianna first drove me to see her. But today is the first time I did not initiate the visit. I have been summoned. Madge's grounds-keeper and friend Melville greeted me and directed me here to the courtyard.

"She'll just be a minute," he says, wiping dirt from his hands, and walks toward the sprawling stucco home to tell her I've arrived.

I should probably be shaking in my boots; who knows how many clerics of the Anglican/Episcopal ilk have been relieved of their post at some country estate? Madge's sandy courtyard is almost like an art gallery; through years of attention and nurture, she and Melville have been able to call forth stunning examples of certain native species. I might feel more trepidation, but... Holy Toledo! What is that?!

I stand speechless before what I think is a six foot tall common evening primrose.

Towering above asters and now-rusty goldenrod, it thrusts a pine-colored, phallus-shaped stock skyward that is peppered with delicate, yellow flowers shaped like the paper flycatchers we made as schoolgirls. Some spent flowers, still vivid yellow, lie at the base of the plant, like offerings at a shrine to Shiva. I am entranced as if staring at a Goldsworthy or a Brancusi, when I hear Madge enter the space.

In town, she usually wears pearls as she's worn since age ten, pulling at them like they are a burdensome responsibility. But here, in her true home, she wears army trousers and a straw hat with some holes and boots worn soft like an aviator jacket. With Madge on the farm, it's like being airlifted back in time to a visit with Isaak Denison or Amelia Earhart. Melville is helping her across the gravel. She has—a recent addition—a cane to steady her other side. Madge is definitely weakening, and my heart sinks to see it. I begin to wonder if my visit isn't part of Madge "putting things in order."

That day isn't today is it...please... that's not why she asked me to come?

I don't think I could bear that...

...not on top of losing Henry.

I am surveying Madge with a pastoral eye. She is weaker, but despite the cane I feel sure her hands are still too flexible, her eyes too fresh, her skin too radiant for that kind of news. But she is undeniably compromised.

"Thank you, Brigid, for coming out to me here. Especially with Henry Jones, and his funeral tomorrow...I was so sorry to get that news. These floods take a terrible toll."

I step over and gently hug her and hear a car pulling onto the gravel just outside the walled garden. A door slams. As measured a gait as Madge took, her brother Max instead races in kicking up pebbles. As at home as she looks in this setting, he looks foreign: high thread count shirt, tweed jacket, and loafers—fine dust already whitening the leather slots where the pennies would go. Though no bow tie. I note that fact.

"Here, Melville...I'll help Madge," he says, moving to take her arm. "I came as quickly as I could extricate myself from the Trustees. Are you all right? Is there a change?"

That's when Max sees me.

He halts. His eyes squint, focusing on me as one does when seeing a mirage on a summer highway. By the expression on his face I can tell he did not expect to find me at his sister's home. Max, it appears, has been summoned just as I have been.

"Dean Brigid? What are you doing here?" Now he turns on his sister, "Madge...are you kidding me? Madge, goddamit... ploys and surprises...you have been doing this kind of thing to me since I was a little boy."

"Well, if you'd ever quit acting like one, maybe I'd stop."

Suddenly, perhaps it is my sense of rootedness, the whole thing seems vaguely hilarious. Next to *The Sound of Music, My Fair Lady* was my family's cult film. Upon being confronted with me, Max still looks like Andy Warhol but acts totally like Prof. Henry Higgins discovering the newly galvanized Eliza ensconced in his mother's parlor. Like Higgins, frustration pours from his silk and tweed pores. His silver curl looks vaguely moist and gets ruffled as he runs his hands through it.

"You," he points a finger at me, "you brazen, brainless clerical upstart! You have no idea what you are doing, not a business bone in your body!"

"And you," he turns to his sister, "encouraging all this prairie romanticism. In case you've forgotten, Frank Lloyd Wright and the 'prairie school' all ended in bankruptcy and disaster. You, and that Marianna, have filled Brigid's head with ludicrous regionalist notions."

"Max, I've heard the woman preach, seen her address city council, present a budget. As have you. I would say Brigid has her own ideas in her own mind. You yourself have commented how she has more degrees than you and I put together."

His expression sours: his older sister conveying that he has some esteem for me opens a chink in his armor.

"Madge, you don't give a damn do you? Don't give a damn that because of this young woman Chase Enterprises will lose millions over time? Well, we care. Gwen and I plan to walk two blocks down to the Methodists on Sundays, where the pastor is a good business person. I can't give any more wisdom to a board that ignores it, nor any more thousands of dollars to support such silliness."

Madge doesn't answer. With the help of her cane, she walks to the evening primrose and plucks one of its star-shaped petals. She gazes at it before she speaks.

"Max," Madge says, "You're right. I probably don't care. Not really. I can't take it...the millions with me...and I have come to care more and more about the place I leave behind."

Max looks at his feet and kicks more gravel.

"Brigid," Madge looks at me, "Max knows this, but you don't: I am dying. Blood disease. I might make three years; it may be only a few months..."

So it is true. I look down—the gravel swims as if in a pool.

"I want to be buried from St. Aidan's Cathedral," she says, then turns a very serious gaze on each of us in turn, "Max, Peter and I took our own hiatus. You and Gwen may need yours too. So it may be unfair to ask...but I am trusting you and Brigid not to allow division to destroy that community nor its house of worship before they sing my final *Ave Maria.*"

"Madge, Dean Brigid is the one choosing the wreckage! If our father were here..."

Max's frustration seems to be turned inside himself now... some invisible battle he is losing with his vision of his own father.

"Max, father erected his skyscrapers. Symbols of his maleness from Des Moines to Grinnell. But you know yourself, that with all his power, he couldn't find harmony, nor relationship...you were one of the people he brushed aside most."

At this, Madge hobbles over and hands her younger brother the flower. He is so tender with her, he accepts it.

"The evening primrose is a giant, climbing skyward on nothing but sand. But its flowers, they open in the evening and only last twenty-four hours, then drop. Max, Dad was like that... he was a tower of money and influence but then he faded. No one remembers him, really. Things move on. You and I and Brigid...we're no different. We must simply each do our best with the short time we have."

Madge's face registers that she feels suddenly spent. We have taken all her energy.

"Melville..." her friend and groundskeeper has stayed near, but scarce, clipping a huge, fountain-like, red-twigged dogwood—it will be the glory of the courtyard in the winter snow.

He comes and offers Madge his shoulder for support.

"I am sorry to have asked each of you to make such a long trip for such a short visit. I'm afraid I get weak quickly. But, I haven't been able to sleep and there's seemed to be no cure for it but to see the two of you together. My affection for you? Boundless... I know you will both steward what has been put in your hands..."

I look at Madge and realize that during the whole visit, I

haven't said a word! A first in this preacher's life.

With that, Melville accompanies Madge from the walled garden.

Max stands twirling the primrose. He twirls and twirls it like a kid with a dreidel. Max spins the flower in his hand one more time and looks at me, shaking his head as if it still is inconceivable. Madge and me and the whole thing is inconceivable.

"I love the cathedral," I tell him, as if to answer his expression. "I don't want to see people stressed, or the building cave in...I lie awake at night imagining people arguing and gossiping and at each other's throats, see the cathedral taken by flood, Roosevelt's organ floating away like some dinghy at sea..."

"Oh, you say that Brigid, but there's scant evidence. You want me to support the prairie, but what will you do to save the building?!"

He kicks some gravel that ricochets off the tiles. "I've been in the real estate and development business for forty years... But this is, of all, the damnedest development..."

With high energy, Max moves toward the exit. As he goes, he gently tosses the primrose at the foot of the towering stalk.

He's right. At least half-right.

I stay in the courtyard as the sun sets and the plants and tiled walls slip from fuchsia-light into shadow. Eventually, only the top of the primrose plant holds the light. The plant is almost like Jack's beanstalk or the century plant I once saw pushing through the glass roof of the Chicago Botanical Garden. Its top branches are higher than the garden walls. Three luna moths incredibly hover and swoop around the plant. Eventually they land; they look like bows on a Christmas tree.

Finally, my flesh holds the chill and I go to my car and turn to face the next task ahead: finishing my eulogy for Henry. His funeral is tomorrow—almost as if he had scheduled it himself— Holy Cross Day, his favorite festival in the church calendar. All of the liturgy the staff planned for the Sunday after Holy Cross we will offer on the holy day itself, as part of Henry's memorial.

Yes, I must go home and write "Henry and the Holy Cross,"

and I also need to give Grandma Helen a call. Max has presented me with a truth. I ask for him to do so, but won't compromise myself. I want him to support my calling, but I haven't done much to support his passion for the building. Yes... I have to give Grandma Helen a call. I have an idea.

32

PRAIRIE ROSE

Rosa pratincola or wild prairie rose is the state flower of Iowa. Prairie rose usually has three leaflets, but may have five. The stems are bright green to reddish green and clambering. They use adjacent vegetation and fences for support. Flowers on prairie rose are about 3 inches across, with five light pink petals and a yellow center. Prickles are few and far apart on the stem. As the name suggests, prairie rose is a species occurring in and at the edge of prairies, woodlands and savannas. Of course, we planted them in front of the cathedral's rose window.

–Note from Dean Brigid Brenchley's Prairie Journal

Des Moines, Iowa 2003

"Is it really necessary?" I asked.

Standing in the cathedral nave, Bishop Farnon was to the right side of me, Merlin to the left, and we were pouring over the plans for a rather ornate public worship event in which I would officially be named dean of the Cathedral Church of St. Aidan.

"The Investiture and Seating of the Dean?" I looked at them with some incredulity. "It sounds so royal family! I'm just not sure my Franciscan heart can do it. Do I actually actively have to sit? In front of about five hundred people? I get nervous if someone pulls out a chair for me at a restaurant—afraid I'll miss the mark."

Merlin actually laughed out loud, "We've got seventy-two hours and I can help you practice. I'll show you tricks for that sort of thing: how you look back a minute, where to place your hand as you sit...I'll have you ready to do the whole thing in eight-inch platform shoes if you want. Besides, Artemis will be verger that day and she'd never let you fall and crumple your new cope."

Bishop Farnon didn't say it, but gave me a Yorkshire look that said, "Just shut up and do as you're told."

As one of his youngest priests, I always had questions and contentions, and high energy. In the film *The Darkest Hour*, as he's about to be made Prime Minister, Winston Churchill says to his wife: "It's not a gift; it's revenge," and I sometimes wonder if this wasn't partially Bishop Farnon's motive when he made me provost of the terribly divided cathedral a year before. But after a year of healing, with a sort of rent-with-the-option-to-buy arrangement, the people of St. Aidan's told the bishop they wanted Provost Brenchley to be made their dean, permanently.

"Well," Bishop James replies, "I would rather have you with your hippy hesitations, than a number of ambitious ones who can't wait to clamber into a dean's seat or better yet a bishop's cathedral...But, yes you have to do it. Besides, I think you are already finding that it is a rather large responsibility. Saturday you will take public vows to pray and care for, not only the people of the congregation, but the people of this city, and—as I have need of you—of the diocese as well. We never know what will unfold in our days of leadership. Believe me, sometimes you will be so exhausted you'll need to sit down. So, yes, Merlin can help you with the etiquette, but the dean *will* be ceremonially seated."

I was still a bit self-conscious about this part of the service. For one, my extended family had flown in for "yet another Quirky event" and were teasing me mercilessly about all this pomp and circumstance and about how they should have paid me a little more respect when they were pulling my Pippi-Longstocking-braids and making fun of my freckles. They are in a festive mood taking up three front pews, with Grandma Helen a leader in the frivolity.

"It really is life in the theater after all..." she said later. "What costumes!"

Yet, when the time actually came—not unlike lying face down on white marble to be ordained—the ritual was full of grace.

For one thing, I never imagined the view from the dean's chair. Like repayment for all the hard work and tough decisions, I had the best seat in the house. Better even than the bishop who was directly behind the altar. From my chair I saw the beautiful faces of all the people, saw the worry lines and smiles, the stories behind each set of eyes...and above them, like the large orb of the sun rising over the horizon, our St. Aidan's Rose Window shimmered just above their heads. The centerpiece of William Foster's cathedral design, the Arts and Crafts style rose window is bolder and more sinuous than the geometry of old Gothic windows, and with its American breadth allows more light into the cathedral.

That's the view I saw during those first moments as dean: our rose window's traceries casting splinters of light all over the gathered people below. I saw how their lives reflect bits of the Light of God.

After communion, the civic element of the investiture was like a final exclamation mark.

I would not understand why until years later, but it moved me most of all. Maximillian and Madge Chase, Phillip Morrow, and Mayor Frances Burnish, along with a cadre of clergy and non-profit leaders, proceeded up to where I was seated and presented to me a Des Moines City Flag. The modern design features three white bridges—Walnut, Locust, and Grand Streets—crossing the swelling blue background of the Des Moines River.

"Dean Brenchley," Mayor Burnish said as Max Chase handed me the flag, "may you work with us to strengthen the important bridges that unify the people of this city."

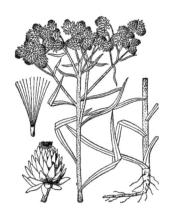

33

COMMON PEARLY EVERLASTING

Anaphalis margaritacea, or common pearly everlasting, is a North American native plant that grows to 3 feet tall and typically occurs on dry, sandy or gravelly sites. An upright, clump-forming plant that features attractive, narrow, woolly, silver-gray foliage and tiny, white, globular flowers with yellow center stamens arranged in flattish clusters on erect stems. Late-summer bloom. Fluffy flower heads are valued for dried flower arrangements. Genus name comes from the classical Greek name for another of the everlastings.

–Note from Dean Brigid Brenchley's Prairie Journal

Holy Cross Day, Thursday

I look out from the pulpit, and it's like gazing across a small sea of humanity washed into the bay of the cathedral. The usual parish suspects are here: Merlin and Ivan and Samuel are in the choir wearing burgundy cassocks and white surplices. In the pews: Burton and Maxine, Marianna, Max and Gwen, Phil, Elena balancing Ana on her knee, Simon, and all the other familiar faces old and young. Jason and Delilah are up near the altar serving as acolytes.

But we are just a sprinkling in the crowd. Everyone, it seems, loved and respected Henry! The guys at the plant, his extended family from Albia who are mainly farmers, people from the Marshland Neighborhood, the local Lions Club.

Today, as his funeral ends it's as if he orchestrated it all.

Every Holy Cross day we unhook St. Aidan's elm-like crucifix from its transparent cables and carry it in procession. Now it sits, propped in the middle of the chancel, because today Marianna has organized Henry and Pearl's grandchildren to come forward.

With ribbons, they tie onto the cross amber Indian grass, blonde switch grass, and teal bluestem as well as common pearly everlasting (the white flower that blooms and blooms until the snow flies).

The chubby hands cover the nailed feet of Jesus.

The children keep tying, and the grasses grow up the vertical wood. The children tie more, and Jesus' straining ribs disappear in grasses.

Finally, wiping a few tears, I stand, holding Henry's urn. When the children finish, I walk down the marble steps and place the urn in Henry's son's hands.

Delilah and Jason lift the cross, heavy-laden with grasses and pearly everlasting.

They move forward.

Behind the cross, Pearl and her family, then the congregation. I am last.

We all slowly follow the cross out to the prairie. Paradisio as Delilah calls it.

On my way out the door between the nave and the narthex, I fumble through the layers of my robes and into my pocket. We sing *The Pange, Lingue* and I move past the offering plate, where the gifts for Henry's memorials are placed.

I add a twenty thousand dollar check to help fix the roof in Henry's honor.

Three days ago the gallery owner came, and Grandma Helen and I together sold off most of the Ward and Brenchley artwork and antiques. We had a ball and agreed that the bungalow is much calmer and more beautiful with just the wingback chairs and a few choice pieces of art.

My check balances atop another check: two hundred fifty thousand dollars from Max and Gwen Chase. In the memo line: *In memorium, Henry Jones. To repair the stones. Our calling.*

All together, we process onto our land, my glebe, an icon for the city. The ground is charred, and yet, like a pointillist painting, dots of green can be seen piercing through the ashen crust. As we process, Nicholas Jones, Henry's youngest grandchild, rides on the shoulders of his father, who mingles Henry's ashes with the prairie.

ACKNOWLEDGMENTS

Of Green Stuff Woven comes from the amalgamation of two surprises.

As a Colorado native, albeit with Kansas roots, 1 never anticipated falling in love with the sweep of diverse plants that make up the tall grass prairie. 1 thank my in-laws Charles and Kay Bascom for three years in their log home in the Flint Hills, years that first immersed me in the grasses which grew over my head. For those who have taught me plant names and their ways: Elvin McDonald, Joanna Hebberger, Marcia Bascom, and Paul Bartelt, among others.

As an agnostic, 1 never expected to meet the Divine on a ski trip, and to have the ways of Jesus usher me into the cadre of earthy, colorful souls who are the Episcopal Church. Even less imaginable that 1 would become a priest or a bishop! Yet, the beautiful human diversity 1 have known in community rivals that of the prairie species. All of the characters in this book are fictionalized and exaggerated for the sake of a good story. But almost all have their roots in good people 1 have been blessed to know, especially those at the Cathedral Church of St. Paul in Des Moines where 1 served as dean.

This book was written during a hiatus from ecclesiastical life. 1 owe much to my professors at Iowa State University's Creative Writing and Environment MFA. For Iowa's poet laureate and then director of the program Debra Marquart, and most especially to current directors, playwright Charissa Menefee and novelist, story-cyclist Kenny Cook who believed in this book and tried to teach a preacher about plot. And to my early tutor at Exeter University, poet and critic Ron Tamplin, who returned as a kind of muse.

Above all, to my sons Conrad and Luke Bascom and my author, husband Tim Bascom for literary insights, editing help, and sustaining love.

ABOUT THE AUTHOR

Of Green Stuff Woven is the debut novel by Cathleen Bascom who was recently elected the first woman Bishop of Kansas in the Episcopal Church.

An assistant professor of religion for four years at Waldorf University and a priest of twenty-eight years in various Episcopal parishes between the Great Lakes and the Rockies, Cathleen served most recently as dean of the Cathedral Church of St. Paul in Des Moines, Iowa. She and the cathedral aided in recovery efforts during the flood of 2008 and were named Urban Stewards of the Year for the installation of an urban prairie green-space. These experiences are imaginatively tapped in *Of Green Stuff Woven*. Passionate about saving the threatened tallgrass prairie, Cathleen founded Iowa Creation Stewards, helping other churches plant postage stamp prairies and organize around environmental concerns, and was appointed by Presiding Bishop Michael Curry to the Episcopal Church's Task Force on Creation Care.

Cathleen, who recently completed an MFA in Creative Writing and Environment at Iowa State University and tends to collect degrees in English Literature and Theology, has contributed chapters to the books *Hungry Heart* and *Expressions of Religious Experience in C.S. Lewis' Chronicles of Narnia*.

Cathleen intends to be a writing bishop, with more stories to come. Connect with Cathleen at Greenstuff-Bascom.com.

LIST OF ILLUSTRATIONS

CHAPTER 1: USDA-NRCS PLANTS Database / Hitchcock, A.S. (rev. A. Chase). 1950. *Manual of the grasses of the United States.* USDA Miscellaneous Publication No. 200. Washington, DC.

Chapter 2: USDA-NRCS PLANTS Database / Hitchcock, A.S. (rev. A. Chase). 1950. *Manual of the grasses of the United States.* USDA Miscellaneous Publication No. 200. Washington, DC.

Chapter 3: USDA-NRCS PLANTS Database / Hitchcock, A.S. (rev. A. Chase). 1950. *Manual of the grasses of the United States.* USDA Miscellaneous Publication No. 200. Washington, DC.

Chapter 4: USDA-NRCS PLANTS Database / USDA NRCS. *Wetland flora: Field office illustrated guide to plant species.* USDA Natural Resources Conservation Service.

Chapter 5: USDA-NRCS PLANTS Database / Britton, N.L., and A. Brown. 1913. *An illustrated flora of the northern United States, Canada and the British Possessions. 3 vols.* Charles Scribner's Sons, New York. Vol. 3: 486.

Chapter 6: USDA-NRCS PLANTS Database / Britton, N.L., and A. Brown. 1913. *An illustrated flora of the northern United States, Canada and the British Possessions. 3 vols.* Charles Scribner's Sons, New York. Vol. 1: 386.

Chapter 7: Adobe Stock Images. stock.adobe.com.

Chapter 8: Adobe Stock Images. stock.adobe.com.

Chapter 9: USDA-NRCS PLANTS Database / Britton, N.L., and A. Brown. 1913. *An illustrated flora of the northern United States, Canada and the British Possessions. 3 vols.* Charles Scribner's Sons, New York. Vol. 1: 141.

Chapter 10: USDA-NRCS PLANTS Database / Hitchcock, A.S. (rev. A. Chase). 1950. *Manual of the grasses of the United States.* USDA Miscellaneous Publication No. 200. Washington, DC.

Chapter 11: USDA-NRCS PLANTS Database / Britton, N.L., and

A. Brown. 1913. *An illustrated flora of the northern United States, Canada and the British Possessions. 3 vols.* Charles Scribner's Sons, New York. Vol. 1: 166.

Chapter 12: USDA-NRCS PLANTS Database / Britton, N.L., and A. Brown. 1913. *An illustrated flora of the northern United States, Canada and the British Possessions. 3 vols.* Charles Scribner's Sons, New York. Vol. 3: 38

Chapter 13: USDA-NRCS PLANTS Database / USDA NRCS. *Wetland flora: Field office illustrated guide to plant species.* USDA Natural Resources Conservation Service.

Chapter 14: USDA-NRCS PLANTS Database / Britton, N.L., and A. Brown. 1913. *An illustrated flora of the northern United States, Canada and the British Possessions. 3 vols.* Charles Scribner's Sons, New York. Vol. 1: 634.

Chapter 15: USDA-NRCS PLANTS Database / Britton, N.L., and A. Brown. 1913. An illustrated flora of the northern United States, Canada and the British Possessions. 3 vols. Charles Scribner's Sons, New York. Vol. 1: 461.

Chapter 16: Adobe Stock Images. stock.adobe.com.

Chapter 17: USDA-NRCS PLANTS Database / Britton, N.L., and A. Brown. 1913. An illustrated flora of the northern United States, Canada and the British Possessions. 3 vols. Charles Scribner's Sons, New York. Vol. 2: 273

Chapter 18: USDA-NRCS PLANTS Database / Hitchcock, A.S. (rev. A. Chase). 1950. Manual of the grasses of the United States. USDA Miscellaneous Publication No. 200. Washington, DC.

Chapter 19: USDA-NRCS PLANTS Database / Britton, N.L., and A. Brown. 1913. An illustrated flora of the northern United States, Canada and the British Possessions. 3 vols. Charles Scribner's Sons, New York. Vol. 2: 268.

Chapter 20: Flint, Charles L. *Grasses and Forage Plants*(Boston, MA: William F. Gill & Company, 1874). ClipArt ETC. Florida Center for Instructional Technology, College of Education,

University of South Florida. https://etc.usf.edu/clipart.

Chapter 21: Chandler B. Beach *The New Student's Reference Work for Teachers Students and Families* (Chicago, IL: F. E. Compton and Company, 1909). ClipArt ETC. Florida Center for Instructional Technology, College of Education, University of South Florida. https://etc.usf.edu/clipart.

Chapter 22: USDA-NRCS PLANTS Database / Hitchcock, A.S. (rev. A. Chase). 1950. *Manual of the grasses of the United States.* USDA Miscellaneous Publication No. 200. Washington, DC.

Chapter 23: USDA-NRCS PLANTS Database / Britton, N.L., and A. Brown. 1913. *An illustrated flora of the northern United States, Canada and the British Possessions. 3 vols.* Charles Scribner's Sons, New York. Vol. 3: 26.

Chapter 24: Hippolyte Coste. *Flore descriptive et illustrée de la France, de la Corse et des contrées limitrophes,* 1901-1906.

Chapter 25: Adobe Stock Images. stock.adobe.com.

Chapter 26: USDA-NRCS PLANTS Database / Britton, N.L., and A. Brown. 1913. *An illustrated flora of the northern United States, Canada and the British Possessions. 3 vols.* Charles Scribner's Sons, New York. Vol. 2: 717.

Chapter 27: USDA-NRCS PLANTS Database / Britton, N.L., and A. Brown. 1913. *An illustrated flora of the northern United States, Canada and the British Possessions. 3 vols.* Charles Scribner's Sons, New York. Vol. 3: 55.

Chapter 28: Adobe Stock Images. stock.adobe.com.

Chapter 29: USDA-NRCS PLANTS Database / Britton, N.L., and A. Brown. 1913. *An illustrated flora of the northern United States, Canada and the British Possessions. 3 vols.* Charles Scribner's Sons, New York. Vol. 1: 41.

Chapter 30: USDA-NRCS PLANTS Database / USDA NRCS. *Wetland flora: Field office illustrated guide to plant species.* USDA Natural Resources Conservation Service.

Chapter 31: USDA-NRCS PLANTS Database / Britton, N.L., and A. Brown. 1913. *An illustrated flora of the northern United States, Canada and the British Possessions. 3 vols.* Charles Scribner's Sons, New York. Vol. 2: 595.

Chapter 32: USDA-NRCS PLANTS Database / Britton, N.L., and A. Brown. 1913. *An illustrated flora of the northern United States, Canada and the British Possessions. 3 vols.* Charles Scribner's Sons, New York. Vol. 2: 284.

Chapter 33: USDA-NRCS PLANTS Database / Britton, N.L., and A. Brown. 1913. *An illustrated flora of the northern United States, Canada and the British Possessions. 3 vols.* Charles Scribner's Sons, New York. Vol. 3: 453.

YOU MIGHT ALSO LIKE

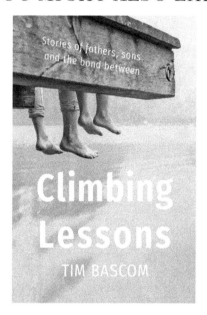

When Doc Bascom tries to show his grade school sons how to climb a huge sycamore, he ends up dropping twelve feet flat-out on his back. Stunned, he finally gasps, "So that's how it's done." And in that moment, he becomes an emblem for all fathers—trying to lead the way, failing, then getting up and trying again.

This "climbing lesson" is just one of forty playful, sometimes poignant stories by award-winning author Tim Bascom, who illustrates the special bond between fathers and sons—and how that relationship must change with time. When Tim takes his own turn at fathering, he realizes that his devoted toddlers are turning into unimpressed teenagers. No longer the hero he had hoped to be, he must accept a new, flawed version of himself, not unlike his father before him.

These brief inter-linked stories show that abiding affection can still prevail, bringing fathers and sons closer, even as they tackle the steepest parts of the climb.

YOU MIGHT ALSO LIKE

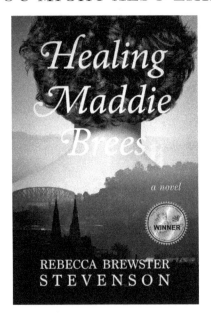

"A gorgeous meditation on broken bodies, fractured faith, and the soul-wrenching path to serenity." *–Kirkus Reviews*

Maddie Brees has been given bad news: She is seriously ill. But she also has an old friend, an ex-boyfriend who might be able to heal her. She was witness to Vincent Elander's so-called miracles in the past. But that was a long time ago, a memory that she would rather stay buried. Now she is happily married to Frank and mother of their three young boys. The religion of her past is behind her, along with any confidence she once had in it. With the onset of her cancer, the memories of Vincent won't leave Maddie alone, and before long they are affecting everything else: her marriage, her husband, the things they thought they agreed on, the beliefs they thought they shared. Soon Frank, who was to be Maddie's rock throughout her treatment, is finding fault-lines of his own. In this exquisitely written narrative, Stevenson explores the questions of honesty and commitment, of disease and isolation, and of the many shapes healing takes.

Printed in the USA
CPSIA information can be obtained
at www.ICGtesting.com
CBHW021417241223
2917CB00005B/24